Praise for *Principles of Web API Design*

"I've had the good fortune to work alc
His varied institutional knowledge, al
application, makes him unique among l
nity, in this book, to benefit from Jame.   .... now to make better
APIs. *Principles of Web API Design* surveys the gamut of available techniques and sets forth a
prescriptive, easy-to-follow approach. Teams that apply the guidance in this book will create
APIs that better resonate with customers, deliver more business value in less time, and require
fewer breaking changes. I cannot recommend *Principles of Web API Design* enough."

—*Matthew Reinbold, Director of API Ecosystems, Postman*

"James is one of the preeminent experts on API design in the industry, and this comprehensive
guide reflects that. Putting API design in the context of business outcomes and digital capabilities makes this a vital guide for any organization undergoing digital transformation."

—*Matt McLarty, Global Leader of API Strategy at MuleSoft,*
a Salesforce company

"In modern software development, APIs end up being both the cause of and solution to many of
the problems we face. James's process for dissecting, analyzing, and designing APIs from concepts
to caching creates a repeatable approach for teams to solve more problems than they create."

—*D. Keith Casey, Jr., API Problem Solver, CaseySoftware, LLC*

"Following James's clear and easy-to-follow guide, in one afternoon I was able to apply his
process to current real-world use cases. I now have the practical guidance, techniques, and
clear examples to help me take those next vital steps. Recommended reading for anyone connected to and working with APIs."

—*Joyce Stack, Architect, Elsevier*

"*Principles of Web API Design* uncovers more than principles. In it, you'll learn a process—a
method to design APIs."

—*Arnaud Lauret, API Handyman*

"This insightful playbook guides API teams through a structured process that fosters produc-
tive collaboration, valuable capability identification, and best-practice contract crafting.
James distills years of experience into a pragmatic roadmap for defining and refining API
products, and also provides a primer for API security, eventing, resiliency, and microservices
alignment. A must-read for architects either new to the API discipline or responsible for
onboarding new teams and instituting a structured API definition process."

—*Chris Haddad, Chief Architect, Karux LLC*

Principles of Web API Design

Principles of
Web API Design

Delivering Value with
APIs and Microservices

James Higginbotham

✦✦ Addison-Wesley

Boston • Columbus • New York • San Francisco • Amsterdam • Cape Town
Dubai • London • Madrid • Milan • Munich • Paris • Montreal • Toronto • Delhi • Mexico City
São Paulo • Sydney • Hong Kong • Seoul • Singapore • Taipei • Tokyo

Pearson's Commitment to Diversity, Equity, and Inclusion

Pearson is dedicated to creating bias-free content that reflects the diversity of all learners. We embrace the many dimensions of diversity, including but not limited to race, ethnicity, gender, socioeconomic status, ability, age, sexual orientation, and religious or political beliefs.

Education is a powerful force for equity and change in our world. It has the potential to deliver opportunities that improve lives and enable economic mobility. As we work with authors to create content for every product and service, we acknowledge our responsibility to demonstrate inclusivity and incorporate diverse scholarship so that everyone can achieve their potential through learning. As the world's leading learning company, we have a duty to help drive change and live up to our purpose to help more people create a better life for themselves and to create a better world.

Our ambition is to purposefully contribute to a world where:

- Everyone has an equitable and lifelong opportunity to succeed through learning.
- Our educational products and services are inclusive and represent the rich diversity of learners.
- Our educational content accurately reflects the histories and experiences of the learners we serve.
- Our educational content prompts deeper discussions with learners and motivates them to expand their own learning (and worldview).

While we work hard to present unbiased content, we want to hear from you about any concerns or needs with this Pearson product so that we can investigate and address them.

- Please contact us with concerns about any potential bias at https://www.pearson .com/report-bias.html.

To my wife,
whose support and encouragement
makes everything possible.

To my grandfather, J.W.,
who gave me a Commodore 64 when I was eight years old
because he believed "computers are going to be big someday,
and my grandson should know how to use one"
and who inspired me to follow in his footsteps as an author.

To my dad,
who continued the work
of J.W. I miss you.

To my son,
who continues the tradition with
his endless coding in Minecraft.

And to my daughter,
who inspires me every day
to write better copy.

Contents

Series Editor Foreword

My signature series emphasizes organic growth and refinement, which I describe in more detail below. Before that, I will tell you a little about how organic reactions brought the author and I together for the first time.

If you've ever spent a summer in a desert, you know that your flesh-and-blood organism becomes very uncomfortable with the heat. That's certainly the case with summer in the Sonoran Desert of Arizona. Temperatures can rise to near 120°F, or 49°C. At 118°F/47.8°C, the Phoenix Sky Harbor Airport shuts down operations. So, if you are going to break free from the heat, you get out before you are stuck in the desert. That's what we did in early July 2019, when we escaped to Boulder, Colorado, where we had previously resided. Knowing that the author of this book, James Higginbotham, had relocated to Colorado Springs, Colorado, gave us the opportunity to meet up for a few days in that nearby Colorado city. (In the western US, 100 miles/160 km is considered to be nearby.) I'll tell you more about our collaboration once I've introduced you to my signature series.

My Signature Series is designed and curated to guide readers toward advances in software development maturity and greater success with business-centric practices. The series emphasizes organic refinement with a variety of approaches—reactive, object, as well as functional architecture and programming; domain modeling; right-sized services; patterns; and APIs—and covers best uses of the associated underlying technologies.

From here I am focusing now on only two words: *organic refinement*.

The first word, *organic*, stood out to me recently when a friend and colleague used it to describe software architecture. I have heard and used the word *organic* in connection with software development, but I didn't think about that word as carefully as I did then when I personally consumed the two used together: *organic architecture*.

Think about the word *organic*, and even the word *organism*. For the most part these are used when referring to living things, but are also used to describe inanimate things that feature some characteristics that resemble life forms. *Organic* originates in Greek. Its etymology is with reference to a functioning organ of the body. If you read the etymology of *organ*, it has a broader use, and in fact organic followed suit: body organs; to implement; describes a tool for making or doing; a musical instrument.

We can readily think of numerous organic objects—living organisms—from the very large to the microscopic single-celled life forms. With the second use of organism, though, examples may not as readily pop into our mind. One example is an organization, which includes the prefix of both *organic* and *organism*. In this use of *organism*, I'm describing something that is structured with bidirectional dependencies. An organization is an organism because it has organized parts. This kind of organism cannot survive without the parts, and the parts cannot survive without the organism.

Taking that perspective, we can continue applying this thinking to nonliving things because they exhibit characteristics of living organisms. Consider the atom. Every single atom is a system unto itself, and all living things are composed of atoms. Yet, atoms are inorganic and do not reproduce. Even so, it's not difficult to think of atoms as living things in the sense that they are endlessly moving, functioning. Atoms even bond with other atoms. When this occurs, each atom is not only a single system unto itself, but becomes a subsystem along with other atoms as subsystems, with their combined behaviors yielding a greater whole system.

So then, all kinds of concepts regarding software are quite organic in that nonliving things are still "characterized" by aspects of living organisms. When we discuss software model concepts using concrete scenarios, or draw an architecture diagram, or write a unit test and its corresponding domain model unit, software starts to come alive. It isn't static, because we continue to discuss how to make it better, subjecting it to refinement, where one scenario leads to another, and that has an impact on the architecture and the domain model. As we continue to iterate, the increasing value in refinements leads to incremental growth of the organism. As time progresses so does the software. We wrangle with and tackle complexity through useful abstractions, and the software grows and changes shapes, all with the explicit purpose of making work better for real living organisms at global scales.

Sadly, software organics tend to grow poorly more often than they grow well. Even if they start out life in good health they tend to get diseases, become deformed, grow unnatural appendages, atrophy, and deteriorate. Worse still is that these symptoms are caused by efforts to refine the software that go wrong instead of making things better. The worst part is that with every failed refinement, everything that goes wrong with these complexly ill bodies doesn't cause their death. (Oh, if they could just die!) Instead, we have to kill them and killing them requires nerves, skills, and the intestinal fortitude of a dragon slayer. No, not one, but dozens of vigorous dragon slayers. Actually, make that dozens of dragon slayers who have really big brains.

That's where this series comes into play. I am curating a series designed to help you mature and reach greater success with a variety of approaches—reactive, object, and functional architecture and programming; domain modeling; right-sized services; patterns; and APIs. And along with that, the series covers best uses of the associated underlying technologies. It's not accomplished at one fell swoop. It requires organic refinement with purpose and skill. I and the other authors are here to help. To that end, we've delivered our very best to achieve our goal.

When James and I got together for a few days in July 2019, we covered a lot of ground on APIs and Domain-Driven Design, along with related subjects. I'd consider our conversations organic in nature. As we iterated on various topics, we refined our knowledge exchange, gauged by our level of interest in whatever direction our hunger led us. Feeding our brains resulted in growing our own desire and determination to extend our software building approaches in order to help others expand their skills and grow toward greater successes. Those who read our books, as well as our consulting and training clients, are the ones who have gained the most.

To say the least, I was impressed by James's encyclopedic knowledge of everything APIs. While we were together, I asked James about writing a book. He informed me that he had self-published one book but wasn't at that time intent on writing another book. That was approximately nine months before I was offered the Signature Series. When the series planning was in the works, I immediately approached James about authoring in the series. I was so happy that he accepted and that he proposed organic software design and development techniques, such as with Align-Define-Design-Refine (ADDR). When you read his book, you will understand why I am so pleased to have James in my series.

—*Vaughn Vernon*

Foreword

According to a recent IDC report on APIs and API management, 75 percent of those surveyed were focused on digital transformation through the design and implementation of APIs and more than one half expected call volume and response time to grow dramatically. And most organizations admitted they faced challenges in meeting expectations for both internally and externally facing APIs. At the heart of all of this is the need for consistent, reliable, and scalable API design programs to help lead and transform existing organizations. As James Higginbotham puts it in this book: "The biggest challenge for today's API programs continues to be successfully designing APIs that can be understood and integrated by developers in a consistent and scalable fashion."

It was for this reason that I was so happy to have this book cross my desk. I've had the pleasure of working with James over the years and, knowing his work and his reputation, was very happy to hear he was writing a book that covers Web API design. Now, after reading through this book, I am equally happy to recommend it to you, the reader.

The field of Web APIs and the work of designing them has matured rapidly over the last few years, and keeping up with the latest developments is a major undertaking. Issues like changing business expectations for the role of APIs; maturing processes for gathering, recording, and documenting the work of API design; as well as evolving technology changes and all the work of coding, releasing, testing, and monitoring APIs make up an API landscape large enough that few people have been able to successfully tackle it. Through his Align-Define-Design-Refine process, James offers an excellent set of recommendations, examples, and experience-based advice to help the reader navigate the existing space of Web APIs and prepare for the inevitable changes ahead in the future.

One of the things about James's work that has always stood out is his ability to reach beyond the technical and into the social and business aspects of APIs and API programs within organizations. James has a long list of international clients across the business sectors of banking, insurance, global shipping, and even computer hardware providers, and the material in this book reflects this depth of experience. The techniques and processes detailed here have been tried and tested in all sorts of enterprise settings, and James's ability to distill what works into this one volume is impressive. Whether you are looking for advice on general design, business-technology alignment, or implementation details for various technologies such as REST, GraphQL, and event-driven platforms, you'll find important and actionable advice within these pages.

In particular, I found the material on how to refine your API design and implementation efforts within an ever-growing enterprise API program particularly timely and especially valuable. For those tasked with launching, managing, and expanding the role of Web-based APIs within a company, *Principles of Web API Design* should prove to be a welcome addition to your bookshelf.

As the aforementioned IDC report indicates, many companies around the globe are faced with important digital transformation challenges, and APIs have a major role to play in helping organizations meet the needs of their customers and in continuing to improve their own bottom line. Whether you are focused on designing, building, deploying, or maintaining APIs, this book contains helpful insights and advice.

I know this book will become an important part of my toolkit as I work with companies of all stripes to continue to mature and grow their API programs, and I expect you, too, will find it useful. Reading this book has reminded me of all the opportunities and challenges we all have before us. To borrow another line from James: "This is only the beginning."

—*Mike Amundsen, API Strategist*

Preface

It's hard to pinpoint the beginning of the journey to writing this book—perhaps it started about ten years ago. It is the result of thousands of hours of training, tens of thousands of miles traveled, and too many written words and lines of code to count. It comprises insights from organizations across the globe that were just starting their API journey or had already begun the adventure. The book incorporates the insights of API practitioners across the world whom I have had the pleasure to meet.

Or perhaps the journey started almost twenty-five years ago, when I first entered the software profession. So many advisors provided their insight via books and articles. Mentors along the way helped to shape my way of thinking about software. They laid the foundation of how I prefer to realize software architecture.

Maybe the journey really started almost forty years ago, when my grandfather gifted me with a Commodore 64. He was a civil engineer and cost engineer who attended night school while working to support his family during the day. He was thirsty for knowledge, reading and absorbing everything he could. He always made us laugh when he said, "I'm still amazed at how television works!" after seeing a computer operate. Yet, he was the one who gifted me that magical computer, saying "computers are going to be big someday, and my grandson should know how to use one." This single action started my lifelong love of software development.

In reality, the journey started more than seventy years ago when the pioneers of our current age of computing established many of the foundational principles we still use today to construct software. Though technology choices change, and the trends come and go, it all builds on the work of so many in the software industry and beyond. Countless people have helped to carve the way for what we do today.

What I am saying is that APIs would not be what they are today without all the hard work that came before us. Therefore, we must thirst for understanding the history of our industry to better understand "the how" and "the why" behind what we do today. Then, we must seek to apply these lessons to all that we do tomorrow. Along the way, we need to find ways to inspire others to do the same. This is what my grandfather and father taught me, so I pass this lesson on to you. This book reflects the things I've learned thus far in my journey. I hope you gain some new insights by building upon what is presented here while you seek to prepare the next generation.

Who Should Read This Book

This book is for anyone who wants to design a single API or a series of APIs that will delight humans. Product owners and product managers will gain a deeper understanding of the elements that teams need to design an API. Software architects and developers will benefit from learning how to design APIs by applying principles of software architecture. Technical writers will identify ways that they not only can contribute to the clarity of API documentation but also can add value throughout the API design process. In short, *Principles of Web API Design* is for everyone involved in API design whether they are in a development or nondevelopment role.

About This Book

This book outlines a series of principles and a process for designing APIs. The Align-Define-Design-Refine (ADDR) process featured in this book is designed to help individuals and cross-functional teams to navigate the complexities of API design. It encourages an outside-in perspective on API design by applying concepts such as the voice of the customer, jobs to be done, and process mapping. Although *Principles of Web API Design* walks through a greenfield example from the ground up, the book may also be used for existing APIs.

The book covers all aspects of API design, from requirements to arriving at an API design ready for delivery. It also includes guidance on how to document the API design for more effective communication between you, your team, and your API consumers. Finally, the book touches on a few elements of API delivery that may have an impact on your API design.

The book is divided into five parts:

- **Part I: Introduction to Web API Design**—An overview of why API design is important and an introduction to the API design process used in this book.

- **Part II: Aligning on API Outcomes**—Ensures alignment between the team designing the API and all customers and stakeholders.

- **Part III: Defining Candidate APIs**—Identifies the APIs, including the API operations required, necessary to deliver the desired outcomes into API profiles.

- **Part IV: Designing APIs**—Transforms the API profiles into one or more API styles that meet the needs of the target developers. Styles covered include REST, gRPC, GraphQL, and event-based asynchronous APIs.

- **Part V: Refining the Design**—Improves the API design based on insights from documentation, testing, and feedback. It also includes a chapter on decomposing APIs into microservices. Finally, the book closes with tips on how to scale the design process in larger organizations.

For those who need a refresher on HTTP, the language of the Web used for Web-based APIs, the appendix provides a nice primer to help you get started.

What's Not in the Book

There are no code listings, other than some markup used to capture API design details. You don't need to be a software developer to take advantage of the process and techniques described in this book. It doesn't dive into a specific programming language or prescribe a specific design or development methodology.

The scope of the full API design and delivery lifecycle is big. While there are some insights provided that extend beyond API design, it is impossible for me to capture every detail and situation that could occur. Instead, this book tackles the challenges teams encounter when going from an idea to business requirements and, ultimately, to an API design.

Let's get started.

Register your copy of *Principles of Web API Design* on the InformIT site for convenient access to updates and/or corrections as they become available. To start the registration process, go to informit.com/register and log in or create an account. Enter the product ISBN (9780137355631) and click Submit. Look on the Registered Products tab for an Access Bonus Content link next to this product, and follow that link to access any available bonus materials. If you would like to be notified of exclusive offers on new editions and updates, please check the box to receive email from us.

Acknowledgments

First, I would like to thank my wife and kids who have supported me in so many ways throughout the years. Your prayers and encouragement have meant so much to me.

Special thanks to Jeff Schneider, who suggested that we should write the first enterprise Java book in 1996, before Java was enterprise. Your insights and endless hours of coaching set me on an amazing career path. Your friendship guided me along the way.

Keith Casey, thank you for inviting me to coauthor a book and deliver API workshops to people all over the world. This book wouldn't have been written without your friendship, encouragement, and insight.

Vaughn Vernon, who sent me a message years ago asking how we could collaborate, which ultimately turned into this book—thank you for inviting me on your journey.

Mike Williams, who encouraged me to risk it all to realize my dreams, you have been an inspiration and a great friend.

A special thank you to the many reviewers of this book. Your dedication to reviewing the chapters, often under a time crunch, to help produce this book is appreciated: Mike Amundsen, Brian Conway, Adam DuVander, Michael Hibay, Arnaud Lauret, Emmanuel Paraskakis, Matthew Reinbold, Joyce Stack, Vaughn Vernon, and Olaf Zimmermann.

To all API evangelists and influencers, thank you for the personal and professional discussions. Here are just a few of the many people I've had the pleasure of meeting: Tony Blank, Mark Boyd, Lorinda Brandon, Chris Busse, Bill Doerfeld, Marsh Gardiner, Dave Goldberg, Jason Harmon, Kirsten Hunter, Kin Lane, Matt McLarty, Mehdi Medjaoui, Fran Mendez, Ronnie Mitra, Darrel Miller, John Musser, Mandy Whaley, Jeremy Whitlock, and Rob Zazueta. And to those on the Slack channel, thanks for your support!

I would like to acknowledge everyone at Pearson who supported me throughout the process. Haze Humbert, thank you for making this process as easy as it can be for an author. And thank you to the entire production team: your hard work is greatly appreciated.

Finally, to my mom, thank you for spending endless hours at the library while I researched computer programming books before I was old enough to drive.

About the Author

James Higginbotham is a software developer and architect with over twenty-five years of experience in developing and deploying apps and APIs. He guides enterprises through their digital transformation journey, ensuring alignment between business and technology through product-based thinking to deliver a great customer experience. James engages with teams and organizations to help them align their business, product, and technology strategies into a more composable and modular enterprise platform. James also delivers workshops that help cross-functional teams to apply an API design-first approach using his ADDR process. His industry experience includes banking, commercial insurance, hospitality, travel, and the airline industry where he helped to get an airline off the ground—literally. You can learn more about his latest efforts at https://launchany.com and on Twitter @launchany.

Part I

Introduction to Web API Design

APIs are forever. Once an API is integrated into a production application, it is difficult to make significant changes that could potentially break those existing integrations. Design decisions made in haste become future areas of confusion, support issues, and lost opportunities far into the future. The API design phase is an important part of any delivery schedule.

Part 1 examines the fundamentals of software design and how it produces a positive or negative impact on API design. It then examines the API first design process and presents an overview of an API design process. This process incorporates an outside-in perspective to deliver an effective API to meet the needs of customers, partners, and the workforce.

Chapter 1

The Principles
of API Design

All architecture is design, but not all design is architecture. Architecture represents the set of significant design decisions that shape the form and the function of a system.

— Grady Booch

Organizations have been delivering APIs for decades. APIs started as libraries and components shared across an organization and sold by third parties. They then grew into distributed components using standards such as CORBA for distributed object integration and SOAP for integrating distributed services across organizations. These standards were designed for interoperability but lacked the elements of effective design, often requiring months of effort to successfully integrate them.

As these standards were replaced by Web APIs, only a few APIs were needed. Teams could take the time to properly design them, iterating as needed. This is no longer the case. Organizations deliver more APIs and at greater velocity than ever before. The reach of Web APIs goes beyond a few internal systems and partners.

Today's Web-based APIs connect organizations to their customers, partners, and workforce using the standards of the Web. Hundreds of libraries and frameworks exist to make it cheap and fast to deliver APIs to a marketplace or for internal use. Continuous integration and continuous delivery (CI/CD) tools make it easier than ever to build automation pipelines to ensure APIs are delivered with speed and efficiency.

Yet, the biggest challenge for today's API programs continues to be successfully designing APIs that can be understood and integrated by developers in a consistent and scalable fashion. Facing this challenge requires organizations to recognize that Web APIs are more than just technology. Just as works of art require the balance of color and light, API design benefits from the blending of business capabilities, product thinking, and a focus on developer experience.

The Elements of Web API Design

An organization's collection of APIs provides a view into what the business values in the marketplace. The design quality of its APIs provides a view into how the business values developers. Everything an API offers—and doesn't offer—speaks volumes about what an organization cares most about. Effective Web API design incorporates three important elements: business capabilities, product thinking, and developer experience.

Business Capabilities

Business capabilities describe the enablers an organization brings to market. They may include external-facing capabilities, such as unique product design, amazing customer service, or optimized product delivery. They may also include internally facing capabilities such as sales pipeline management or credit risk assessment.

Organizations deliver business capabilities in three ways: directly by the organization, outsourced via a third-party provider, or through a combination of organizational and third-party processes.

For example, a local coffee shop may choose to sell custom coffee blends. To do so, it sources coffee beans through a third-party distributor, roasts the coffee beans in-house, then utilizes a third-party point-of-sale (POS) system for selling its coffee blends in a retail store. By outsourcing some of the necessary business capabilities to specialized third parties, the coffee shop is able to focus on delivering specific business capabilities that differentiate them from others in the marketplace.

APIs digitize the business capabilities that an organization brings to a marketplace. When embarking on designing a new API or expanding an existing API, the underlying business capabilities should be well understood and reflected into the API design.

Product Thinking

Organizations were integrating with partners and customers prior to the growth of Web APIs. The challenge most organizations face, however, is that each integration has been custom made. For each new partner or customer integration, a dedicated team consisting of developers, a project manager, and an account manager were tasked with building a custom integration. This involved tremendous effort and was often repeated, with per-partner customizations.

The growth of the software-as-a-service (SaaS) business model, along with the increase in demand for Web APIs, have shifted the discussion from one-off integration with partners and customers to a focus on product thinking.

Applying product thinking to the API design process shifts the team focus from a single customer or partner to an effective API design that is able to handle new automation opportunities with little to no customization effort for a given customer segment. It also enables a self-service model for workforce, business-to-business, and customer-driven integration.

The focus of an API product becomes less on custom implementations and more on meeting market needs in a scalable and cost-effective way. Reusable APIs emerge from considering multiple consumers at once. When embarking on the design of a new API, use a product thinking approach to obtain feedback from multiple parties that will consume the API. Doing so will shape the API design early and lead to increased opportunities for reuse.

Developer Experience

User experience (UX) is the discipline of meeting the exact needs of users, from their interactions with the company to their interactions with its services and with the product itself. Developer experience (DX) is just as important for APIs as UX is for products and services. The DX focuses on the various aspects of engagement with developers for an API product. It extends beyond the operational details of the API. It also includes all aspects of the API product, from first impressions to day-to-day usage and support.

A great DX is essential to the success of an API. When a great DX is delivered, developers quickly and confidently consume a Web API. It also improves the market traction of productized APIs by moving developers from being integrators to becoming experts on the API. The expertise translates directly into the ability to deliver real value to their customers and their business quickly and with reduced effort.

As API teams seek to understand how to design a great experience for their API, remember that DX is an important factor for internal developers, also. For example, great documentation enables internal developers to understand and consume an API quickly, whereas an API that has poor documentation requires contacting the internal team responsible for the API to learn how to use it properly. While they may be able to gain direct access to the developers that designed and implemented an API, it adds unnecessary communication overhead. Internal developers benefit from great DX because they can create business value faster.

CASE STUDY
APIs and Product Thinking Meets Banking

Capital One started its API journey in 2013 with the goal of developing an enterprise API platform. The initial set of platform APIs focused on delivering automation throughout the organization to increase velocity of delivery while breaking down siloed barriers.

As the number of digital capabilities in its API platform grew, Capital One's focus shifted from internal APIs to several product opportunities in the marketplace. It launched its public-facing developer portal called DevExchange at South by Southwest (SXSW)[1] with several API products. These product offerings included bank-grade authorization, a rewards program, credit card prequalification, and even an API to create new savings accounts.

Capital One extended the idea further by leveraging its digital capabilities to develop an omnichannel presence. APIs used to power its Web site and mobile app formed a foundation for a voice-based interactive experience[2] using Amazon's Alexa platform and interactive chat using a chatbot named Eno (the word *one* spelled backwards).

Taking a product-based approach to its APIs, along with a robust API portfolio of digital capabilities, allowed Capital One to explore opportunities with its customers and partners. It didn't happen overnight, but it did happen because of an API focus that started with an executive vision and execution by the entire organization.

API Design Is Communication

When developers think of software design, thoughts of classes, methods, functions, modules, and databases likely spring to mind. UML sequence and activity diagrams, or simple box and arrow diagrams if preferred, are used to convey understanding across a codebase. All these elements are part of the communication process development teams use for understanding and future developer onboarding.

---

1. "Capital One DevExchange at SxSW 2017," March 27, 2017, https://www.youtube.com/watch?v=4Cg9B4yaNVk

2. "Capital One Demo of Alexa Integration at SXSW 2016," September 6, 2016, https://www.youtube.com/watch?v=KgVcVDUSvU4&t=36s

Likewise, API design is a communication process. Rather than communicating inwardly between the members of a single team, APIs shift the communication outward. The lines of communication are extended in three distinct ways:

1. **Communication across network boundaries:** An API's design, including its choice of protocol, has an impact on the chattiness of the API. Network protocols, such as HTTP, are better for coarse-grained communication. Other protocols, such as Message Queuing Telemetry Transport (MQTT) and Advanced Message Queuing Protocol (AMQP), often used for messaging APIs, are better suited for fine-grained communication within a defined network boundary. The API design reflects the frequency of communication between systems and the impact it may have on performance because of network boundaries and bottlenecks. The API design process has a heavy impact on performance of the client and server.

2. **Communication with consuming developers:** API design and associated documentation are the user interface for developers. They inform developers how and when they are able to use each API operation. They also determine whether and how developers can combine operations to achieve more complex results. Communication early and often during the API design process is essential to meet the needs of developers consuming the API.

3. **Communication to the marketplace:** API design and documentation inform prospective customers, partners, and internal developers what outcomes the APIs make possible through the digital capabilities they offer. Effective API design helps to communicate and enable these digital capabilities.

API design is an important part of communication. An API design process helps us to consider these aspects of communication during the design phase.

Reviewing the Principles of Software Design

Software design focuses on the organization and communication of software components within a codebase. Techniques such as code comments, sequence diagrams, and the judicious use of design patterns help improve the communication effort among team members.

Web API design builds on these principles of software design, but with a broader audience that extends beyond the team or organization. The scope of communication expands beyond a single team or organization to developers all over the world. Yet, the same principles of software design apply to Web-based

API design: modularization, encapsulation, loose coupling, and high cohesion. While these may be subjects familiar to most developers, they are fundamental to API design and need review before approaching any API design process.

Modularization

Modules are the smallest atomic unit within a software program. They are composed of one or more source files that contain classes, methods, or functions. Modules have a local, public API to expose the functionality and business capabilities that they offer to other modules within the same codebase. Modules are sometimes referred to as *components* or *code libraries*.

Most programming languages support modules through the use of namespaces or packages that group code together. Grouping related code that collaborates into the same namespace encourages high cohesion. Internal details of a module are protected through access modifiers provided by the programming language. For example, the Java programming language has keywords such as `public`, `protected`, `package`, and `private` that help to encourage loose coupling through limited exposure of a module.

As more and more modules are combined, a software system is created. A subsystem combines modules into a larger module in more complex solutions, as shown in Figure 1.1.

Applying the same concepts of modularization to Web-based API design helps to reveal the boundaries and responsibilities of every API. This ensures clear responsibilities across complementary APIs that focus on externalizing digital capabilities while hiding the internal implementation details. Consuming developers benefit by understanding the API quickly and effectively.

Encapsulation

Encapsulation seeks to hide the internal details of a component. Scope modifiers are used to limit access to a module's code. A module exposes a set of public methods or functions while hiding the internal details of the module. Internal changes may

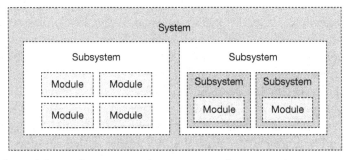

Figure 1.1 *Modules combine into ever-larger units, resulting in a software system.*

occur without impacting other modules that depend on its public methods. Sometimes encapsulation is referred to as *information hiding,* a concept applied to software development since the 1970s by David Parnas.

Web APIs extend this concept a bit further. They hide the internal details of programming language, choice of Web framework, the classes and objects of a system, and database design behind an HTTP-based API. Internal details, encapsulated behind the API design, encourage a loosely coupled API design that depends on messages rather than underlying database design and models for communication. No longer do organizations need to understand all the internal implementations details, such as for a payment gateway. Instead, they only need to understand the operations that the API offers and how to use them to achieve the desired outcomes.

High Cohesion and Loose Coupling

High cohesion is a term used when the code within a module is all closely related to the same functionality. A highly cohesive module results in less "spaghetti code," as method calls aren't jumping all over the codebase. When code is scattered across the entire codebase, calls frequently jump across modules and back again. This style of code is considered to exhibit low cohesion.

Coupling is the degree of interdependence between two or more components. Tightly coupled components indicates that the components are very constrained by the implementation details of the other. Loosely coupled components hide the components' internal details away from others, restricting the knowledge between modules to a public interface, or programming language API, that other areas of the code can invoke.

Figure 1.2 demonstrates the concepts of high cohesion and loose coupling within and across modules.

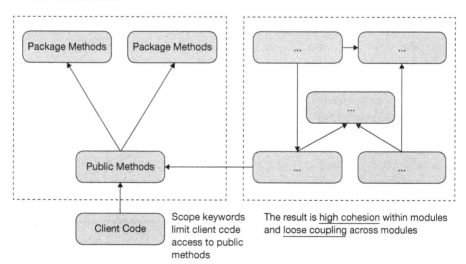

Figure 1.2 *Loose coupling and high cohesion are fundamentals of modular API design.*

Web APIs extend these concepts by grouping related API operations for high cohesion while ensuring that the internal details are encapsulated to encourage a loosely coupled API design.

Resource-Based API Design

A resource is a digital representation of a concept, often an entity or collection of entities that may change over time. It consists of a unique name or identifier that can reference documents, images, collections of other resources, or a digital representation of anything in the real world such as a person or thing. Resources may even represent business processes and workflows.

Resource-based APIs focus on interactions across a network, independent of how they are stored in a database or manifested as objects. They offer different operations, or affordances, as possible interactions with a specific resource. In addition, resources support multiple representations that allow a Web app, mobile app, and reporting tool to interact with the resource using different media formats such as JSON or XML.

Resources Are Not Data Models

It is important to recognize that resources are not the same thing as a data model that resides with a database. The data model, often reflected as a schema design in a database, is optimized for the read and write interactions necessary to support the required I/O performance and reporting needs of a solution.

While data may be part of an API, the data model should not be used as the basis of API design. Data models meet a specific set of requirements, including read and write performance, optimized data storage, and optimized query support. Data models are optimized for the internal details of an application.

Like the choice of programming languages and frameworks, the choice of database types and vendors changes over time. APIs designed to directly map to a data or object model expose these internal implementation details to API consumers. The result is a more fragile API that must introduce significant design changes when the data model changes.

Web API design seeks to achieve a different set of goals, including delivering outcomes and experiences, optimized network access, and programming language independence. Because APIs involve integration between systems, they should remain stable over a long period of time, whereas data models may change to accommodate new or changing data access requirements.

While APIs may have an impact on the data model, an API design should evolve independently from the latest database trends.

What Happens When Teams Expose a Data Model as an API?

Constant code changes: Database schema changes will result in a constantly changing API, as the API must keep in lockstep with the underlying database. This change to the data model forces consumers into a complex conformist relationship in which they must rewrite their API integration code every time the underlying data model changes. This hindrance may be overcome by an anticorruption layer that isolates a unit of code from these changes. However, the constant flux of the API creates a high cost of development as downstream developers maintain the anticorruption layer.

Create network chattiness: Exposing link tables as separate API endpoints causes API "chattiness," as the consumer is forced to make multiple API calls, one for each table. It is similar to how an n+1 query problem degrades database performance. While an n+1 problem can be a performance bottleneck for databases, API chattiness has a devastating impact on API performance.

Data inconsistencies: Not only does performance suffer from network chattiness, but the n+1 problem also results in data inconsistencies. Clients are forced to make multiple API calls and stitch the results together into a single unified view. This may result in incomplete or corrupted data due to inconsistent reads, perhaps across transactional boundaries, that occur from multiple API requests necessary to obtain necessary data.

Confuse API details: Columns optimized for query performance, such as a `CHAR(1)` column that uses character codes to indicate status, become meaningless to API consumers without additional clarification.

Expose sensitive data: Tools that build APIs that mirror a data model expose all columns with a table using `SELECT * FROM [table name]`. This also exposes data that API consumers should never see, such as personally identifiable information (PII). It may also expose data that helps hackers compromise systems through a better understanding of the internal details of the API.

Resources Are Not Object or Domain Models

API resources are not the same as objects in an object-oriented codebase. Objects support collaboration within a codebase. Objects are often used to map data models into code for easier manipulation. They suffer from the same issues as exposed data models: constant code changes, network chattiness, and data inconsistencies.

Likewise, domain models, typically comprised of objects, represent the specific business domain. They may be used in a variety of ways to address the needs of the system. They may even traverse different transactional contexts based on how they are applied. Web APIs, however, are most effective when they take transactional boundaries into consideration rather than directly exposing internal domain or object model behavior.

Keep in mind that API consumers don't have the luxury of seeing the details of a data model and all the code behind an API. They didn't sit in on the endless meetings that resulted in the multitude of decisions that drove a data model design. They don't have the context of why data model design decisions were made. Great API designs avoid leaking internal details, including database design choices, by shifting from data design to message design.

Resource-Based APIs Exchange Messages

Resource-based APIs create a conversation between the business and a user or remote system. For example, suppose a user of a project management application was conversing with the API server. The conversation may look something like what's shown in Figure 1.3.

Does it seem strange to think about APIs as a chat session? It isn't far off from what Alan Kay originally intended when he coined the term *object-oriented programming*. Rather than a focus on inheritance and polymorphic design, he envisioned object-oriented programming as sending messages between components:

> I'm sorry that I long ago coined the term "objects" for this topic because it gets many people to focus on the lesser idea.
> The big idea is "messaging."[3]

Like Kay's original vision for object-oriented programming, Web APIs are message based. They send request messages to a server and receive a response message as a result. Most Web APIs perform this message exchange synchronously by sending a request and waiting for the response.

API design considers the conversational message exchange between systems to produce desired outcomes by customers, partners, and the workforce. A great API design also considers how this communication evolves as requirements change.

---

3. Alan Kay, "Prototypes vs Classes was: Re: Sun's HotSpot," Squeak Developer's List, October 10, 1998, http://lists.squeakfoundation.org/pipermail/squeak-dev/1998-October/017019.html.

Figure 1.3 *An example interaction between an API client and API server, as if the user was talking to the server in conversational terms.*

The Principles of Web API Design

An API design approach must include a balance between robust digital capabilities and a focus on a great developer experience that supports quick and easy integration. It must be rooted in a series of principles that create a solid foundation. These five principles establish the necessary foundation and are detailed throughout this book:

> **Principle 1:** APIs should never be designed in isolation. Collaborative API design is essential for a great API. (Chapter 2)

Principle 2: API design starts with an outcome-based focus. A focus on the outcome ensures the API delivers value to everyone. (Chapters 3–6)

Principle 3: Select the API design elements that match the need. Trying to find the perfect API style is a fruitless endeavor. Instead, seek to understand and apply the API elements appropriate for the need, whether that is REST, GraphQL, gRPC, or an emerging style just entering the industry. (Chapters 7–12)

Principle 4: API documentation is the most important user interface for developers. Therefore, API documentation should be first class and not left as a last-minute task. (Chapter 13)

Principle 5: APIs are forever, so plan accordingly. Thoughtful API design combined with an evolutionary design approach makes APIs resilient to change. (Chapter 14)

Summary

Web API design incorporates three important elements to deliver a successful API: business capabilities, product thinking, and developer experience. These cross-functional disciplines mean that organizations cannot ignore the process of API design. Developers, architects, domain experts, and product managers must work together to design APIs that meet the needs of the marketplace.

In addition, Web API design builds on the principles of software design, including modularization, encapsulation, loose coupling, and high cohesion. API designs should hide the internal details of the systems they externalize. They should not expose underlying data models but rather focus on a system-to-system message exchange that is both flexible in design and resilient to change over time.

So, how do teams go from business requirements to an API design that is evolvable while delivering the desired outcomes to customers, partners, and the internal workforce? That is the subject of the next chapter, which introduces a process that bridges business and product requirements into an API design. The process is explored in detail in subsequent chapters.

Chapter 2

Collaborative API Design

Big design up front is dumb but doing no design up front is even dumber.

— Dave Thomas

An API design that looks good to the designer may not be the best design to solve the problems at hand. The initial assumptions about an API design may be incorrect as the API encounters the real world of customer, partner, and workforce needs.

API contract design is a separate and critical step of software delivery. Following an API design process encourages communication internally within the organization and externally between the organization and the developers ultimately tasked with integrating the API. It helps to identify incorrect assumptions and validate the assumptions that are correct. Finally, it encourages collaboration between API designers and the developers that will integrate the API.

This chapter presents a design process that is flexible to meet the needs of a single API product or mid- to large-scale enterprise API platform. Organizations from as small as 10 employees to those with a staff of more than 10,000 developers have used this collaborative design process. Ultimately, it delivers business value with a customer-centric focus by applying outside-in design using the five principles outlined in Chapter 1, "The Principles of API Design."

Why an API Design Process?

Before presenting the design process overview, it is important to recognize that teams can design and deliver an API successfully without the need for a formal API design process. I have worked with many companies across the world that have managed to deliver an API into production without any kind of consistent approach to API design. However, the APIs they produced took longer to deliver, as they required multiple iterations of breaking design changes. The APIs that weren't properly designed lacked sufficient insights into how to use the API compared to those designed with an API design process.

An API design process encourages efficiency throughout the delivery process. By focusing on the API contract first, the design represents the needs of users and developers as a primary concern. Also, implementation details are less likely to leak into the API design, resulting in a fragile API design that must introduce breaking changes as implementation details change over time.

A backend API is the primary blocker for any frontend delivery schedule. If frontend developers are forced to wait until the backend developers have completed the API implementation, the end-to-end delivery process will take too long. Any errors in design won't be identified until the frontend developers start to integrate the API. Customer feedback isn't available until all of the integration work has been completed. Figure 2.1 visualizes this problem and the impact it has on the delivery schedule.

An API design process encourages an iterative, team-oriented design effort that allows for greater overall efficiency. The frontend and backend API teams work together to arrive at a design, then parallelize their specific tasks. Customer feedback may be incorporated earlier as well, avoiding last-minute rework efforts. As depicted in Figure 2.2, the process is repeated for each release, ensuring the design process becomes more rapid while incorporating feedback iteratively. Remember that the sooner that API design mistakes are caught, the cheaper they are to fix.

API Design Process Antipatterns

Failing to adopt an API design process or adopting a process that is less than effective can lead to the antipatterns that result in negative impacts for the team and the entire organization. Review the common API design antipatterns detailed here and see if any of them resonate.

The Leaky Abstraction Antipattern

API designers without a formal API design process will start with code and work backward into an API design. The API design will incorporate internal technology decisions, sometimes to the point of requiring familiarity with a particular database or cloud vendor.

For example, a public API product for a recommendation engine required the understanding of Apache Lucene to use the API. The API accepts configuration files via an HTTP POST using the Lucene configuration file format to manage the

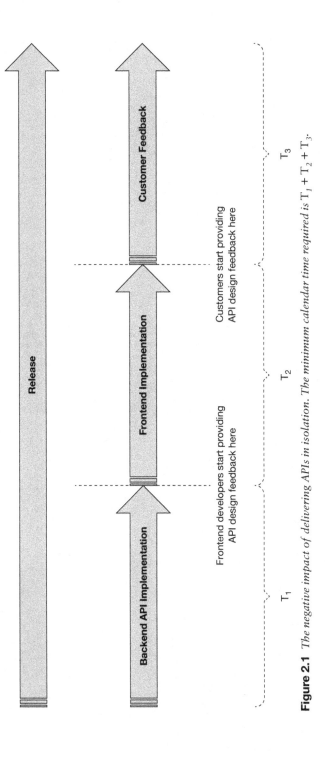

Figure 2.1 *The negative impact of delivering APIs in isolation. The minimum calendar time required is $T_1 + T_2 + T_3$.*

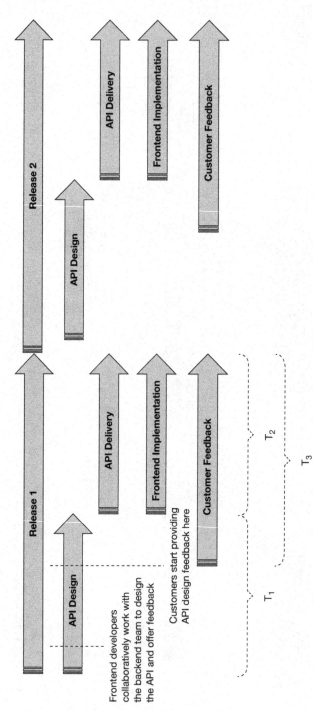

Figure 2.2 *The positive impact of delivering APIs with a design process that optimizes for efficiency and repeatability. The minimum calendar time required is* $T_1 + max(T_2 + T_3)$.

recommendation engine. The leaking of internal implementation details to API consumers resulted in the need to become Apache Lucene experts rather than experts in using the recommendation engine API.

There is value in prototyping APIs or producing evolutionary API design through a mixture of code and design. However, this approach requires a focused effort to find the right balance of prototyping, followed by an outside-in design effort that incorporates the lessons learned. An effective API design process supports this iterative learning approach.

The Next Release Design Fix Antipattern

Teams without an API design process may find themselves already planning the next API release, perhaps before the current version has been pushed to production. This is a result of API design decisions that become unchangeable with the current release. Design improvements that would result in breaking changes get moved as technical debt to the backlog.

This antipattern starts as an innocent design decision due to the complexity of the underlying code change. Perhaps the code change will take too long. Teams are forced to push an inadequate API design into production and support it for the foreseeable future. The needed change can be something as small as a spelling mistake or a minor typo that has to remain part of the API to avoid introducing a breaking change to a large number of developers.

An API design process, combined with an API stability contract, as discussed in Chapter 14, "Designing for Change," can mitigate this kind of problem.

The Heroic Design Effort Antipattern

Those more familiar with the business domain incorporate their understanding of customer and market needs to deliver an API that meets the needs of their target market. This approach may work well for small teams with a deep understanding of the customer and the market.

However, it doesn't offer a predictable way to engage in emerging areas where subject matter expertise is in short supply, resulting in the need for heroic API design efforts. Long days of chaotic development that are filled with multiple design changes per day during the march to production are the signs of the heroic design effort antipattern. Last-minute calls with pilot customers that result in discovering significant design flaws are commonplace. Teams scramble to find a design solution that addresses the flaws before the release. Code is quickly patched to "make it work" with the limited time available.

While an API design process does not guarantee a perfect design the first time, it helps challenge assumptions quickly. It also encourages early communication with subject matter experts and customers to address flawed design issues before they are too expensive to rectify.

The Unused API Antipattern

Teams do not want their project to be considered a failure, or worse, to languish with little to no use in production. Yet, this is often the case, as API designs may miss the underlying goals and desires of the target audience. An API may be released to great fanfare, only to languish with few, if any, integrations. When an integration is finally started, bugs are encountered due to brittleness of the design and implementation. Rather than designing in isolation, an API design process should encourage validation early and often from stakeholders to avoid an API going unused.

The API Design-First Approach

An API design process is a predictable method of moving from business requirements to an API design. The goal of API design is to make it easier to discover, integrate, and deploy solutions in a way that is scalable for the organization and external parties.

An API design-first approach is important, as APIs last forever. Once an API has at least one integration in production, it is nearly impossible to migrate consumers to the next version of an API.

Taking an API design-first approach starts by identifying the capabilities to deliver, then moves toward an API design to meet the desired outcomes—all before writing a line of production code.

Of course, reality doesn't work exactly in this way. Code and data may already exist and must be leveraged from an existing system. API design-first doesn't require strict adherence to a greenfield process that assumes no preexisting code or data. It should, however, emphasize the API design effort as a separate and critical step of software delivery.

An API design-first approach has five rapidly executed, iterative phases, as shown in Figure 2.3:

1. **Discover:** Determine the digital capabilities the API needs to deliver, searching for APIs that may already exist to meet the requirements.

2. **Design:** Produce an initial API design or improve an existing API design to address the digital capabilities required but not available.

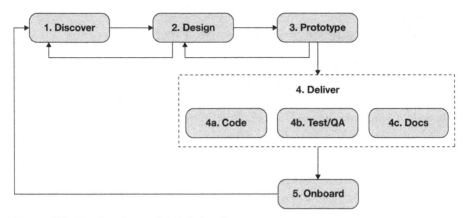

Figure 2.3 *The five phases of API design-first*

3. **Prototype:** Produce a prototype or mock API to gain feedback from stakeholders regarding the current design. Revisit previous steps based on the feedback.

4. **Deliver:** Deliver the API through a parallelized effort across developers, quality assurance, operations, and documentation teams. API capabilities are released iteratively rather than through a single release, driven by the agreed-upon API design.

5. **Onboard:** Ensure customers, partners, and/or internal developers are onboard with the API, integrating it with their solutions. Support is critical at this stage to help teams with complex integration needs.

Notice the iterative design process that occurs as stakeholder input is gathered. Feedback is incorporated early and often, making design changes along the way. This results in an API contract, which provides the specific details of how the design is realized. Prototypes or mock implementations demonstrate the API in action, prior to the full delivery process. Once delivery begins, the effort is parallelized across all teams, with the API contract as the primary communication artifact. After developers are onboarded with the API, additional feedback results in a new design effort.

> ### Principle 1: APIs should never be designed in isolation
> Collaborative API design is essential for a great API. Both technical and nontechnical participants should be involved throughout the API design process. Leaving the API design effort only to development teams will greatly reduce the chances of maximizing the API's potential.

Remaining Agile with API Design-First

An API design-first approach is focused on frequent feedback and opportunities to make adjustments throughout the design and delivery process. An API design-first approach does not specify that all design work must be complete before proceeding into code. To understand how, it is time to revisit the Agile Manifesto and see how it can be applied to an API design-first approach.

The Agile Manifesto Revisited

A quick review of the Agile Manifesto principles helps to help us to better understand how API design-first fits with agile development. Following are a few principles relevant to the concerns of API design-first:[1]

- Our highest priority should be to satisfy the customer.
- We should welcome changing requirements, even late in development.
- We must strive to deliver working software frequently.
- Business people and developers must work together daily.
- Working software is the primary measure of progress.
- Be attentive to technical excellence and good design, as this enhances agility.
- Seek the simple by maximizing the amount of work not done.

Keeping these principles in mind, teams have the opportunity to remain agile while communicating early and often with stakeholders on the API design. These stakeholders may include internal development teams, channel partners, and the developers tasked with integrating the API.

Delivering an API design progressively, rather than all at once, allows teams to meet the principle of welcoming changing requirements and delivering working software frequently. It also helps teams avoid last-minute scrambles that can negatively impact API design.

The "seek the simple" principle encourages teams to design in a simple way. Teams should design an API that avoids clever designs that require a higher cognitive load to understanding. Instead, designs should be intuitive based on the use cases it addresses and should use vocabulary that is appropriate for the solution domain. They should offer only the necessary information to support the use case.

---

1. Kent Beck, et al., "Principles behind the Agile Manifesto," https://agilemanifesto.org/principles.html.

The Agility of API Design-First

The goal of API design-first should be to gather sufficient details to limit the risk of a breaking change in the future. It doesn't mandate that an entire design process must be completed before development begins. Agile development and API design-first make terrific companions.

> **Remember**
>
> Teams can always add to an API design, but it is impossible to take things away without breaking integrations that depend on them. Take advantage of agile software development to incrementally design APIs with the needs of customers, partners, and the workforce in mind.

An API design-first process enables teams to move quickly, thoughtfully, and with the agility to make changes early in the process. It is the complete opposite of a waterfall approach to API design.

The Align-Define-Design-Refine Process

One of the biggest challenges most API design teams encounter is how to deliver an API design from business requirements in any variety of forms: use cases, spreadsheets, wireframes, and so on. Those with a background in software business analysis may find this to be an easier task. However, there are still challenges when it comes to mapping a domain model and capabilities into a Web-based API design. One of those challenges is the need to ensure alignment of scope and deliverables among all technical and nontechnical team members.

As the name suggests, the Align-Define-Design-Refine (ADDR) process[2] guides teams through an API design-first approach. The process groups the step-by-step process into four distinct phases:

1. **Align:** Ensures alignment of understanding and scope across business, product, and technology around a set of desired outcomes

2. **Define:** Maps business and customer requirements into digital capabilities that will form the basis of one or more APIs to deliver the desired outcomes

---

2. The ADDR process is based on the many lessons learned during my years of experience in API design coaching.

3. **Design:** Applies specific design steps for each API to meet the desired outcomes using one or more API styles

4. **Refine:** Refines the API design through feedback from developers, in addition to documentation, prototyping, and testing efforts

There are seven steps across the phases, which are explored in-depth for the remainder of this book:

1. **Identify digital capabilities:** Identify the customer needs and desired outcomes, including the corresponding digital capabilities that are required.

2. **Capture activity steps:** Expand the digital capabilities to include a unified understanding and clarity through collaborative API design sessions.

3. **Identify API boundaries:** Group the digital capabilities into API boundaries and determine whether the APIs already exist or new APIs are required.

4. **Model API profiles:** Use a collaborative API modeling session to define the high-level API design, including resources and operations into an API profile.

5. **High-level API designs:** Select one or more API styles that each API profile will offer and document the high-level design elements.

6. **Refine the design:** Incorporate design feedback from API consumers using techniques that encourage improvement in the developer experience.

7. **Document the API:** Complete the API documentation, including reference documentation and getting started guides, to accelerate integration.

Figure 2.4 summarizes the ADDR process that supports an API design first approach.

The process achieves the following goals:

- Deliver an API design that emphasizes and solves the customer problems using a vocabulary they understand.

- Reduce the constant design churn common with informal design processes.

- Optimize the entire organization, not just developers, for API design and delivery.

- Avoid unnecessary steps whenever possible to expedite delivery.

- Create a repeatable process that delivers an API design with a mixture of technical and nontechnical roles, some of whom don't fully understand the nuances of API design but are able to contribute their insights.

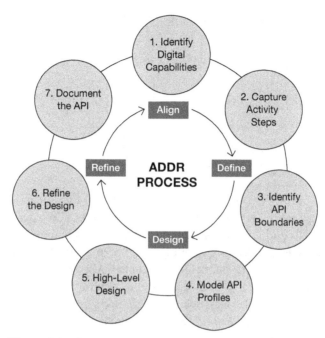

Figure 2.4 *The ADDR process overview*

- Produce artifacts that may be referenced within the team and shared across the organization rather than some scribbles on a whiteboard that fail to communicate reason and intent about the resulting API design.

These outcomes contribute to a healthy, sustainable, and successful API program. The remainder of this book examines the ADDR process in detail and applies each step using a real-world design project:

- Aligning and defining the APIs required to deliver desired outcomes based on the jobs to be done by developers and end users (Chapters 3–6)

- Designing APIs that help meet the desired outcomes of the target audience using the appropriate API styles along with common patterns and practices (Chapters 7–9)

- Decomposing APIs into smaller services to shift complexity when needed (Chapter 10)

- Improving the developer experience through a combination of robust documentation, helper libraries, command-line interfaces, and testing strategy to ensure consumers get up and running quickly and with confidence (Chapters 11–13)

- Evolving the API design, which is critical to sustainable, long-lived APIs (Chapter 14)

- Protecting APIs to ensure that data is not leaked to unauthorized parties (Chapter 15)

- Scaling the API design effort, which is important for larger initiatives (Chapter 16)

The Role of DDD in API Design

As mentioned, an API design process should emphasize and solve the customers' problems using a vocabulary they understand. This requires a deep understanding of how the API will address market and customer needs, combined with business strategy. If the design and development of an API occurs without factoring in these concerns, it will often miss the mark for being a great API that is a joy to use.

Domain-driven design (DDD) is an approach to software development that encourages collaboration between business domain experts and software developers to address complex solutions. DDD's core principles include discussion, listening, understanding, discovery, and delivering differentiating, strategic business value. Every member of the team across technical and nontechnical roles contributes to the insightful depth of business innovations in the software solutions. Those new to DDD may wish to refer to the seminal book on DDD by Eric Evans[3] and Vaughn Vernon's *Implementing Domain-Driven Design,*[4] which provides insights on implementing DDD in an organization.

The ADDR process is built loosely on concepts and practices found in DDD. However, organizations do not need to be practicing DDD, or even familiar with it, to be effective at applying the process. Those familiar with DDD may recognize some of the concepts and techniques used. However, it is important to recognize that the ADDR process may deviate from DDD practices when necessary to ensure that it remains approachable and repeatable in a variety of situations. As such, those familiar with DDD may wish to make adjustments to the process to best fit their needs and preferences.

API Design Involves Everyone

Most software development involves several people across a variety of roles. Business leaders and product owners analyze market needs. Software architects and technical leads map out the important design decisions for the solution.

---

3. Eric Evans, *Domain-Driven Design: Tackling Complexity in the Heart of Software* (Boston: Addison-Wesley, 2003).

4. Vaughn Vernon, *Implementing Domain-Driven Design* (Boston: Addison-Wesley, 2013).

Developers design and write the code that makes it all work. Designers and user experience (UX) experts pull everything together as a user interface, with an eye toward usability.

Each person contributes their experience and can leverage their strengths and skills as part of the API design process. For smaller organizations, a single person may be required to fill multiple roles. Whenever possible, assign the more technical roles separately from the product and business roles to ensure a healthy balance of perspectives when designing APIs.

The roles typically involved in API design sessions may include, but are not limited to, the following:

- **API designers and architects** help facilitate the design process and bring in API design expertise.

- **Subject matter experts (SMEs) and domain experts** help to clarify requirements and shape the vocabulary used in API design.

- **Technical leads** are responsible for guiding implementation efforts and may require additional clarifying questions for estimation purposes.

- **Product managers** incorporate market opportunities and customer needs into the API design.

- **Technical writers** ask clarifying questions during scope and design sessions that will impact the capabilities delivered and drive the production of API documentation and getting started guides.

- **Scrum Masters and project managers** provide input to assist in scheduling and identifying risks.

- **QA teams** can provide input on designing testable APIs, determine how and when to test Web APIs, and design test plans in parallel with development efforts.

- **Infrastructure and operations** ensure network, server, container platforms, message brokers, streaming platforms, and other necessary resources are available for the teams that are building and consuming APIs.

- **Security teams** review API designs for personally identifiable information (PII) and nonpublic information (NPI) concerns, identify risks, limit the surface area of attacks, and help to design APIs that will access sensitive data.

An API design process integrates perspectives from each of these roles to align the business with development teams, define the clear goals and outcomes of an API, and design the API to meet the defined goals. Upcoming chapters explore this process in further detail.

Applying the Process Effectively

The ADDR process may be integrated with any existing process. However, be prepared that some steps may seem uncertain or awkward at first. Over time, the processes will become more familiar, and the labor will be rewarded. Give the organization time to become familiar with the process. It may also be useful to spend time listing previous challenges and how the process seeks to address them.

Organizations may wish to incorporate this process incrementally. In this case, it is recommended to start with identifying the activities and steps needed for an API, as detailed in Chapter 4, "Capture Activities and Steps," then proceed with Chapter 6, "API Modeling." Additional steps may be introduced over time as they are needed.

Summary

The design of an API's contract is a separate and critical step of software delivery. API design requires communication within the organization and with the developers using the API. It helps to course-correct wrong assumptions. It also encourages communication between business, product, and technology teams.

An API design-first approach takes an outside-in perspective on the design of an API by focusing on the customers and developers who are building the solution. Combined with design techniques that take a bottom-up approach, APIs will have a more balanced design that both reflects the domain and the needs of customers and developers. An API design process requires a variety of roles that help to align, define, and design the capabilities and outcomes that APIs will provide.

With the introduction to the art and fundamentals of API design complete, it is time to dive into the details of the ADDR process with the first phase: Align.

Part II

Aligning on API Outcomes

One of the challenges teams face when designing an API is determining how to move from business requirements into an API design. Teams want to have the confidence that the API they plan to deliver meets stakeholder needs. In addition, they want to know that business and tech teams are aligned to prevent last minute overhauls of the API design and underlying implementation.

Part 2 addresses these concerns by introducing the Align phase of the ADDR process. The process and techniques presented in Chapter 3, "Identify Digital Capabilities," and Chapter 4, "Capture Activities and Steps," guide teams through the process of translating business requirements into digital capabilities required by customers, partners, and the workforce. After teams have applied the recommended steps of the process, they will have the confidence of scope and alignment with stakeholders to proceed into defining and designing the necessary APIs.

Chapter 3

Identify Digital Capabilities

When we buy a product, we essentially "hire" it to help us do a job. If it does the job well, the next time we're confronted with the same job, we tend to hire that product again. And if it does a crummy job, we "fire" it and look for an alternative.

— Clayton M. Christensen, Taddy Hall, Karen Dillon, and
David S. Duncan

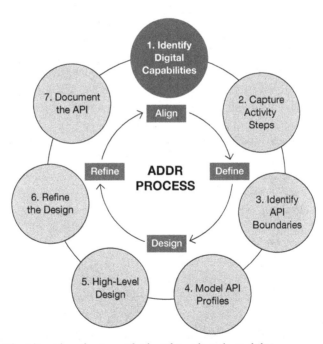

Figure 3.1 *The Align phase begins with identifying digital capabilities.*

APIs are the most common manifestation of digital capabilities, as they power Web and mobile apps, partner integrations, and workforce solutions. They allow the casual or expert developer to take advantage of data, business processes, and internal systems programmatically to produce desired outcomes. Organizations must develop the skills to identify digital capabilities (see Figure 3.1) and use them to shape the API design to help users produce results.

The ADDR process starts with defining the digital capabilities necessary to deliver customer outcomes. It also elaborates on the specific activities and steps needed to deliver the outcomes, prior to designing the APIs.

This chapter introduces the concepts of digital capabilities, explains how they relate to APIs, and outlines an approachable method for mapping requirements into a format that identifies necessary digital capabilities. These digital capabilities are then used to inform the design of product and platform APIs.

Ensuring Stakeholder Alignment

As discussed in Chapter 2, "Collaborative API Design," API design is a communication process. It communicates the digital capabilities offered by an API to external and internal developers across team and organizational boundaries. Those outside of the API-producing team that will consume the API cannot, and should not, be required to read the actual code of the API to fully understand how it works. In fact, external developers may not have access to the source code at all. Therefore, the API design and any subsequent documentation should strive to communicate with developers in the simplest way.

Effective API design incorporates the needs of customers. In this context, customers are defined as a segmented group of developers and end users whose experience will be shaped, for better or worse, by the API design. Keeping an API design in alignment with customer needs helps to deliver a great user and developer experience.

An API design that misses the mark will deliver a poor experience, often requiring significant changes that will break existing integrations. Once an API has at least one integration in production, it is very difficult to convince internal or external teams to spend the time and money necessary to upgrade to the next version of an API. This leaves no room for an API design that breaks existing integrations. Therefore, arriving at an API design that meets the needs of customers requires focused effort rather than guesswork.

Unless the organization is small enough to support direct communication between developers and customers, multiple roles often are involved with product definition: product owners, product managers, business analysts, software analysts, and account managers, to name just a few. These roles represent the needs of the customers. An effective API design includes input from many roles across the organization, not just the technical details of how to push data in and out of a data store or legacy system.

It is also necessary to create alignment between stakeholders and the development teams responsible for implementing the API. If the API lacks business context, it may meet the needs of customers but lack sufficient factors to meet business goals. If the API lacks a customer context, it may meet the needs of business but fail to deliver the desired outcomes of customers. If it lacks both, the API will serve no real purpose and efforts will have been wasted. In the ADDR process, digital capabilities are used to create alignment between business, customers, and technology to avoid these negative consequences.

What Are Digital Capabilities?

Business capabilities describe the enablers an organization brings to market. Examples of business capabilities include consumer product design, product manufacturing, and customer support.

Digital capabilities are assets that turn desired outcomes into reality through automation. They offer the workforce, partners, and customers the ability to interact with the organization digitally. Digital capabilities may take the form of one or more technology solutions. Examples include REST APIs, Webhook-based asynchronous APIs for integration, SOAP services, message streams, and bulk data exchange through a nightly, weekly, or monthly file-based export process.

Reviewing the digital capabilities offered by an in-house or competitor's product or service provides greater insights into what the organization values, including the market segments they address.

A digital capabilities portfolio is the collection of digital capabilities offered by a product or organization. For organizations building a platform to connect two or more parties within a marketplace, the terms *digital platform* and *platform capabilities* may be more familiar.

While digital capabilities may be mapped to business capabilities, they operate at different levels of concern. Business architects define business capabilities, such as customer service, and may associate key performance indicators (KPIs) or objectives and key results (OKRs) to track growth. Digital capabilities focus on producing outcomes and include the activities required to deliver the business capabilities of the organization. Business capabilities describe the "what" of the organization; digital capabilities describe the "how."

Table 3.1 *Digital Capabilities Realized by a REST-Based Project Management API*

Digital Capability	Example REST-Based API Design
Manage project from start to finish	`POST /projects`
Add collaborators to a project	`POST /projects/{projectId}/collaborators`
Subdivide a project into issues	`POST /issues`
Mark issue complete	`POST /issues/{issueId}/completed`
View incomplete issues	`GET /issues?status=incomplete`
View active projects	`GET /projects?status=active`

Table 3.1 provides an example for a typical project management application to demonstrate the differences between digital capabilities for a project management application and how they may be realized through a REST-based API.

Notice how the digital capabilities are written with a focus on customers and their desired outcomes. The choice of API design style, such as REST, GraphQL, or gRPC (detailed in Chapters 7 and 8), is not explicitly part of a digital capability but rather a part of how the digital capability is manifested. In some cases, multiple API design styles may be offered for a single digital capability.

There are a few ways that business and product requirements may be captured and used to drive the design of digital capabilities as APIs. The ADDR process recommends using job stories, which are rooted in the jobs to be done approach to design.

Focusing on the Jobs to Be Done

Jobs to be done (JTBD) are the identified needs fulfilled by a product or service offering. JTBD includes capturing how a customer problem, the task to be performed, and the desired outcome that should result.

JTBD[1] was formulated by Clayton Christensen, author of *The Innovator's Dilemma,*[2] as a method of taking the viewpoint of the customer when designing a product or service. JTBD ensures that the product addresses a specific need and therefore has a better chance of gaining market adoption. It starts by identifying the needs of customers, the job, and then defining how a product or service will fill that need.

---

1. Christen Institute, "Jobs to Be Done," accessed August 12, 2021, https://www.christenseninstitute.org/jobs-to-be-done.

2. Clayton M. Christensen, *The Innovator's Dilemma: When New Technologies Cause Great Firms to Fail* (Boston: Harvard Business Review Press, 2016).

In JTBD, jobs are more than just functions that need to be performed. Jobs are really about the desired outcome or accomplishment. Jobs may be new and unsolved or may be solved in some way that doesn't quite meet the customers' needs. A product that produces the desired outcome is one that considers all of these factors about the jobs to be done. JTBD applies to APIs as well as all other aspects of product and software design with the organization.

The idea behind JTBD is rooted in the voice of the customer (VOC)[3] from the mid-1980s, where product managers attempted to improve product performance by getting into the mindset of the customer. VOC combines market research data with specific wants and needs that have been identified through surveys and customer interviews.

Christensen also reminds us that there is an emotional and social side to the jobs that a product attempts to solve. The job extends beyond the immediate problem to include a reduction or removal of the anxiety involved. The product should provide a positive experience while producing progress toward the desired outcome. Some may even go so far as to offer enjoyment while completing the job.

> **Principle 2: API design starts with an outcome-based focus**
>
> A focus on the outcome ensures the API delivers value to everyone. This requires a product-thinking approach to API design rather than one that is driven purely by data and systems integration. The ADDR process is focused on identifying and realizing these outcomes.

What Are Job Stories?

Customers and users don't care about APIs, microservices, serverless, or the flavor of frontend framework used. They want a solution to a problem. They care about outcomes.

Job stories capture the jobs to be done for any product, including the customer motivations, events, and expectations for a new product, service, or API. They frame every design problem from the perspective of the customer. Job stories seek to identify the problems that customers have and the eventual outcome they wish to achieve. Jobs are identified that will solve these problems. APIs will offer digital capabilities that will power these JTBD to produce the desired outcome.

---

3. Wikipedia, s.v. "Voice of the Customer," last modified July 15, 2021, 12:112, https://en.wikipedia.org/wiki/Voice_of_the_customer.

Job stories were created by Alan Klement[4] and are based on JTBD formulated by Christensen. They offer a simple framework to capture all of the aspects of the job to be done.

Teams producing job stories will find that their API designs focus more on the desired outcomes of the audience. They will also have the details necessary to create acceptance criteria for automated tests. It is important to note that job stories shouldn't contain implementation specifics. Instead, they should elaborate on what needs to happen to make the necessary progress to deliver the outcome.

The ADDR process leans heavily on job stories to capture business requirements in a customer-centric way. Job stories express customer requirements in a simple format and provide a natural way to identify digital capabilities that will drive API design.

The Components of a Job Story

Job stories are composed of three components using the "When, I want to, so I can" format:

1. **When:** The *triggering event* to establish causality is the situation or reason why the customer desires the outcome. Triggering events are key indicators for when an API will be used.

2. **I want to:** The *capability* is what the customer has identified as the action that needs to be taken. The capability identifies the important role that the API will play to deliver the desired outcome. It is also used to deconstruct the operations that the API will deliver.

3. **So I can:** The *outcome* is the desired end state. It is the result of applying the capability when the triggering event occurs. The outcome drives the acceptance criteria for the API design.

Figure 3.2 shows an example Forgot Password job story, highlighting its three components.

The example job story in Figure 3.2 demonstrates how a job story may be used to inform the design of a digital capability. In this case, it captures a digital capability titled Reset My Password. This is one of many digital capabilities the API must offer to meet the needs of the target customers.

---

4. Alan Klement, "Replacing the User Story with the Job Story," JTBD.info, November 12, 2013, https://jtbd.info/replacing-the-user-story-with-the-job-story-af7cdee10c27.

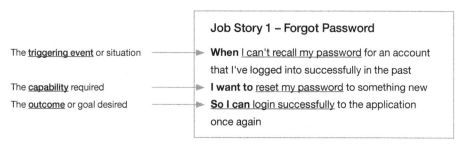

Figure 3.2 *A job story and its three components.*

Writing Job Stories for APIs

The details used to create job stories may exist in different forms. Some details may identify a problem that needs to be solved. Other details may indicate the desired outcome but lack other information.

Because there is no right or wrong way to approach creating job stories, three methods are provided here to help teams navigate the many situations that are encountered in the real world. Apply one, two, or all three methods to compose job stories that capture customer needs. Then formulate the insights into the job story format of "When, I want to, so I can."

Method 1: When the Problem Is Known

This method is the most common, as customers are usually good at identifying the problems that they need resolved. In this case, use some or all of the following questions to explore the problem space and identify the remaining two components necessary to compose the job stories:

- What is the desired outcome that the customer wish to experience to solve the problem?

- What is the job required to achieve the outcome?

- Given these two answers, does the original problem best describe the triggering situation, or is there a better way to express the problem in job story format?

Method 2: When the Desired Outcome Is Known

There are times when the desired outcome is understood, but the triggering situation is not. This may be the case when customers have a desired outcome in mind but may not be sure why they need it. Use the following questions to guide the discussion and help to formulate job stories based on their desired outcomes:

- What is the problem, as described by the customer, that drives the desired outcome?

- What is the job required to achieve the outcome? If multiple tasks are identified, summarize them into a single job description.

- Does the desired outcome still best express their need, or should it be rewritten?

Method 3: When the Digital Capability Has Been Identified

There may be times when a customer has identified the digital capability that they desire. This is common when customers are subject matter experts or have spent considerable time thinking about the problem. In this case, ask the following questions to help validate the digital capability that they identified and fill in the missing pieces of the job stories:

- What is the desired outcome that the customer wishes to experience?

- What is the problem or triggering situation that demands the outcome, as described by the customer or stakeholder?

- Does the identified digital capability help to produce the desired outcome? If not, is there a better way to word the digital capability or one better suited to solve the problem?

Overcoming Job Story Challenges

When teams begin to construct job stories, they may encounter three issues: the job stories become too detailed, they become feature centric, or they may need additional user context. All of these issues may be resolved using the suggestions that follow.

Challenge 1: Job Stories Are Too Detailed

Job stories should contain enough context to enable future deconstruction of the job story into independent tasks (more on this in Chapter 4). However, job stories may become littered with all kinds of details that will be important in the near future. This is a common occurrence when job story authors are concerned about losing track of specific details that have been previously discussed. Consider the following example that has too many details:

When *I find a product I want to buy,*

I want to *provide the quantity, color, and style of the product*

So I can *add it to my shopping cart and see the current subtotal, shipping costs, and estimated sales tax.*

When a job story contains too many details, extract the details as additional items below the job story. Doing so ensures the details are not lost and keeps the job story clear and focused. Here is the same job story, rewritten with the details moved outside of the job story narrative:

When *I find a product I want to buy,*

I want to *add the product to my shopping cart*

So I can *include it in my order.*

Additional details:

- *The following fields will be required when adding an item to a cart: quantity, color, and style.*
- *The shopping cart will then show the current subtotal, shipping costs, and estimated sales tax.*

These details can be extracted into bullet points in a document or Markdown file or added as an additional notes column in a spreadsheet.

Challenge 2: Job Stories Are Feature Centric

Those familiar with writing user stories tend to craft job stories with a focus on features rather than outcomes. This challenge may be encountered for existing products that already have a user interface or high-fidelity wireframes. Instead of focusing on the problem and desired outcome, the author of the job story immediately jumps to the solution.

The following is an example of a job story that focuses on feature details:

When *I find a product I want to buy,*

I want to *add the product to my shopping cart by clicking a yellow button*

So I can *include it in my order.*

Consider adjusting job stories that contain features into a standard job story structure. If the team is concerned about losing details about the feature in the job story, move feature details into an "additional details" section of the job story. The feature details can then be referenced at a later point in the design process.

For example:

When I find a product I want to buy,

I want to add the product to my shopping cart

So I can include it in my order.

Additional details:

- The button to add a product to a cart should be yellow.
- The label should say "Add to Cart."

Challenge 3: Additional User Context Is Needed

User stories have the benefit of the "As a" phrase used to start the story. This phrase helps to identify the persona that the user story is designed to address. However, some products may end up with a long list of user stories that start with the same prefix—for example, "As a user, . . .". If this is the case, then the persona isn't a necessary detail after all and just clutters the user story.

The job story format by default doesn't concern itself with the persona. However, there are times when the details about a persona help to shed additional context in a job story. In this case, substitute the persona name in the "I want to" clause, as demonstrated in this example:

When a decision is needed on the dates for a special sale,

A manager wants to produce a sales report with customized criteria

So the manager can view the sales history and determine the best days to run the sale.

This approach provides a nice blend between job stories and user stories.

Techniques for Capturing Job Stories

Currently, there is no tool designed specifically for capturing job stories, so teams have the flexibility to select a tool that works best for them. Following are a few recommendations, but feel free to use anything that enables communication and collaboration within and across teams.

- **Spreadsheets:** Spreadsheets are the universal tool and are quite useful for capturing job stories. One job story per row in a spreadsheet will suffice. The first column should be a job story identifier. Dedicate the next columns to each of the three components, "When," "I want to," "so I can." Finally, add a fifth column for notes. Many spreadsheets support collaborative editing, enabling multiple people to review, comment, and contribute as needed.

- **Documents:** Documents are also useful, though they are a bit less structured. They are useful when teams wish to mimic an index card style for capturing job stories. Start with a heading that indicates the job story identifier, such as a number or brief description. Place each of the three components of a job story, "When," "I want to," "so I can," on a separate line for readability. Leave room for capturing additional insights or details as a list of bulleted items. Add a blank space between each job story to help separate each one, or assign one job story per page.

- **Markdown files:** Markdown is a text file with an approachable syntax useful for capturing job stories. Markdown files may be used to export job stories into HTML, PDF, and other formats. Use a single Markdown file with all job stories, or create a Markdown file for each job story. Combine with a version control system, such as git, to view a history of changes to the job stories. Of course, this approach is targeted at teams with deeper technical expertise.

A Real-World API Design Project

To explore the API design process, a fictitious bookstore called JSON's Bookstore is used. The bookstore is a SaaS-based online book company that ships books from its warehouse to customers all over the world. This fictitious business derives from many consulting engagements I have had over the years. It opens the opportunity to better explore and apply the various concepts of API design with a real-world context. Teams will see the various challenges involved with designing APIs that are meant to support different audiences and to support operations, commerce, and partner integration. The bookstore project will also help teams explore the challenges involved with applying design techniques to existing APIs.

JSON's Bookstore must design a series of APIs to support online commerce, order fulfillment, inventory management, and catalog management. The company also needs to support integration with partners and customers. Along the way, the API surface area will increase, requiring JSON's Bookstore to find ways to manage and govern the APIs in a scalable way that doesn't slow down its development velocity.

Job Story Examples

The job stories in Table 3.1 were identified to support the shopping and purchase experience for JSON's Bookstore. As an exercise, review the job stories and try writing some additional ones to practice the job story format.

Refer to the full list of job stories using the API workshop examples[5] available on GitHub.

Summary

APIs are digital capabilities that help turn desired outcomes into reality through automation. An API designed with these outcomes will help to deliver a better API design for the target audience.

Table 3.2 *Job Stories for JSON's Bookstore*

ID	When. . .	I want to. . .	So I can. . .
1	I want to see the new books that have been released	List recently added books	Keep up with the latest watercooler talk
2	I want to find a book that will be entertaining or teach me something new	Search for a book by topic or keyword	Browse related books
3	I encounter an unfamiliar book	View a book's details and reviews	Determine if the book is of interest to me
4	I find one or more books that I wish to buy	Place an order	Buy the books and have them shipped to my preferred address
5	I am uncertain of when my order will arrive	View the status of an order	Confirm the date that the order will arrive

---

5. https://bit.ly/align-define-design-examples

Job stories offer contextual understanding of the desired outcomes and the digital capabilities that will be necessary to make them a reality. Through the process of composing job stories, a shared understanding of business and customer needs for all stakeholders is established. The more effort that is placed into composing job stories, the more likely the API will meet the needs of customers. Job stories are the first artifact needed to align all stakeholders prior to API design. The next chapter discusses how to expand job stories into the activities and activity steps that will be the foundation for API design.

Chapter 4

Capture Activities and Steps

The real story is that software developers are spending a relevant amount of their time learning, in order to do things they don't have a clue about. Differently from other professions, we're doing things for the first time, most of the time (even if it looks like the same old typing from the outside).

— Alberto Brandolini

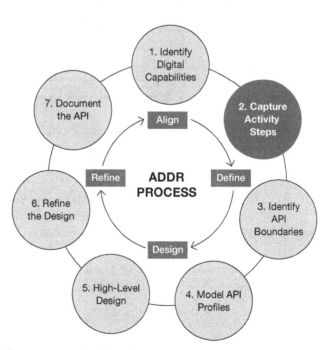

Figure 4.1 *The next step in the Align phase is to capture activity steps.*

This quote from Alberto Brandolini resonates with many teams that are faced with building software in less familiar domains. While some developers can stay in the same business vertical for most or all of their career, most do not have that luxury. Developers are required to understand a new domain quickly, translate it into software, and repeat throughout their career. They must quickly become familiar with a domain such that they are able to turn it into working software that includes user interfaces, APIs, and data models.

The ADDR process helps to bridge this gap through a series of rapid design steps. Chapter 3, "Identify Digital Capabilities," detailed the first step of the API design process through the understanding of desired outcomes. The next step is the gathering of details from stakeholders, development teams, and business domain experts to better understand the concepts, processes, and workflows of the domain.

This chapter addresses how to capture domain details and expected behavior using an activity-based structure (see Figure 4.1). It also introduces the EventStorming framework as a collaborative way to explore the domain. The result is a deeper understanding of the domain, alignment between all team members, and a foundation for defining and designing the APIs that will deliver the necessary digital capabilities.

Extending Job Stories into Activities and Steps

Creating job stories helps identify the desired outcomes along with the digital capabilities necessary to produce the outcomes. This topic was covered previously in Chapter 3. The next step is to detail the digital capabilities as the activities and activity steps required to achieve these outcomes.

An activity is work that contributes toward a desired outcome. Activities may be performed by only one participant or by a combination of multiple participants that collaborate together. A participant may be a person, an internal system, or a third-party system.

Activity steps decompose activities into individual tasks that need to be performed to complete the activity. Once all necessary activities are completed, the job story outcome will be met.

There are two quick steps to capture these details: identify the activities for each job story, then decompose each activity into individual steps. The results are then used to identify API boundaries, which is detailed in Chapter 5, "Identifying API Boundaries."

During this part of the process, all team members gain deeper understanding and alignment on the solution. If requirements are vague or uncertainty remains, the team may choose to proceed into a collaborative EventStorming session to explore the solution further. EventStorming is detailed later in this chapter.

Identify the Activities for Each Job Story

Start by identifying any activities to be performed that produce the desired outcome for each job story. The goal is to find the bigger units of work that will contribute to the outcome.

Examples of activities for the JSON's Bookstore Place an Order job story 4, identified in Table 3.2 of Chapter 3, are shown in Table 4.1.

Notice that the activities are high level and will often require one or more steps to accomplish the activity. If individual activity steps are identified during this step, go ahead and note it. Then seek to determine the activity that it belongs to and capture that as well.

Decompose Each Activity into Steps

Activities are composed of steps, with each step captured at a level of granularity that ensures it is executed by one participant at a time. If an activity step requires two or more participants to execute it simultaneously, continue to decompose the activity step into smaller, independent steps for each participant.

Decomposing an activity into its individual steps requires a deeper understanding of how the API will solve real-world problems. This requires the insights of a domain expert or subject matter expert (SME). Include SMEs in the process of capturing activities and activity steps. If an SME is unavailable, spend some time interviewing SMEs and customers to better understand the needs. Be sure to allow sufficient time for this research to ensure all questions have been addressed, leaving no room for making assumptions about the problem space. When available, the product manager should be responsible for the interview process.

Table 4.1 *Example Activities for JSON's Bookstore Place an Order Job Story*

Digital Capability	Activity	Participants	Description
Place an Order	Browse for Books	Customer	Browse or search for books
Place an Order	Shop for Books	Customer, Call Center	A customer adds books to a cart
Place an Order	Create an Order	Customer, Call Center	A customer places the order using the contents of the shopping cart

Table 4.2 *Example Activity Steps for JSON's Bookstore*

Digital Capability	Activity	Activity Step	Participants	Description
Place an Order	Browse for Books	List Books	Customer, Call Center	List books by category or release date
Place an Order	Browse for Books	Search for Books	Customer, Call Center	Search for books by author, title
Place an Order	Browse for Books	View Book Details	Customer, Call Center	View the details of a book
Place an Order	Shop for Books	Add Books to Cart	Customer, Call Center	Add a book to the customer's cart
Place an Order	Shop for Books	Remove Books from Cart	Customer, Call Center	Remove a book from the customer's cart
Place an Order	Shop for Books	Clear Cart	Customer, Call Center	Remove all books from the customer's cart
Place an Order	Shop for Books	View Cart	Customer, Call Center	View the current cart and total
Place an Order	Create an Order	Checkout	Customer, Call Center	Create an order from the contents of the cart
Place an Order	Create an Order	Pay for Order	Customer, Call Center	Accept and process payment for the order

Table 4.2 decomposes the activities for JSON's Bookstore into activity steps.

Notice that some activities may have only a single step, whereas others may have multiple steps. This is common, as some activities are more complex than others.

Repeat this process for each job story. Review the activities and steps with SMEs to gain feedback and to ensure proper alignment. Once completed, proceed to the Define phase detailed in Chapter 5. If requirements are not clear enough to produce activities and steps, more work will need to be done. The API workshop examples,[1] available on GitHub, provide templates and examples for capturing job story activities.

What If Requirements Aren't Clear?

The activities and activity steps examples detailed in Table 4.1 and Table 4.2 are easily understood, as most people have experienced an online ecommerce Web site. For domains not familiar to the team, it may be necessary to explore the problem space further before the activities and activity steps are clear. Event-Storming is the recommended technique to understand and align on requirements in a collaborative way.

---

1. https://bit.ly/align-define-design-examples

Using EventStorming for Collaborative Understanding

EventStorming[2] is a collaborative process to help surface the business processes, requirements, and domain events as a visual model. It is a tool designed by Alberto Brandolini that has been adapted in different ways to fit the needs of organizations around the world.

EventStorming is most effective when conducted as an in-person session. Remote sessions may be used, when necessary, though they result in limited dynamic conversation. A facilitator helps the group navigate the process and helps to keep the session on track. Everyone is expected to contribute throughout the entire session by offering insights, asking clarifying questions, and identifying missing facts that require follow-up research.

Unlike other techniques that focus on the software design of a solution, EventStorming seeks to create a shared understanding of all or a portion of a domain. Artifacts and learnings from EventStorming sessions are used as input to the software design process, including the API design process.

CASE STUDY
EventStorming for International Wire Transfers

A recent EventStorming session was conducted for a group developing support for sending international wire transfers. The team was very familiar with the mechanics of performing the wire transfer but wished to explore the process leading up to the transfer. It was decided that EventStorming would be a useful tool for the exploration process.

In the weeks leading up to the EventStorming session, job stories were used to capture the requirements. A specific set of job stories was selected for the upcoming EventStorming session. The selected job stories expressed jobs to be done for the areas the group wished to explore. The participant list was selected, and the team met for a remote session.

During the remote session, several insights were achieved:

1. Team alignment regarding the overall process to support international wire transfers

2. Identification of open questions regarding some fundamental business policies

3. Clear definitions of key terminology, referred to as *ubiquitous language* in domain-driven design, that included input from business

---

2. https://www.eventstorming.com

The most valuable insight, however, was the number of unknowns around the specifics of currency conversion. No one was familiar with the internal policies regarding when a currency conversion was conducted. There were several options, from performing the conversion at the time of wire initiation to waiting until the wire transfer process started. The gap in knowledge was identified within an hour of starting the session. It was decided that further investigation was necessary. Domain experts were brought into the session to clarify the matter.

With better knowledge at hand, some significant decisions needed to be made. The session was halted to gain further clarification on the scope of the release. The EventStorming was concluded at a future time when more information was known, ensuring that the initial release met all business and customer needs.

Had the EventStorming session not been conducted, developers would have assumed a specific set of business policies with regard to currency conversion. SMEs would have required a different set of business policies, forcing developers to make last minute changes and incur significant technical debt to deliver on time.

How EventStorming Works

EventStorming sessions are very interactive. They benefit from a dedicated facilitator to ensure the sessions make the most effective use of the attendees' time. In-person sessions require a large wall space, called the EventStorming canvas, where color-coded sticky notes are placed and moved around to construct a narrative of how the solution will work. Remote sessions are also possible when teams are distributed or unable to locate a single room of sufficient size or duration.

The ADDR process separates the EventStorming session into five distinct steps. Each step seeks to add more detail and understanding until a better understanding of the domain is gained. Along the way, assumptions are clarified to ensure greater alignment between the team and the SMEs. The resulting output of an EventStorming session is used immediately to capture activities and steps. It is also used later in the process to help identify API boundaries, as detailed in Chapter 5.

Step 1: Identify Business Domain Events

Scheduled Time: 30–60 minutes

The EventStorming process starts by identifying business domain events for a job story or group of job stories. Everyone captures these events on stickies, all of the same color (typically orange), and places them on the canvas. (Brandolini recommends using consistent colors for specific items. See color list under "Step 4: Expand Domain Understanding.")

Domain events are phrased in the past tense to indicate that something has already happened. Phrasing domain events in the past tense can be challenging for some attendees. Help them rephrase the domain events until the habit is built. Being consistent in this effort pays off during subsequent steps. Table 4.3 demonstrates the preferred naming conventions for domain events and those to avoid.

This step should offer two passes of 15 to 30 minutes each. For a session with a larger scope, more passes may be required. The result is a large number of unordered sticky notes scattered all over the canvas.

As events are placed, attendees may start to slow down. This is common and easily remedied. Between each pass, review some areas of the canvas to identify missing domain events. Ask attendees to review all domain events and identify causation events that may come before a business domain event. If the causation event is missing, have them add it as a new domain event sticky note.

Figure 4.2 demonstrates what this would look like when capturing the business domain events for JSON's Bookstore job stories 1 and 4 captured in Chapter 3, Table 3.2.

Once the session is complete, take a brief break, then proceed to the next step.

Step 2: Create an Event Narrative

Scheduled Time: 90–120 minutes

Next, the domain event stickies are ordered into a narrative from beginning to end. Along the way, duplicate events are removed, and clarifications are made to ensure the events start to frame the narrative.

Table 4.3 *Domain Event Past-Tense Naming Examples*

Avoid	Preferred
User Authentication Successful	User Authenticated
Place an Order	Order Placed
Print Shipping Label	Shipping Label Printed

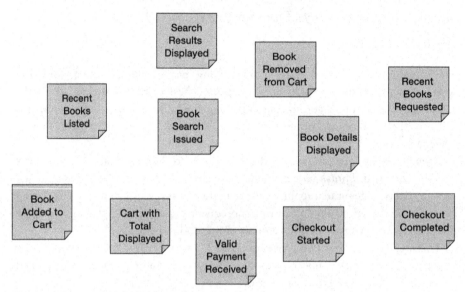

Figure 4.2 *An example of domain event sticky notes for the JSON's Bookstore online store. The events have now been captured and will be organized in the next step.*

The facilitator is responsible for asking the group clarifying questions to ensure the narrative is composed properly. Find the starting domain event for the narrative, then seek to find the next domain event and place it after the first. Leave plenty of space on the canvas to insert domain events as needed.

It is common for sessions to become stuck if there are branching or parallel narratives. To help expedite the session, select a single narrative and order the domain events accordingly. Branching or parallel narratives may be captured below the primary narrative, if desired.

Figure 4.3 illustrates creating a narrative from the business domain events previously identified.

While this step may appear to require very little time, expect conversations to emerge as the narrative is established. Therefore, allocate between one and two hours minimum. If necessary, turn some of the domain events to a 45-degree angle to note that they need to be revisited and proceed with the remainder of the narrative. Once the overall narrative is established, revisit the domain events in question or mark them with hotspot (typically hot pink) stickies for follow-up.

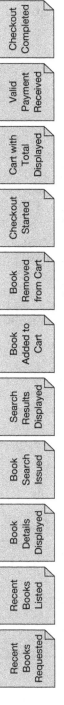

Figure 4.3 *Business domain event sticky notes arranged into a linear narrative for JSON's Bookstore.*

Step 3: Review the Narrative and Identify Gaps

Scheduled Time: 60–90 minutes

Once all events have been cleaned up and grouped in a general timeline, the group seeks to ensure that no events are missing. To do this, the group starts to walk from left to right to tell the full narrative. If events are missing or need clarification, they are changed immediately. It is at this step that a large surface area is beneficial to ensure sticky notes may be moved around and for filling in gaps in the narrative.

It is also at this step that all domain concepts need to be unified to establish a common vocabulary. This vocabulary will evolve into the ubiquitous language for each bounded context that will be identified in the next step of the ADDR process. Figure 4.4 demonstrates cards that may be attached to the EventStorming canvas to unify common vocabulary. If necessary, rewrite existing domain events to use the new vocabulary. It won't take long for the group to start adopting the new terminology.

Expect this step to take at least an hour as questions are raised and discussions emerge.

Step 4: Expand Domain Understanding

Scheduled Time: 30–60 minutes

After the events have been ordered, additional sticky note colors are used to expand domain understanding. Figure 4.5 illustrates a portion of the Place Order job story for JSON's Bookstore using these additional types of sticky notes.

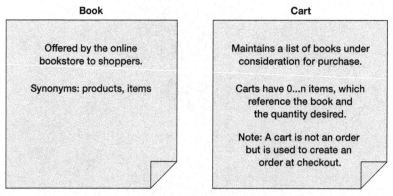

Figure 4.4 *Two examples of cards used to capture vocabulary clarifications during a session. These cards will become part of the ubiquitous language for a bounded context identified in the next step of the process.*

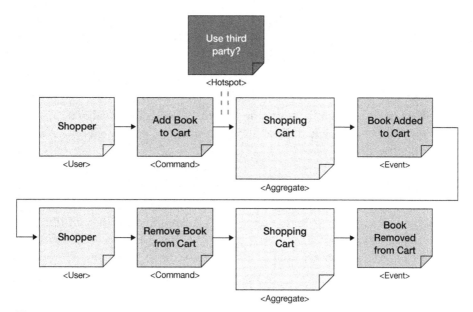

Figure 4.5 *The Place Order job story for JSON's Bookstore, expanded to include additional color-coded sticky notes for commands, aggregates, and users. There is also a hotspot sticky with an open question to resolve after the session.*

Following is a summary of the common sticky note types—and the colors typically designated for each type—that are used throughout an EventStorming session:

- **Business event (orange):** The result of an action or policy that indicates forward progression through a workflow or process
- **Hotspot (bright pink):** Unknown or missing data that requires research and follow-up after the session.
- **Command (dark blue):** An action taken by a user or system.
- **Aggregate (large, pale yellow):** Behavior or logic that executes as a result of a command and behavior and often results in one or more events. In domain-driven design (DDD), Aggregates are defined as units of transactional consistency. In EventStorming, this is a higher-level representation of workflows, state machines, and other behavior.
- **Policy (lilac):** The triggering event or motivation for why a new command is executed and is always required. It acts as the bridge or glue between an event and a command. Policies may start with the word *when* or *whenever*.

- **External system (pale pink):** Systems outside of the solution. These may be external to the team but internal to the organization or a third-party system. They are best thought of as aggregates outside of the group's control.

- **User interface (white):** A user interface that will offer one or more roles the capability to execute a command against an aggregate.

- **User (yellow, small):** A specific role that is interacting with the system, typically via a UI, but also perhaps as a result of an automated call, email, or other mechanism.

Start by adding commands (blue stickies) to capture what actions are taken by a system or user that will result in one or more of the identified business domain events. Commands are sent to aggregates, so capture those as well. Business rules, often phrased as "when xyz happens, . . ." may be captured as policies (lilac). Hot pink stickies are used as hotspot indicators where more information is required.

Step 5: Review the Final Narrative

Scheduled Time: 30 minutes

Finally, the narrative is reviewed from both directions, start to end and end to start, to ensure all elements have been captured. Important events and triggers are clearly marked to denote key transitions between steps. Figure 4.6 shows a fully explored Place an Order job story using the sticky notes necessary to express the understanding gained during the session.

This completes the EventStorming session. The canvas should be saved for future reference, as it will be useful for informing future steps in the API design process. Consider taking photos of the canvas and sharing them with the team. Rolling the canvas up or relocating it to a shared space is helpful for team members colocated in the same office space. If the team used a digital tool, such as Miro,[3] export the work as a PDF or image for sharing on a wiki or as part of other project assets.

Finally, write the activities and activity steps identified during the session using the format outlined previously.

---

3. https://miro.com

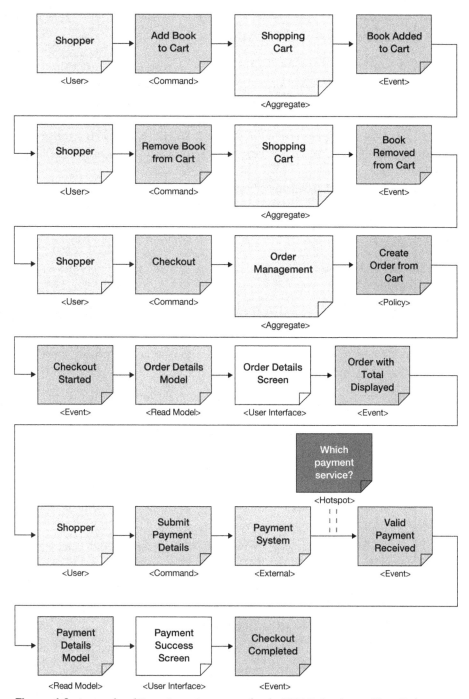

Figure 4.6 *A completed EventStorming canvas for the JSON's Bookstore Place Order job story. Because of space limitations, the single line of sticky notes is wrapped into two additional lanes.*

The Benefits of EventStorming

Alignment between stakeholders and development teams is achieved through a shared understanding of terminology, processes, goals, and required integrations with other internal and external systems. Questions are surfaced for follow-up after the session to prevent assumptions or misunderstandings from being captured into the API design and code. An EventStorming session helps everyone to surface these insights and communicate effectively through a fun and effective exercise.

There are five additional benefits of conducting an EventStorming session:

1. Shared understanding of requirements and scope of the problem being modeled

2. Shared understanding of the workflow processes, business rules, and constraints

3. Establishment of a shared domain vocabulary, replacing multiple terms with a ubiquitous language

4. Identification of unknowns that require follow-up and clarification prior to software design and development

5. Identification of boundaries within the solution, useful for scoping team efforts and division of labor to minimize cross-team dependency coordination

There are circumstances when EventStorming is most effective:

- Prior to API and microservice design and implementation to help establish outside-in design thinking

- Prior to software design and development to clarify assumptions and address open questions

- After clearly documenting desired outcomes, typically through the use of job stories, discussed in Chapter 3

- When all roles are represented in the session

- When embarking on a significant scope of effort or one that spans multiple teams

There are also circumstances when the value of an EventStorming session may be reduced. To avoid spending unnecessary time in an EventStorming session, consider these factors that contribute to an ineffective session:

- The business process is well known and documented, as results will likely produce the same insights.

- The scope of the problem is small enough that the identified business requirements are sufficient and complete.

- The business requirements have not yet been identified. In this case, start with constructing job stories, covered in Chapter 3, to clearly define the desired outcomes and parties involved.

- Business stakeholders cannot attend or do not see value in the exercise. While development teams may still conduct a session, doing so may lead to modeling a process based on too many technical assumptions that do not meet business needs

- Software delivery has begun, and delivery dates are fixed. If the teams are early enough in the delivery process, the output of the session may be used to make software architectural and design adjustments prior to a release. Otherwise, teams will be forced to proceed with existing decisions rather than the insights obtained through an EventStorming session

Who Should Be Involved?

Including the right mix of attendees is critical for a successful EventStorming session. A session must involve a few representatives from various roles and responsibilities. It should be kept to no more than twelve people to ensure full participation by all attendees. Larger groups can prevent less assertive attendees from engaging in the session.

Optional participants that may raise the group size should be considered for inclusion on a case-by-case basis to avoid overloading the session with too many voices. Sessions with dozens of people often slow down or result in participants looking down at their phone or checking email. Smaller groups benefit from the need for smaller conference space when conducting an in-person session. Avoid observers whenever possible, as they don't add value and may distract from the session. Rarely do observers strictly observe.

When selecting the participants for an EventStorming session, be sure to consider the following roles, in priority order:

1. Business owners, including those helping to define the requirements, such as product managers and product owners

2. SMEs with familiarity of the domain space

3. Technical leads, architects, and senior developers involved in leading the software delivery

4. Security experts, especially when the problem space requires the involvement of privacy or security concerns

5. Individual software developers and contributors not involved with decision making (on a case-by-case basis only)

Facilitating an EventStorming Session

A facilitator familiar with EventStorming is important. Facilitators are responsible for moving the process forward and keeping everyone engaged throughout the process.

Emails and message notifications may lead to distractions, slowing down progress, causing clarifying questions to be missed, or preventing SMEs from answering clarifying questions. Remote sessions only add to the number of distractions possible, as it is easy to task switch. Facilitators must work toward preventing these issues by controlling the pace of the session and the frequency of breaks and providing clear transitions between each step in the process.

When in doubt, facilitators need to evaluate discussions to determine if they are clarifying intent or becoming a digression. If necessary, apply the hotspot sticky to capture an area of contention and revisit. Otherwise, the session will slowly become a forum for opinion by one or two people.

Because EventStorming is relatively new and experienced facilitators are in short supply, this section provides insights and tips from recently conducted sessions.

Prepare: Gathering Necessary Supplies

When conducting an in-person session, EventStorming requires some essential supplies. Be sure to have all the necessary supplies ordered and on hand several days prior to the session. Avoid gathering supplies the day before or the morning of the session.

The session will require a large number of sticky notes that includes a variety of colors. Typically, orange stickies are used the most, so having more of that color is important. Most office supply stores offer boxes of colors that match the needs for EventStorming. However, feel free to adjust colors to team preferences or to what is available. Remember that most attendees will be attending their first EventStorming session, so they won't know the "proper colors" anyway. If experienced participants complain about the wrong colors, request that they be in charge of the supplies for any future sessions.

A large wall is also required for hanging a large paper sheet as a modeling surface where sticky notes are applied and moved around as needed. Some organizations prefer to use paper sheets that are no more than 18 to 24 inches (45–60 cm) to allow two or three lanes of sheets along the wall.

A legend should be visible to ensure that everyone is reminded of each color of sticky note used. Be sure to write out a legend that shows all sticky note colors, their type (e.g., "Business Domain Event" for orange stickies), and arrows that show how they are typically combined to produce a narrative. An example legend is shown in Figure 4.7.

Black markers should be used to write on the sticky notes, ensuring words are easy to read when stepping away from the modeling surface. Ensure there is at least one marker for each participant, with a few extra scattered around the room in case some are lost.

Remote sessions may choose to use a diagramming tool to simulate sticky notes. Another option is to use a shared document that is accessible by each attendee, applying similar color-coding to text as those used with sticky notes. Whatever is chosen, practice using the tool prior to the event to ensure an effective use of time during the session.

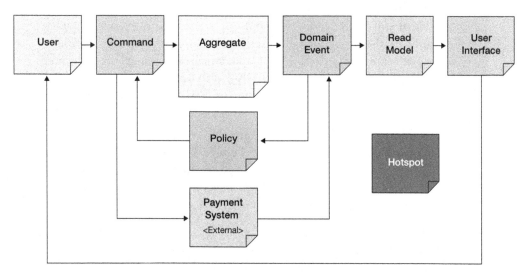

Figure 4.7 *A legend that shows how common color-coded sticky notes work together to capture the domain during an EventStorming session.*

Share: Communicating the EventStorming Session

Achieving a successful EventStorming session requires preparation and effective communication before a session, at the start of a session, and after a session has been completed. The following are suggestions for facilitators to communicate effectively via email, video, and face to face before the session:

- **Product management attendance is essential.** Insist that product owners and product managers attend. A developer-heavy session will focus on how things work today, existing systems, and delivering the status quo. In addition, misalignment will occur, rendering an incorrect understanding of the domain and desired outcomes.

- **Share the purpose and scope of the session.** If the purpose and scope are not shared ahead of time, many will be confused or will fail to participate. Communicating the purpose and scope will also ensure the right people are in the room, which is key for EventStorming to be most effective. Establish expectations initially and reinforce at the start of the session.

- **Establish mutual expectations.** Confusion or unmet expectations will lead to an ineffective session or a poor view of EventStorming. Establish expectations regarding the process, desired outcome, and design assets to be produced. Reiterate these at the start of the session to reinforce the goals and establish a proper mindset.

- **Ensure that API design has not started yet.** Teams that have already started API design will likely ignore the output of the session in favor of moving forward with the current design. The session should be used to guide future vision with immediate execution. Teams unwilling or unable to incorporate the output of the session will likely fail to obtain the highest possible value of an EventStorming session. Ensure team buy-in from everyone before proceeding.

- **Reinforce how EventStorming fits into the overall API design process.** Share a progress indicator or revisit the overall process often to demonstrate where the session fits into the bigger picture. Remind the audience that EventStorming produces valuable insights that will inform the upcoming API modeling and design steps. Otherwise, the session may seem like busy work.

At session kickoff, review the items once more. Reviewing everything the day of the session helps to bring everything top-of-mind and sets the expectations for the session.

Execute: Conducting the EventStorming Session

At the start of a session, review the expectations, process, and scope of the session. Then start with the first step of the session. Most first-time attendees will be a bit uncertain how to get started. Be ready to help them along or allow those more familiar to start the process.

Show how the process works by first demonstrating it. Post the first business domain event by taking input from the group, phrase it into the past tense to demonstrate the expected format, then post it on the timeline at an approximate location. Then request that the group start to create their own independently. Use the same technique for each step in the session.

Establish clear reasons for each step of the process. Most first-time attendees won't fully understand why each step in the process is necessary. Help them understand the value of the time spent. While the process may be obvious to the facilitator, most attendees will need time to adapt to the process of EventStorming.

Wrap-up: Capture Activities and Activity Steps

Once the session is complete, take photos of canvas with the sticky notes for sharing. Before leaving the area, the photos should be checked to ensure that all handwriting is legible. If not, move closer to the board and take more photos.

To make the canvas available digitally, use a tool to produce a single panoramic photo, or number the photos from left-to-right to ensure they can be reassembled as needed. If the team resides in a shared office space, the canvas may be carefully removed and placed in a new location for reference.

Digital tools, such as Miro, may be helpful for remote sessions and support PDF or image export of the final canvas. It is also possible to use a shared document, such as Google Docs or a Word document hosted on SharePoint, if other tools are not readily available. Experience shows that color-coded text works just as well as virtual sticky notes and is easier to cut-and-paste as the canvas is manipulated.

Finally, use the canvas to identify and capture activities and activity steps, as described at the start of this chapter.

Follow-up: Post-Session Recommendations

The facilitator should send a follow-up email two days after the session. The two-day email should thank everyone for their participation and share the new location of the sticky notes and the digital folder where the photos reside. A survey link may also be provided to gather input for process improvement.

A second email from the facilitator should be sent two weeks after the session. This email should ask how the output of the session is being used by the team. Use this opportunity to find blocking issues that prevent the team from proceeding. Schedule a follow-up discussion to coach the team on next steps if they are blocked.

Finally, consider writing up a case study of the session and including quotes from attendees, if permission is provided. This helps teams uncertain about the EventStorming process understand the value that it provides and increase their willingness to invest the necessary time. It also helps to share team wins across the organizations.

Customizing the Process

Remember that EventStorming is a tool that offers discovery-based learning in a collaborative environment. Customizing the process helps organizations gain the most from sessions. The following additions or modifications have been explored beyond the original process suggested by Brandolini:

- **The three-lane approach:** Rather than a single sheet of paper covering the wall, using narrow paper that allows for creating three separate lanes in parallel. All initial events are attached to the top lane during business event identification. When ordering them into a narrative, the events are moved to the middle lane. The top lane is then used to expand the available space when expanding the canvas with new sticky notes beyond the initial business events. The bottom lane is used as a "parking lot" for events considered out of scope or identified as duplicate. This approach was built out of necessity, as the only available paper rolls from an organization's supply closet were only 12 inches (30 cm) high.

- **45-degree angle sticky notes:** When a note isn't clear, needs to be rewritten into past tense, or is revisited for another reason, anyone is empowered to tilt a sticky note at a 45-degree angle. This flags the note for follow-up before proceeding to the next step of the process.

- **Multipart EventStorming sessions:** With the introduction of remote sessions, fatigue often sets in more quickly than with high-energy in-person sessions. In this case, consider breaking an EventStorming session into multiple parts that take no more than two hours before a minimum of a one-hour break. If necessary, a session may be spread across two days as long as all attendees will be available to participate both days.

- **Shared facilitation:** The facilitator is encouraged to ask different people to lead the narration/storytelling effort. Shared facilitation encourages co-ownership of the session, keeps team members engaged and away from email, and helps cross-train others in the EventStorming process. The facilitator demonstrates what is expected, facilitates for a time, then asks for a volunteer or selects someone to facilitate a portion of the process. This continues throughout the session until everyone has had a chance to facilitate some portion of the session. During the activity, the original facilitator remains available and coaches everyone as needed.

Summary

It is essential for teams to establish a detailed understanding of domain concepts, processes, and workflows. Capturing these details as activities and activity steps helps to align all team members and establish a foundation for future API design work. The EventStorming framework may be used as a collaborative method for exploring the domain concepts in detail alongside domain and subject matter experts.

The next step in the API design process is to start defining the bounded contexts and APIs needed to realize the digital capabilities offered by an API product or API platform.

Part III

Defining Candidate APIs

At this point in the API design process, digital capabilities have been identified using job stories. Activities required to produce the outcomes have been captured and are based on insights from an EventStorming session. By starting with a focus on outcomes and activities, teams remain aligned with the needs of customers and business goals.

The next step in the API design process is to identify candidate APIs. These candidate APIs will reflect one or more boundaries that are identified using an EventStorming canvas or list of activities produced from the previous step. As the boundaries are identified, one or more API profiles begin to emerge.

Each API profile provides more detailed clarity about the API and informs the eventual API design. It reflects the API resources that need to be designed, along with the operations to be offered. This definition step is essential in designing an API that is focused on delivering the desired outcomes of customers, partners, and the workforce.

Chapter 5

Identifying API Boundaries

Total unification of the domain model for a large system will not be feasible or cost-effective.

—Eric Evans, *Domain-Driven Design*

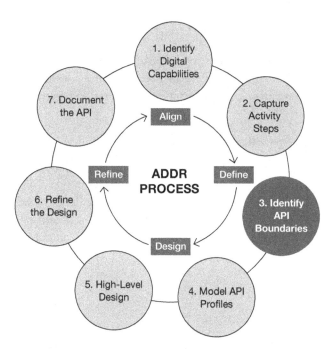

Figure 5.1 *The first step in the Define phase is to identify API boundaries.*

Every API provides a mental model for how developers will integrate with it to produce the desired outcomes. Establishing the scope and responsibilities of an API also helps guide the design of this mental model, contributing to a more positive developer experience. By borrowing techniques from domain-driven design (DDD) used in identifying bounded contexts, candidate APIs are identified and the responsibility of each API is clearly defined from the artifacts produced in the Align phase (see Figure 5.1).

Output from activity step identification, as detailed in Chapter 4, "Capture Activities and Steps," is useful in finding boundaries and therefore candidate APIs. These candidate APIs realize the digital capabilities that will produce the desired outcomes captured in job stories, as detailed in Chapter 3, "Identify Digital Capabilities." Before getting started with the process, it is important to understand how some mistakes in defining API boundaries can lead to a poor developer experience.

Avoiding API Boundary Antipatterns

It is important to clarify the intent and scope of an API. Identifying the scope of an API helps developers find the right one for the job. Without a clear scope and set of associated responsibilities, APIs will suffer from common API boundary antipatterns.

The Mega All-in-One API Antipattern

Even the most experienced API designers are faced with challenges when trying to determine how many separate API products they need.

Creating a single, large API product makes it difficult for developers to find what they need quickly. Likewise, many small API products, perhaps as a result of externalizing microservices individually, may result in fragmentation and frustration. Applying clear API boundaries helps to reduce confusion around very large or many small APIs.

The Overloaded API Antipattern

Organizations with multiple products or that offer a platform comprised of multiple APIs have additional challenges ahead. All too often, organizations want to design the perfect Accounts API or Customer API that will be the single place to find out all the details about an account or customer. What starts as a well-intentioned goal eventually leads to a single API that tries to do everything but ultimately does nothing well.

In the bookstore example, *books* could imply one of several contexts:

- Books that are entries in the catalog of available products to purchase
- Books available as part of the warehouse inventory
- Books added to a shopping cart
- Books that are part of a placed order
- Books that have been shipped as part of an order

Creating a single Books API is likely not the best route to clarity or sanity. API changes would be constant as new contexts around the term *books* are introduced. The result would be operations that mix and match the term in different ways until the API becomes a confusing mess. Not only does this lead to a poor developer experience, it also contributes to significant delays when delivering new enhancements in the future.

In larger organizations, a single team may become responsible for most of the API through this incorrect assumption that a single Books API is the best way to organize support across the book catalog, inventory, shopping, and fulfillment processes of the organization. The velocity of delivery is greatly reduced as the remainder of the organization waits for the single team to add the operations needed to support new functionality.

Instead, seek to clarify single-word terms such as *book* with more context. For example, a Books Catalog API helps to limit the scope of API operations to those involved to catalog management. Within this clearly defined scope are additional responsibilities, including managing public descriptions, associated author metadata to each book, book covers, sample chapters, and more. Only those interested in catalog management need to work with this API.

The Helper API Antipattern

Nearly every development team has at one time built a helper library. This library has a mixture of little utilities that are scattered all around the codebase. The namespace used to store the helpers (e.g., `com.mycompany.util`) is referenced all over the codebase.

Some APIs suffer the same challenges as the sad, overused helper API. These are APIs that have a mixture of uses but aren't cohesive as a unit. Developers integrating with the API struggle to understand when and where to apply each one. The lack of scope and responsibility of the API makes the developer confused and unable to use it effectively.

Bounded Contexts, Subdomains, and APIs

The goal of an API boundary is to unify on the ubiquitous language while reducing overall coordination between teams as much as possible. In the case of Web APIs, boundaries may offer one or more network interfaces to support all the operations within the bounded area. Each boundary should be owned by a single team that is empowered to build and own everything within the boundary.

Defining clear boundaries is an important factor for APIs, as it helps to accelerate the API design and development process by scoping APIs to a specific set of responsibilities. The terminology used for API operations and resources should reflect the bounded context's ubiquitous language as well. For larger or more complex boundaries, further decomposition may be required, perhaps resulting in additional APIs and/or services hidden behind the API. Over time, boundaries may shift as more is learned about the solution.

The challenge most teams face is how to identify bounded contexts for their APIs. Team members may just know it when they see it, whereas others may place boundaries around a specific portion of a domain model. Neither of these methods results in a repeatable, teachable process that clearly identifies the scope of an API. Instead, it is recommended to use the EventStorming canvas and activity steps artifacts from the Align phase to help identify boundaries.

A Note about API Boundaries and DDD

While this chapter seeks to incorporate common DDD terminology and practices for identifying API boundaries, it is also meant to support organizations that have not adopted common DDD practices.

This chapter seeks to find a middle ground that supports practitioners familiar with the intricacies of DDD as well as those less familiar. In either case, there are many useful lessons within DDD that still apply to organizations not fully engaged in DDD practices. Organizations more familiar with DDD may wish to introduce additional practices that go beyond the scope of this chapter.

As teams complete their API design, refer to Vaughn Vernon's excellent book, *Implementing Domain-Driven Design*,[1] for further details on implementing DDD.

---

1. Vaughn Vernon, *Implementing Domain-Driven Design* (Boston: Addison-Wesley, 2013).

Finding API Boundaries Using EventStorming

As mentioned in Chapter 4, EventStorming helps to unify terminology while aligning teams with an understanding of processes, business policies, and system interactions. By examining the language used throughout the EventStorming canvas, developers find hints about possible API boundaries begin to emerge as terms and focus shift. This is demonstrated by language pattern shifts, as indicated in Figure 5.2.

As terminology shifts, boundaries start to emerge. Identify and name each of the boundaries. Then, assign a Web-based API for each boundary as a starting point. The API will offer the API operations necessary to deliver the digital capabilities for that boundary.

Teams may also choose to use the aggregates identified in EventStorming as hints to API scope. While this offers some additional insights into API boundaries, it may not always be the case. Aggregates that were captured on the basis of fine-grained responsibilities and focused on a single responsibility are more useful for identifying internal modules or services behind the API. However, if aggregates were grouped at a more coarse-grained level, they may succeed in identifying an API that is responsible for orchestrating outcomes.

For some EventStorming sessions exploring a limited scope, there may be only a single boundary. For most solutions, however, there will be at least two boundaries identified on an EventStorming canvas.

Figure 5.3 highlights three specific boundaries that qualify as separate APIs, based on the insights provided from EventStorming.

Finding API Boundaries through Activities

While EventStorming helps to find boundaries by design, it isn't the only method for guiding the identification process. The same approach may be used by reviewing the activities and activity steps produced by subject matter experts already familiar with the necessary processes and workflows, as described in Chapter 4. This is a particularly effective approach when considerable effort has already been invested in capturing requirements.

Look for shifts in language like what was described previously using EventStorming. Often, the activity step names and/or descriptions have a basic sentence structure with nouns and verbs. Make note of where the nouns shift in the activity steps. The nouns acted upon may offer clues to where boundaries exist. When steps shift to a new set of nouns, mark the location and use it as the starting point of a new boundary. While not as comprehensive as EventStorming, the activities and activity steps will offer insights into shifts in language that demonstrate a shift in a boundary.

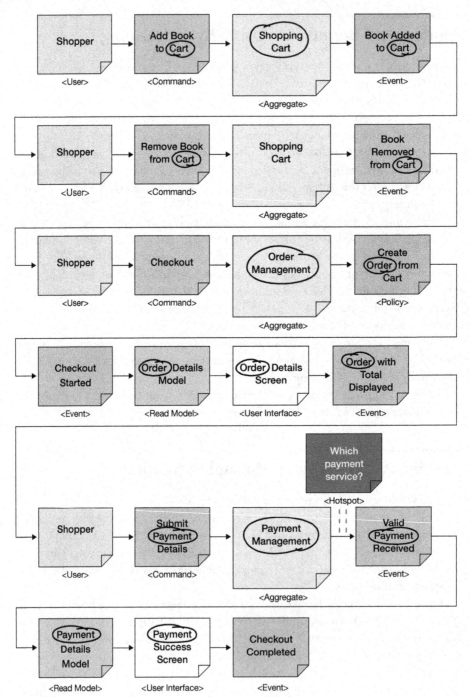

Figure 5.2 *An EventStorming canvas is helpful in finding shifts in language, leading to the identification of bounded contexts.*

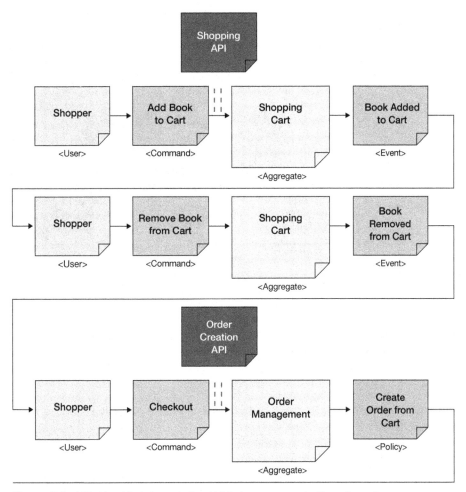

Figure 5.3 *APIs identified through the shift in language on the EventStorming canvas.*

As an example, the activities and activity steps from Table 4.2 in the previous chapter are presented in Table 5.1. Notice the shift from Books to Cart, then to Order and Payment. These shifts provide a starting point for identifying boundaries, from which APIs are formed.

Naming and Scoping APIs

Next, the boundary is given a name to represent the API that will be designed. Seek to assign a name that includes the scope, outcome, or target audience. Examples of well-known API names include Twitter's Followers API and eBay's Seller API.

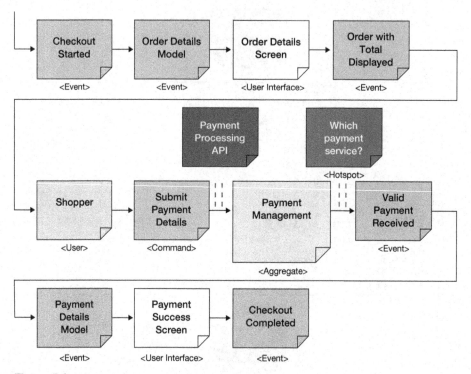

Figure 5.3 *(continued)*

Table 5.1 *Activity Steps for JSON's Bookstore; Separators Indicate Shifts in Vocabulary That Identify Boundaries*

Digital Capability	Activity	Activity Step	Participants	Description
Place an Order	Browse for Books	List Books	Customer, Call Center	List books by category or release date
Place an Order	Browse for Books	Search for Books	Customer, Call Center	Search for books by author, title
Place an Order	Browse for Books	View Book Details	Customer, Call Center	View the details of a book
Place an Order	Shop for Books	Add Books to Cart	Customer, Call Center	Add a book to the customer's cart
Place an Order	Shop for Books	Remove Books from Cart	Customer, Call Center	Remove a book from the customer's cart
Place an Order	Shop for Books	Clear Cart	Customer, Call Center	Remove all books from the customer's cart
Place an Order	Shop for Books	View Cart	Customer, Call Center	View the current cart and total
Place an Order	Create an Order	Checkout	Customer, Call Center	Create an order from the contents of the cart
Place an Order	Create an Order	Pay for Order	Customer, Call Center	Accept and process payment for the order

Avoid using the terms *service* and *manager,* as they are generally not useful in understanding the purpose of the API.

The APIs in Figure 5.3 are named Shopping API, Order Creation API, and Payment Processing API. This is a good start and clearly articulates the scope and responsibility of each API.

> **Note**
>
> Some API designers may prefer to combine the Order Creation and Payment Processing APIs, as they could be considered cohesive and therefore should exist as a single API. They are separated in this simple example for instructional purposes. However, field insights dictate that separating order creation and payment through clearly defined boundaries allows for more complex payment processing at a future time without burdening the order creation boundary with the added complexity.

Finally, separate the activity steps into the corresponding API based on the boundary it represents. Table 5.2 captures the Shopping API, including the activity steps relevant to the API.

Table 5.3 captures the checkout process for the Place an Order digital capability.

Finally, Table 5.4 captures the payment step as part of the Place an Order digital capability.

Table 5.2 *Shopping API, Discovered through Boundary Identification, with Corresponding Activity Steps from JSON's Bookstore*

Digital Capability	Activity	Activity Step	Participants	Description
Place an Order	Browse for Books	List Books	Customer, Call Center	List books by category or release date
Place an Order	Browse for Books	Search for Books	Customer, Call Center	Search for books by author, title
Place an Order	Browse for Books	View Book Details	Customer, Call Center	View the details of a book
Place an Order	Shop for Books	Add Books to Cart	Customer, Call Center	Add a book to the customer's cart
Place an Order	Shop for Books	Remove Books from Cart	Customer, Call Center	Remove a book from the customer's cart
Place an Order	Shop for Books	Clear Cart	Customer, Call Center	Remove all books from the customer's cart
Place an Order	Shop for Books	View Cart	Customer, Call Center	View the current cart and total
Place an Order	Create an Order	Checkout	Customer, Call Center	Create an order from the contents of the cart
Place an Order	Create an Order	Pay for Order	Customer, Call Center	Accept and process payment for the order

Table 5.3 *Order Creation API, Discovered through Boundary Identification, with Corresponding Activity Steps from JSON's Bookstore*

Digital Capability	Activity	Activity Step	Participants	Description
Place an Order	Create an Order	Checkout	Customer, Call Center	Create an order from the contents of the cart

Table 5.4 *Payment Processing API, Discovered through Boundary Identification, with Corresponding Activity Steps from JSON's Bookstore*

Digital Capability	Activity	Activity Step	Participants	Description
Place an Order	Create an Order	Pay for Order	Customer, Call Center	Accept and process payment for the order

With the boundaries clearly defined, API modeling can begin. This effort leads to API profiles that define the operations and events each API will offer. API modeling is detailed in the next chapter.

Summary

APIs benefit from careful scoping and assignment of responsibilities. Applying boundaries helps to identify one or more APIs that will be required to deliver the desired outcomes captured as job stories. This prepares the way for the next step, API modeling, in which a blueprint of the API is formed and the foundation is laid for API design.

Chapter 6

API Modeling

You can use an eraser on the drafting table or a sledgehammer on the construction site.

— Frank Lloyd Wright

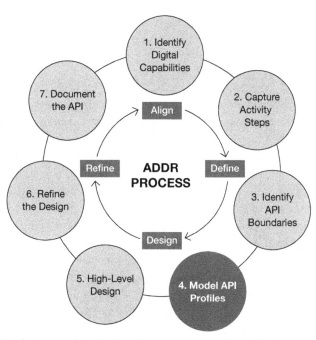

Figure 6.1 *The final step of the Define phase is to create API profiles in preparation for transitioning to the Design phase.*

Developers are often tempted to start writing code immediately. Code is the primary tool for developers. It is everything—the hammer, screwdriver, ruler, and saw. When code is seen as the one and only tool to design an API, the quality of the API design can suffer. The march to produce code for production becomes more valued than the outcomes the API is meant to produce.

Of course, code produces value when it is used to explore a specific area of a solution to reduce risk. It is also valuable to use code to experiment, surface unknowns, or explore a new technology. The term *tracer bullet* was applied to software by David Thomas and Andrew Hunt in their book *The Pragmatic Programmer*.[1] The term describes the use of code as a means of exploration and risk reduction. Tracer bullet code delivers value through learning rather than through production-ready code.

API modeling is a tracer bullet for API design. It is a technique for exploring the necessary elements of an API prior to the design and delivery process. API modeling (see Figure 6.1) helps to bring together the insights and artifacts from the previous steps into an API profile that describes the scope and intent of the APIs needed to deliver the desired outcomes of end users.

What Is API Modeling?

Just as a beautiful Web design begins from a wireframe, a great API design begins with an API model that helps define its scope and responsibilities. The goal of API modeling is to fully understand and validate the needs of developers and end users. Unlike a wireframe, which focuses strictly on end user interaction, API modeling focuses on both developer and end user goals. Often, these goals are aligned, but sometimes they are not. API modeling helps to surface issues quickly so that they may be resolved prior to writing code.

API modeling uses job stories, activities, and activity steps as inputs to produce a cohesive view of each API, called an *API profile*. An API profile captures characteristics about the API, including its name, scope, operations, and emitted events that will be used to deliver desired outcomes. API modeling is done before designing and developing begins—while the cost of change is significantly lower.

After completing API modeling, teams will be ready to migrate the API profiles produced into an API design. API modeling can be used as input for a single API design style of choice, such as REST, GraphQL, or gRPC. It may also be used to

---

1. David Thomas and Andrew Hunt, *The Pragmatic Programmer: Your Journey to Mastery*, 20th Anniversary Edition, 2nd ed. (Boston: Addison-Wesley, 2020).

inform the design of an API that uses a combination of these API styles to support the various digital channels for customers and partner integration needs.

The API Profile Structure

API profiles capture all necessary information about an API, independent of the API style or styles that it will expose (e.g., REST and GraphQL). The API profile is used to drive the design of an API, but also provides the beginnings of the API documentation effort during the early stages of API definition.

An API profile captures the following details about each API:

- The name and a short description of the API
- The scope of the API (internal, public, partner, etc.)
- API operations with input and output message details
- Participants allowed to perform each operation, in preparation for securing the API
- Events generated by each API operation, to drive extensibility beyond the API's original intent
- (Optional) architectural requirements identified, such as a service-level agreement (SLA)

A spreadsheet or document is sufficient to capture each API profile. Using a collaborative spreadsheet allows teams to capture and refine API profiles without the need to email changes among team members. Some teams prefer to use tools such as wikis for capturing API profiles. No matter what tool is selected, be sure that everyone in the organization has access to read and comment on the API profiles produced. Using a tool that is provisioned for only a subset of the organization is not recommended.

Figure 6.2 shows a template that is easy to read and fits both spreadsheet and document formats.

The API Modeling Process

The goal of the API modeling process is to produce one or more API profiles, one for each API identified during modeling. The modeling process is divided into five quick steps. Each step adds additional detail to the API profile until a blueprint of the API emerges.

My API—Description goes here
API scope (internal, public, partner, etc.)
Architectural requirements (service-level agreements, standards compliance, etc.)

Operation Name	Description	Participants	Resource(s)	Emitted Events	Operation Details
listThingies()	List/search for thingies	Customer, Shopper	Thingy	Thingies.Listed	Request Parameters: vendorId, … Returns: Thingy[]
…	…	…		…	…

Figure 6.2 *A template for capturing API profiles in a spreadsheet or document.*

What about Using the OpenAPI Specification?

The OpenAPI Specification (OAS) is a machine-readable format used to capture the description of REST-based and gRPC-based APIs. The format was designed to aid in the generation of API reference documentation and boilerplate code. As such, the OAS structure is rooted in URL paths. Because API modeling precedes a complete API design that includes resource paths, OAS isn't an appropriate format for API profiles. However, API profiles will help accelerate the creation of OAS-based API descriptions later in the design process.

API teams have found that using the Application-Level Profile Semantics (ALPS) specification, detailed in Chapter 13, "Document the API Design," is a useful way to produce a machine-readable API profile that may be used to accelerate the API modeling and design process independent of the chosen API style(s).

The specifics about using the OAS to capture the API description of a REST-based API design is addressed in Chapter 7, "REST-Based API Design."

Those who have produced the artifacts from the previous Align-Define-Design-Refine (ADDR) process steps will typically complete the API modeling process in under two hours. For those who skipped some of the steps, API modeling may take several hours to complete.

Step 1: Capture API Profile Summary

The first step in the process is to fill out the basic details of the API profile, including the API name, a short description, and the scope of the API. The scope of the API should correspond to the scopes that the organization supports, which are typically internal, public, and partner. Remember that these details can be changed as the team gains more understanding about the purpose and responsibilities of each API.

Next, capture the API operation names and participants based on the activities and activity steps captured previously. For each activity step identified previously, convert it into an operation name that uses a consistent naming format. It is suggested to use lowerCamelCase, which makes it easier for the team to explore the API model using sequence diagrams, as recommended later in this chapter.

Figure 6.3 demonstrates how to capture the start of an API profile using JSON's Bookstore's Shopping API, previously identified during the Align phase of the design process.

Shopping API—Supports the book browsing experience and cart management Public					
Operation Name	**Description**	**Participants**	**Resource(s)**	**Emitted Events**	**Operation Details**
listBooks()	List books by category or release date	Customer, Call Center			
searchBooks()	Search for books by author, title	Customer, Call Center			
viewBook()	View book details	Customer, Call Center			
addBookToCart()	Add a book to the customer's cart	Customer, Call Center			
removeBookFromCart()	Remove a book from the customer's cart	Customer, Call Center			
clearCart()	Remove all books from the customer's cart	Customer, Call Center			
viewCart()	View the current cart and total	Customer, Call Center			

Figure 6.3 *JSON's Bookstore's Shopping API with a name, description, scope, and operation names filled in using the details from the bounded context exercise in Chapter 5, "Bounded Contexts in API Design."*

Step 2: Identify the Resources

The next step is to use the API profile to identify resources for the API. Resources are often domain entities that will be operated upon by the API. Finding the target for each operation helps to identify the initial set of resources. This is often a difficult task when first starting an API design. However, the Align and Define phases of the process provide sufficient understanding to inform designers of an initial set of candidate resources.

Using the Shopping API example to illustrate the resource identification process, Figure 6.4 shows that the Book and Cart resources are used by the operations and are therefore resource candidates.

For each candidate resource, create a table that captures the resource name and any properties that are currently known. Including a description helps to align understanding and is useful when moving into the API design phase.

When creating an API profile, focus on capturing only the properties that are essential to the operation. So doing speeds up the modeling process and ensures the focus remains on the API profile rather than on implementation details.

Figure 6.5 shows the Shopping API resources, including a new resource called Book Author that was discovered while enumerating the properties for the Book Resource.

A Word of Caution on Resource Identification

While it may be tempting to use a database schema as the starting point for resource identification, keep in mind that API designs should not leak internal implementation details. A database schema reflects optimizations for transactional read and write operations rather than exposing business domain concepts over a network API.

It is best to work top-down when modeling an API to avoid leaking internal data model decisions into the API design. If the implementation phase demonstrates a one-to-one relationship between resources and a database schema, then it becomes a "happy accident," as painter Bob Ross[2] would say.

---

2. Bob Ross, "We Don't Make Mistakes," clip from *The Joy of Painting,* season 3, episode 5, "Distant Hills" (Schmidt1942, 2013; originally aired Feb. 1, 1984), https://www.youtube.com/watch?v=wCsO56kWwTc.

Shopping API – Supports the book browsing experience and cart management Public					
Operation Name	Description	Participants	Resource(s)	Emitted Events	Operation Details
listBooks()	List books by category or release date	Customer, Call Center			
searchBooks()	Search for books by author, title	Customer, Call Center			
viewBook()	View book details	Customer, Call Center			
addBookToCart()	Add a book to the customer's cart	Customer, Call Center			
removeBookFromCart()	Remove a book from the customer's cart	Customer, Call Center			
clearCart()	Remove all books from the customer's cart	Customer, Call Center			
viewCart()	View the current cart and total	Customer, Call Center			

Figure 6.4 *Identifying the Book and Cart resources for JSON's Bookstore's Shopping API profile.*

Book Resource	
Property Name	**Description**
title	The book title
isbn	The unique ISBN of the book
authors	List of Book Author resources

Cart Resource	
Property Name	**Description**
books	The books currently in the cart for purchase
subtotal	The total cost of all books in the cart
salesTax	The sales tax to be applied
vatTax	Any value-added tax to be applied
cartTotal	The total cost of the cart

Book Author Resource	
Property Name	**Description**
fullName	The full name of the author

Figure 6.5 *Capturing each resource for the Shopping API, along with some basic details about each one as a starting point.*

Step 3: Define the Resource Taxonomy

Once the resources have been identified, it is time to find the relationships among resources to define the API taxonomy. A taxonomy[3] is a classification of concepts and how they are arranged. An API taxonomy captures the set of resources the API will offer and their relationships to other resources.

There are three relationship types that resources may have between one another:

1. **Independent:** The resources exist standalone and do not require another resource's existence. Independent resources may reference other independent or dependent resources.

2. **Dependent:** One resource cannot exist without the existence of a parent resource. Be sure not to confuse a dependent resource relationship with one resource referencing another. This is a very specific case and not frequently encountered.

3. **Associative:** The resources may exist independently; however, their relationship requires additional properties to describe it. The result is a third resource that represents the relationship between the two resources. The third resource may have an independent or dependent relationship between each of the other two resources.

---

3. Dan Klyn, "Understanding Information Architecture," TUG, https://understandinggroup.com/ia-theory/understanding-information-architecture.

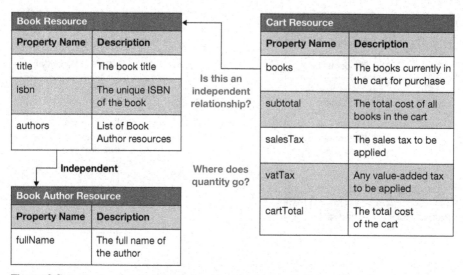

Figure 6.6 *Reviewing the resource relationships introduces a challenge: where does the quantity of books belong?*

Figure 6.6 shows the resources identified for the Shopping API, along with possible relationships. The relationship between a Book resource and Book Author resource is independent. There may be a reference between them, but each one exists independently of the other.

Notice in Figure 6.6 that a question needs to be addressed regarding where the quantity is specified when a book is added to a cart. This issue needs to be explored further. When a book is added to a cart, additional details that may be important include the quantity and the price of each book. This indicates an associative relationship that requires a new resource, in this case a Cart Item. The result is shown in Figure 6.7.

The operation `addBookToCart()` is renamed `addItemToCart()`, and `removeBook-FromCart()` is renamed `removeItemFromCart()` to reflect the introduction of the Cart Item resource, as shown in Figure 6.8.

Step 4: Add Operation Events

When the API taxonomy is completed, expand each API operation with the significant events that it will emit. These events may be used for data analytics purposes or as events that other systems may react to when they occur because of the operation.

The EventStorming canvas, created during the Align phase of the project, provides a starting point for important business events that were captured using the color-coded domain event sticky notes. If you didn't use EventStorming, capture the events as they are identified during the modeling process.

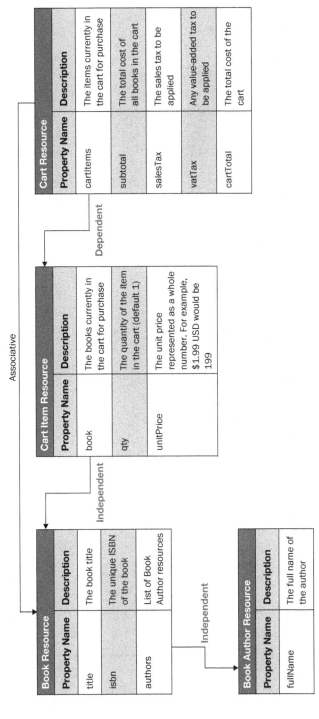

Figure 6.7 *A new resource, Cart Item, is added because of the associative relationship between Book and Cart.*

Shopping API—Supports the book browsing experience and cart management Public					
Operation Name	Description	Participants	Resource(s)	Emitted Events	Operation Details
listBooks()	List books by category or release date	Customer, Call Center	Book, Book Author		
searchBooks()	Search for books by author, title	Customer, Call Center	Book, Book Author		
viewBook()	View book details	Customer, Call Center	Book		
addItemToCart()	Add a book to the customer's cart	Customer, Call Center	Cart Item, Cart		
removeItemFromCart()	Remove a book from the customer's cart	Customer, Call Center	Cart Item, Cart		
clearCart()	Remove all books from the customer's cart	Customer, Call Center	Cart		
viewCart()	View the current cart and total	Customer, Call Center	Cart		

Figure 6.8 *The Shopping API profile, revised to reflect the introduction of the Cart Item resource.*

Event names should be presented in past tense and should apply the preferred standards and practices used within the organization. Figure 6.9 expands the previous model with events that each operation will emit. Notice the past-tense naming in the Emitted Events column.

The API profile now reflects the events that the identified operations will emit. Some operations may emit only one event, some more than one event, and some may not need to emit any event at all.

Step 5: Expand Operation Details

The final step is to expand the details of each operation to include important input and output details. Don't be too concerned with capturing everything at this point, as it is unnecessary. Focus on the essential input and output resources and parameters necessary to convey understanding across the team. There is no need to capture the type of each property or define a schema in the API model at this stage. Avoid being overly concerned with finding every parameter, as there will be plenty of time during the design phase to capture the complete design. If necessary, use a "parking lot" to capture important items that will need to be addressed as the design emerges.

An additional level of detail that is used to inform the upcoming API design is the matter of operations being synchronous or asynchronous. Synchronous APIs operate in a traditional request/response manner common to HTTP. Asynchronous APIs operate in the background rather than providing an immediate result. Asynchronous APIs are discussed in detail in Chapter 9, "Messaging, Streaming, and Event-Based Async APIs." For now, note the synchronous nature of each operation.

An often-overlooked detail for operations is safety. Safety and idempotence are important concerns when selecting the appropriate HTTP method. Each HTTP method specification describes the safety and idempotence that a server must implement. Safety classifications are also important for clients to consider as part of their error-handling code.

There are three classifications of safety for HTTP operations:

1. **Safe:** The operation does not make any state changes to the target resource(s). This safety classification is assigned to all read-based (GET) operations.

2. **Idempotent:** The operation makes state changes to the target resource(s), but if the operation is executed with the same input, it will produce the same result. This is important, as it informs API clients if they can reissue a request that previously failed, without additional side effects. This safety classification is assigned to replace and delete operations (PUT and DELETE).

Shopping API — Supports the book browsing experience and cart management Public					
Operation Name	**Description**	**Participants**	**Resource(s)**	**Emitted Events**	**Operation Details**
listBooks()	List books by category or release date	Customer, Call Center	Book, Book Author	Books.Listed	
searchBooks()	Search for books by author, title	Customer, Call Center	Book, Book Author	Books.Searched	
viewBook()	View book details	Customer, Call Center	Book	Book.Viewed	
addItemToCart()	Add a book to the customer's cart	Customer, Call Center	Cart Item, Cart	Cart.ItemAdded	
removeItemFromCart()	Remove a book from the customer's cart	Customer, Call Center	Cart Item, Cart	Cart.ItemRemoved	
clearCart()	Remove all books from the customer's cart	Customer, Call Center	Cart	Cart.Cleared	
viewCart()	View the current cart and total	Customer, Call Center	Cart	Cart.Viewed	

Figure 6.9 *JSON's Bookstore's Shopping API, now with emitted events added for each operation in the API profile.*

3. **Unsafe:** The operation makes state changes to the target resource(s) and cannot guarantee the same results if called multiple times with the same input. This safety classification is typically assigned to create and update (POST and PATCH) operations.

Review each operation to determine the safety classification type that is required of the operation. Doing so during API modeling provides additional insights during the design process.

Figure 6.10 shows the Shopping API example expanded to include input and output details for each operation, synchronicity, and safety classification.

The API profile may then be finalized by capturing any architectural requirements, such as SLAs, necessary to support consumers and industry standards that may need to be considered during design (e.g., adherence to an open banking standard).

Refer to the API workshop examples repository[4] available on GitHub for API profile templates and examples to help jumpstart the effort.

Validating the API Model with Sequence Diagrams

The API design team has a responsibility to ensure the APIs will meet the requirements of everyone using it. This requires two final actions: validating the API model to ensure no gaps exist and gathering feedback from stakeholders.

Validate the API profiles against the previously produced original job stories and activities to validate that all requirements have been met. To validate the API model, create sequence diagrams that demonstrate typical usage scenarios. These scenarios may be sourced from the EventStorming canvas, job stories, and other sources. Figure 6.11 shows an example scenario that supports a shopping and checkout experience using the modeled APIs.

During the validation process, clarify all details to ensure full alignment and definition of the API scope and operations. If operations are missing to complete the scenario, revisit the modeling steps to capture the missing operations.

Once the model has been validated, share the model with all stakeholders and obtain feedback. If API modeling was performed with the entire team, including business and product stakeholders, then feedback was obtained during the process. Otherwise, share the produced assets and seek to incorporate feedback prior to moving into the design phase of the process.

---

4. https://bit.ly/align-define-design-examples

Shopping API—Supports the book browsing experience and cart management

Public

Operation Name	Description	Participants	Resource(s)	Emitted Events	Operation Details
listBooks()	List books by category or release date	Customer, Call Center	Book, Book Author	Books.Listed	Request Parameters: categoryId, releaseDate Returns: Book[] safe / synchronous
searchBooks()	Search for books by author, title	Customer, Call Center	Book	Books.Searched	Request Parameters: searchQuery Returns: Book[] safe / synchronous
viewBook()	View book details	Customer, Call Center	Book	Book.Viewed	Request Parameters: bookId Returns: Book safe / synchronous
addItemToCart()	Add a book to the customer's cart	Customer, Call Center	Cart Item, Cart	Cart.ItemAdded	Request Parameters: cartId, bookId, quantity Returns: Cart unsafe / synchronous
removeItemFromCart()	Remove a book from the customer's cart	Customer, Call Center	Cart Item, Cart	Cart.ItemRemoved	Request Parameters: cartItemId Returns: Cart idempotent / synchronous
clearCart()	Remove all books from the customer's cart	Customer, Call Center	Cart	Cart.Cleared	Request Parameters: cartId Returns: Cart safe / synchronous
viewCart()	View the current cart and total	Customer, Call Center	Cart	Cart.Viewed	Request Parameters: cartId Returns: Cart safe / synchronous

Figure 6.10 *JSON's Bookstore Shopping API with operation details added to the API profile.*

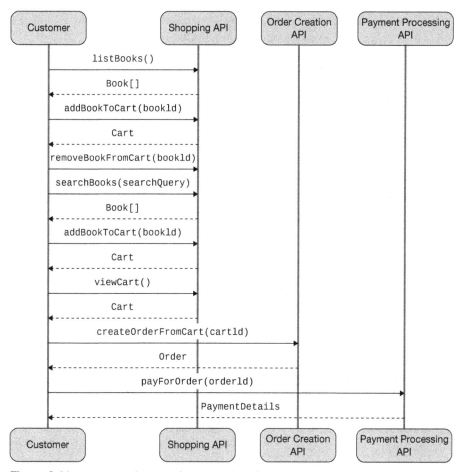

Figure 6.11 *JSON's Bookstore's Place an Order job story, represented as a sequence diagram to ensure all operations were identified as part of the API modeling process to implement job story outcomes and associated activities.*

Evaluating API Priority and Reuse

Not every API has equal weight in the delivery schedule. A sizing exercise is an optional step before moving into API design. The results of this exercise help teams avoid building APIs unnecessarily or in the wrong priority order.

First, assess the business and competitive value that the API offers. Ask the following questions to assess the value that each API brings:

- Does the API help provide a competitive advantage over other market offerings?
- Does the API reduce the cost of doing business, perhaps by reducing manual processes?
- Does the API create a new revenue stream or improve an existing revenue stream?
- Is the API producing business intelligence, market insights, or decisioning factors?
- Does the API automate repetitive tasks that free the organization for more critical business functions?

If the answer to all the questions is no, then the value produced is low. Answering yes to one or more questions results in the API offering value to the business or marketplace.

Next, size the effort to build each API from scratch. One approach is to use a relative sizing approach by classifying the APIs as small, medium, or large. Consider the details surfaced during EventStorming and write activity steps to roughly estimate the size and complexity to build the API from the ground-up.

Finally, determine if there are existing APIs that could be leveraged or extended. These APIs may be commercial off-the-shelf (COTS) APIs, internal APIs produced by another team, or open-source solutions that could be leveraged to speed delivery. Organizations often forget this step, resulting in wasted time and effort building duplicate or noncore APIs. Performing this step encourages organizations to reuse APIs first and build new APIs only when necessary.

Figure 6.12 shows a tabular format that captures examples of these details for JSON's Bookstore API profiles modeled in this chapter.

Summary

API modeling helps to bring together the insights and artifacts produced in the Align phase of the design process into a model that describes the scope and intent of the APIs required. Review the following checklist to ensure nothing was missed:

- **Resource taxonomies** identify the properties of each resource along with the relationships and dependencies among them.

API Profile	Business and Competitive Value	In-House Build Effort	Existing Internal/Third-Party APIs
Shopping API	Medium	Medium	Third-party eStore solutions (high complexity to customize and add our internal recommendation engine support)
Order Creation API	Medium	Medium	Third-party order processing APIs (may include fulfillment support also)
Payment Processing API	Small	Large	Various third-party payment processors

Figure 6.12 *A sizing and prioritization effort for the current set of JSON's Bookstore's API profiles captured during API modeling.*

- **API profiles** are created to offer a high-level specification of each API, independent of how the APIs will be designed and implemented.

- **Sequence diagrams** help to validate how the APIs deliver the outcomes captured in the job stories.

- **Sizing and prioritization** help to ensure that APIs are reused when possible and built when necessary.

By spending time modeling APIs, teams can clearly articulate the needs of each API. They are also able to identify the effort involved in building them from scratch and to consider internal or third-party APIs that may meet requirements. Reusing existing APIs saves weeks or months of delivery effort.

With API modeling complete, the Define phase of the ADDR process has reached an end. The API Design phase is next. This phase migrates the API profiles into a specific API style. Chapter 7 shows how to use API profiles to inform the design of a REST-based API. If the target API style is not REST, feel free to jump to the appropriate chapter.

Part IV

Designing APIs

Now that APIs have been modeled as part of the Define phase, the team has a better understanding of the scope of each API and the operations it needs to support to realize the desired outcomes. The next phase of the Align-Define-Design-Refine (ADDR) process is to migrate the modeled API profiles into API designs.

There are many choices of API styles, from REST to RPC and beyond. This section details a step-by-step process on producing a high-level design using the artifacts created during the Align and Define phases of the process. Feel free to jump to the specific chapter needed to apply the API style of choice.

Chapter 7

REST-Based API Design

The REST interface is designed to be efficient for large-grain hypermedia data transfer, optimizing for the common case of the Web, but resulting in an interface that is not optimal for other forms of architectural interaction.

— Roy Thomas Fielding

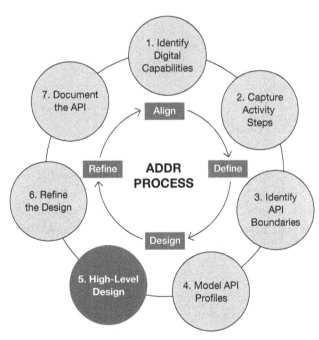

Figure 7.1 *The Design phase offers several options for API styles. This chapter covers REST-based API design.*

As teams move from the modeling to the design phase, they are faced with a variety of decisions. Some of these will resolve easily, while others will take time and deliberation. Just know that it is difficult to get an API design right the first time. Therefore, teams are encouraged to spend time designing and prototyping their APIs to gain feedback from early adopters before coding begins.

This chapter presents an overview of REST, along with a step-by-step process for migrating an API profile, created during the API modeling phase, into a REST-based API design. Along the way, various decisions and common design patterns are explored. The result will be a high-level API design (Figure 7.1) that applies REST-based principles.

> ### Principle 3: Select the API design elements that match the need
>
> Trying to find the perfect API style is a fruitless endeavor. Instead, seek to understand and apply the API elements appropriate for the need, whether that is REST, GraphQL, gRPC, or an emerging style just entering the industry. The next three chapters provide insights into popular API styles to help teams select the right style or styles that fit the need. The chapters discuss when to apply each style, when to select synchronous or asynchronous interaction models, and whether to offer SDK libraries.

What Is a REST-Based API?

Representational State Transfer (REST) is an architectural style for distributed hypermedia systems. Unlike HTTP, REST is not a specification that is managed by a standards group. The term was coined by Roy Thomas Fielding in his PhD dissertation, "Architectural Styles and the Design of Network-based Software Architectures."[1] This paper outlines the core concepts and constraints for understanding an architectural style and how these constraints were applied in varying degrees to architect the World Wide Web.

When discussing REST APIs or REST-based APIs, many people reference Fielding's work without realizing that it extends far beyond Web-based APIs. The paper seeks to establish fundamental constraints for designing evolvable and scalable distributed systems. Those interested in software architecture, particularly distributed software, should read Fielding's paper as part of their studies.

---

1. Roy Thomas Fielding, "Architectural Styles and the Design of Network-based Software Architectures" (PhD diss., University of California, 2000), https://www.ics.uci.edu/~fielding/pubs/dissertation/top.htm.

The paper does not require the use of HTTP as the underlying protocol for REST-based architecture. It does, however, discuss how the authors of the HTTP specification relied on the outlined architectural constraints to make it more evolvable. Because HTTP is the protocol of choice for most network-based APIs, the details offered in this and later chapters rely on HTTP as the protocol of choice.

The set of architectural properties outlined in Fielding's paper serve to establish constraints to create agreement around flexibility and evolvability when applied to distributed systems, including network-based APIs:

- **Client/server:** The client and the server act independently, and the interaction between them is only in the form of requests and responses.

- **Stateless:** The server does not remember anything about the user who uses the API, so all necessary information to process the request must be provided by the client on each request. Note: This isn't about storing server-side state.

- **Layered system:** The client is agnostic as to how many layers, if any, there are between the client and the actual server responding to the request. This is a key principle of HTTP, allowing for client-side caching, caching servers, reverse proxies, and authorization layering—all transparent to the client sending the request.

- **Cacheable:** The server response must contain information about whether or not the data is cacheable, allowing the client and any middleware servers to cache data outside of the API server.

- **Code on demand (optional):** The client can request code from the server, usually in the form of a script or binary package, for client-side execution. This is performed today by browsers requesting JavaScript files to extend the behavior of a Web page. Code on demand is an opportunity for API teams to provide JavaScript files for clients to retrieve that perform form validation and other responsibilities. Thus, evolvability can be extended to clients through code on demand.

- **Uniform interface:** Encourages independent evolvability by leaning on resource-based identification, interaction using representations, self-descriptive messages, and hypermedia controls.

The architectural constraints outlined in Fielding's paper are important when considering the design of a Web-based API. When taken together, these constraints contribute to the design of evolvable Web APIs.

REST Was Never about CRUD

As already mentioned, REST is not a specification or a protocol. Contrary to popular opinion, a REST-based API does not require JSON or the use of the create-read-update-delete (CRUD) pattern of data interaction. REST is simply a set of constraints and agreements on how the individual components should work together. This offers flexibility to address architectural issues. Many of today's Web-based APIs use JSON and the CRUD pattern as design elements.

Unfortunately, a challenge emerges when people apply the REST label to an API that uses CRUD and JSON but may not intentionally apply the constraints as originally described in Fielding's paper. This has resulted in many disagreements on what is "RESTful" and whether something is "REST enough."

Frankly, these disagreements are not beneficial. Instead, it is best to approach an API labeled as RESTful or REST-based with a mindset of grace and understanding that not everyone has read and fully applied the original REST paper. Use the opportunity to gently coach teams on how their architecture and API design can be improved over time. Whatever you do, please don't use the opportunity to show how much more you know about REST than they do.

REST Is Client/Server

The client/server architecture is an essential REST constraint. The server hosts available resources, supporting operations through synchronous, message-based interactions that use one or more representations as the client interacts with it.

Separating the client and server allows the user interface of the client to change over time. New devices and interface styles may be used without requiring changes to the server.

Most important is that the client is able to evolve independently of the server. The server may offer new resources or additional representation formats without negatively impacting the client. This is fundamental to why APIs may be offered as products, with or without a preexisting user interface provided by the vendor.

REST Is Resource-Centric

The key abstraction of information in REST is a resource. As mentioned in Chapter 1, "The Principles of API Design," a resource consists of a unique name or identifier that can reference documents, images, collections of other resources, or a digital representation of anything in the real world, such as a person or thing.

Resource representations capture the current state or intended state of a resource. Every resource must support at least one representation format but may support more than one. These representations may include a data format such as JSON, XML, CSV, PDF, image, and other media types.

The representation formats supported for any given resource may vary depending on the needs of the client. For example, JSON may be a default media format offered by a REST-based API. However, some resources may need to be manipulated in a spreadsheet and therefore offer an alternative CSV-based representation of the same resource.

For example, a resource may represent a person named Vaughn Vernon. The resource may have one or several representations. There may be a JSON-based representation, along with an XML representation. If a historical record is kept of all changes, each change may also exist as a representation that is available in JSON and XML media formats.

REST Is Message Based

Readers of Fielding's dissertation may have noticed that it focuses on the message exchange between client and server. Notice the use of the terms *REST messages* and *self-descriptive messages* in the paper. REST-based API design goes beyond the properties within a JSON or XML representation.

A resource representation is the message body within the overall message. Transport protocol design is also part of a complete REST-based API design. The URL path, URL query parameters, and HTTP request/response headers must all be considered as part of the design process. Focusing only on the message body results in an incomplete design.

The combination of the HTTP method, URL, request headers, and request body is a command message sent from the client to the server. It tells the server what you would like to do. The response headers, response status code, and response payload comprise the reply message to the client. When developers think of REST-based APIs as exchanging messages with clients, their API designs become more capable of evolving over time as the message evolves and the API grows and matures.

REST Supports a Layered System

The REST architecture style is a layered system, which means that a client should not be built on the assumption it is communicating directly with the server. There may be multiple middleware layers between the client and server that offer caching, logging, access controls, load balancing, and other infrastructure needs, as shown in Figure 7.2.

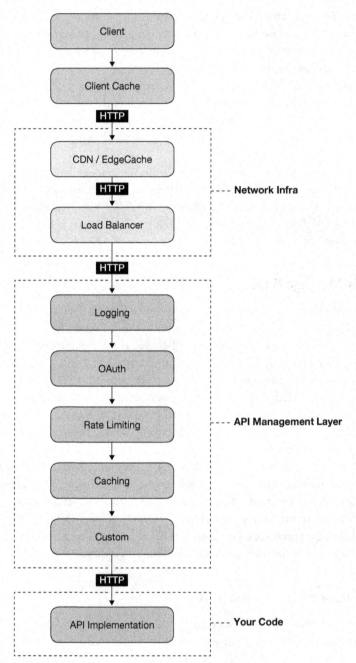

Figure 7.2 *REST supports a layered architecture, allowing middleware servers to exist between the client and server.*

REST Supports Code on Demand

Code on demand is a powerful but underutilized constraint. When a client requests a resource, it may also request code to act upon it. The client does not have to know what is in the code, it just has to understand how to execute it. The primary benefit is that the API can extend itself without requiring the client applications to perform a specific upgrade.

This technique is something that browsers do every day by downloading JavaScript files to execute locally within the browser. The browser does not need to know what is in the JavaScript files it downloads, only that they require the built-in JavaScript engine and therefore may be executed within the confines of the security sandbox offered by the browser. As new features and functionality become available, they are immediately available to the user without requiring a browser upgrade.

While used heavily by Web-based applications, this REST constraint is one of the least utilized for REST-based Web APIs but one of the most powerful. Imagine an API that offers the option of downloading code to create Web forms and client-side validation behavior without the need to code and maintain it on the client side!

Hypermedia Controls

A hypermedia API is one driven by self-descriptive links in the representation. These links point to other, related API operations that reference related resources. They may also be used to reference other possible uses of the API, commonly referred to as *affordances*. Fielding considered hypermedia important to a REST-based architecture.

APIs that use hypermedia controls extend the conversation between client and server by offering runtime discovery of operations. They may also be used to convey server-side state to the client through the presence or absence of links in the representation. This powerful concept is explored later in this section.

Hypermedia controls help connect the dots of various resources within and across APIs, making it operate more like the Web. Imagine using a search engine to find some results, only to never be offered links to click to explore the results. Unfortunately, that is the way most design their APIs, offering only data and not hypermedia controls that afford the client the opportunity to explore the depth of the data and operations offered by the API.

A common use of hypermedia controls includes pagination, as shown in this Hypertext Application Language (HAL)-based response:

```
{
 "_links": {
   "self": {"href": "/projects" },
   "next": {"href": "/projects?since=d266f6cd&maxResults=20" },
   "prev": {"href": "/projects?since=43be807d&maxResults=20" },
   "first": {"href": "/projects?since=ef24266a&maxResults=20" },
   "last": {"href": "/projects?since=4e8c74be&maxResults=20" },
  }
}
```

API clients can be designed to use the next link to follow the search results page by page until the next link is no longer present, indicating all search results have been processed.

APIs that offer hypermedia controls help to create context-driven responses. These controls are able to indicate what operations are possible, or not possible, based on the presence or absence of hypermedia links. This capability avoids the need to send Boolean fields or state-related fields that the client interprets to decide what actions may be taken. Instead, the server determines this ahead of time and conveys what can and cannot be done by the presence or absence of the links provided.

What Is HATEOAS?

Hypermedia as the engine of application state, or HATEOAS, is a constraint within REST that originated in Fielding's dissertation. It describes the absence or presence of links as indicators of what operations the client may perform. Because the server understands both the user executing the operation and the authorization requirements of the operation itself, it is better positioned to determine what the client is able to do. Without this constraint, clients are required to reimplement the same server-side business logic and keep that logic in sync at all times.

It is important to note that Fielding has expressed a preference to use the term *hypermedia controls* rather than HATEAOS. Through the remainder of the book, the term hypermedia controls will be used in place of HATEOAS for clarity.

Following is an example HAL-based response for an article within a content management system that offers hypermedia links to valid operations based on the status of the article and the user's role as an author:

```
{
 "articleId":"12345",
 "status":"draft",
 "_links": [
     { "rel":"self", "url":"..."},
     { "rel":"update", "url":"..."},
     { "rel":"submit", "url":"..."}
],
 "authors": [ ... ],
 ...
}
```

Once the author is ready to submit the article for editorial review, the editor would retrieve the article and receive the following actions based on the submitted status of the article and the editor's role:

```
{
 "articleId":"12345",
 "status": "submitted",
 "_links": [
     { "rel":"self", "url":"..."},
     { "rel":"reject", "url":"..."},
     { "rel":"approve", "url":"..."}
],
 "authors": [ ... ],
 ...
}
```

Hypermedia controls have big implications for API-driven workflows that use context-driven hypermedia controls. They help to reduce the amount of business logic that has to be repeated in the client to mimic intended server behavior. Without them, the client would need to be coded to know what actions are allowed based on the status of the article and the role of the user. Instead, the client may be coded to look for specific hypermedia links that indicate if specific buttons are displayed or disabled for the end user, avoiding the need to keep in sync with the server-side business logic. This ensures the API is evolvable without breaking client code.

REST-based APIs offer four primary hypermedia control types:

1. **Index hypermedia controls:** Offer a list of all available API operations, typically as an API homepage

2. **Navigation hypermedia controls:** Include pagination links within payload responses or by using the `Link` header

3. **Relationship hypermedia controls:** Links that indicate relationships with other resources or for master-detail relationships

4. **Context-driven hypermedia controls:** Server state that informs the client what actions are available

It is important to note that any API style that does not encourage a unique URL per resource is unable to take advantage of hypermedia controls. This is the case for GraphQL and gRPC API styles, detailed in Chapter 8, "RPC- and Query-based API Design," along with older network API styles and messaging specifications such as SOAP and XML-RPC.

Measuring REST Using the Richardson Maturity Model

The Richardson Maturity Model, or RMM for short, is a maturity model created by Leonard Richardson that describes four levels of REST-based API design maturity. The four levels are generally defined as the following:

- **Level 0:** A single API operation, or endpoint, that receives all requests. Further, the name of the desired action is reflected with some sort of action parameter or even embedded within the payload of the request (e.g., `POST /api?op=getProjects`)

- **Level 1:** Incorporation of resource-based design through URL-based naming but with additional action parameters where needed (e.g., `GET /projects?id=12345`)

- **Level 2:** Addition of properly applied HTTP methods, such as `GET`, `POST`, `PUT`, and response codes to improve client/server interaction

- **Level 3:** Self-descriptive APIs that include hypermedia controls to suggest related resources and client affordances based on server-side state

RMM was meant to be used as a general classification of an API's improvement as designers seek to reach a design that uses hypermedia controls. Unfortunately, it has been used to denigrate the efforts of designers by proving that an API labeled as REST-based has not met sufficient criteria to be truly labeled as REST.

Richardson addressed the confusion and intent of RMM in a 2015 REST Fest talk titled "What Have I Done?"[2] Richardson described the whole idea of RMM as "very embarrassing" and said it was meant simply as one possible measurement of improvement and maturity when attempting to target a hypermedia API. It was not meant to be a canonical method of classifying all APIs as REST-compliant. Instead, design to meet the needs of clients rather than trying to measure a specific level of design maturity.

When to Choose REST

Fielding's dissertation explicitly defines REST as an architectural style for course-grained data transfer:

> The REST interface is designed to be efficient for large-grain hypermedia data transfer, optimizing for the common case of the Web, but resulting in an interface that is not optimal for other forms of architectural interaction.

While Fielding doesn't define *large grain* explicitly, the Web is a good example. An HTML page is sent as a single, complete resource. It is not split into separate assets and retrieved separately. Once the HTML resource has been received and parsed, all referenced images, JavaScript, and style sheets are retrieved individually.

REST is a good architectural style choice when the interaction level requires course-grained resources over HTTP. This is common for APIs exposed over the Internet that may encounter additional network latency or unpredictable connectivity.

For finer-grained interaction styles, RPC or other styles may be a better fit. Some RPC styles offer improved performance and long-running connections that do not meet the REST constraints outlined by Fielding. This includes the choice of gRPC and asynchronous API styles, discussed in Chapter 8 and Chapter 9, "Messaging, Streaming, and Event-Based Async APIs," for service-to-service and client-to-service interactions.

---

2. Leonard Richardson, "What Have I Done?" (lecture, REST Fest, Greenville, SC, September 18, 2015).

In addition, many organizations default to REST for their API style choice when offering customer- and partner-facing Web APIs. Most select the REST-based API style internally because of the abundance of tooling, infrastructure, operational, and management support. Because REST builds on the patterns of the Web, it is familiar to developers, easily managed by ops teams, and offers an abundance of tools and libraries for producing and consuming APIs.

REST API Design Process

Now that one or more APIs have been modeled, as described in Chapter 6, "API Modeling," it is time to start the API design process. While the goal of API modeling is to explore and capture the API requirements into a series of API profiles, the API design process maps the API profiles into HTTP using the REST-based principles discussed earlier in this chapter. Because most of the effort involved in API design was focused on modeling the API to produce the API profile, there are five quick steps to a high-level API design.

Step 1: Design Resource URL Paths

The first step uses the API resources and resource relationships identified in the API modeling process, captured previously in Figure 6.7 of Chapter 6. Migrate the list of resources identified in the API profile into a tabular list, as shown in Figure 7.3. For dependent resources, indent the name slightly to denote the relationship. This will help when establishing the URL paths for each resource.

Next, convert each resource name into a URL-friendly name using all lowercase letters and using hyphens in place of spaces. Start the path with a leading slash, followed by the resource name in pluralized form to denote that this is a collection of resource instances.

Resource Path
Books
Book Authors
Carts
Cart Items

Figure 7.3 *Begin by migrating the list of resources from the API profile created during modeling into a preliminary API design. Note that Cart Items is a dependent relationship, as detailed in Chapter 6, so it is indented slightly.*

Dependent resources are nested under the parent, requiring the parent identifier in the path to interact with the dependent resources.

A Warning about Dependent Resources

It is common to see a considerable number of dependent resources when APIs are designed from the bottom up from a relational database or by using a relational style to resource design.

Nesting dependent resources is for constraining the navigability of children to the scope of the parent. While it may be tempting to create dependent resources, keep in mind that each nested level requires the API consumer to include the parent identifier in the path. For example:

```
GET /users/{userId}/projects/{projectId}/tasks/{taskId}
```

For an API consumer to retrieve a task by a given identifier, it also needs to have the parent project and user identifiers. This places additional work on the client to track these parent identifiers.

Nesting dependent resources is a useful design option but should be used only when it improves the usability of the API.

The results are shown in Figure 7.4. Notice that the resource collections are plural names. While not required, this convention is commonly found with REST APIs.

Migrate the list of operations, including their descriptions and request/response details, into a new tabular format designed to capture the high-level design. This is shown in Figure 7.5.

Resource Path
/books
/carts
/carts/{cartId}/Items
/authors

Figure 7.4 *Convert each resource name into a URL-friendly name with dependent resources nested under the parent.*

Resource Path	Operation Name	HTTP Method	Description	Request	Response
/books	listBooks()		List books by category or release date	categoryId/releaseDate	Book[]
/books/search	searchBooks()		Search for books by author, title	searchQuery	Book[]
/books/{bookId}	viewBook()		View book details	bookId	Book
/carts/{cartId}	viewCart()		View the current cart and total	cartId	Cart
/carts/{cartId}	clearCart()		Remove all books from the customer's cart	cartId	Cart
/carts/{cartId}/items	addItemToCart()		Add a book to the customer's cart	cartId	Cart
/carts/{cartId}/items/{cartItemId}	removeItemFromCart()		Remove a book from the customer's cart	cartIdcartItemId	Cart
/authors	getAuthorDetails()		Retrieve the details of an author	authorId	BookAuthor

Figure 7.5 *Migrate the API profile's list of operations, descriptions, and request/response details into a new design-centric tabular format.*

Step 2: Map API Operations to HTTP Methods

The next step is to determine which HTTP method is appropriate for each operation. Chapter 6 outlined three safety classifications that each HTTP method may be assigned: safe, idempotent, or unsafe. Table 7.1 outlines the safety classifications for common HTTP methods based on their intended use.

During modeling, common verbs were likely identified in the operation name and/or description of the API profile. These verbs often provide clues to the HTTP method that best matches the operation. By combining the safety classification of HTTP methods, as outlined in Table 7.1, with the operation mappings listed in Table 7.2, the appropriate HTTP method can be selected.

Using Table 7.2 as a reference, along with the list of resource paths created previously in step 1, assign the appropriate path and HTTP method to each operation based on the intended usage. If the operation is interacting with a specific resource instance, include the resource identifier in the path. The results are shown in Figure 7.6.

Table 7.1 *Safety Classifications for Common HTTP Methods*

HTTP Method	Method Description	Safety Classification	Safety Description
GET	Returns requested data	Safe	No state changes are made
POST	Used in a variety of scenarios, from calculations to creating new resources	Unsafe	Cannot guarantee the same results for multiple calls with the same input
PUT	Representation from client used to replace resource	Idempotent	Guarantees the same results for multiple calls with the same input as the client is providing to the entire resource representation
PATCH	Performs a partial update of a resource	Unsafe	Cannot guarantee the same results for multiple calls with the same input, as the client provides only a partial representation of the resource
DELETE	Deleted a resource from the server	Idempotent	Multiple calls to delete the same resource will still result in the resource being deleted (even if it doesn't exist)

Table 7.2 *Mapping Common Verbs Found in Operation Names/Descriptions to HTTP*

Operation Verb	Typical HTTP Method + Resource with Examples
List, Search, Match, View All	GET resource collection `GET /books`
Show, Retrieve, View	GET resource instance `GET /books/12345`
Create, Add	POST resource collection `POST /books`

Replace	PUT resource instance or collection
	`PUT /carts/123`
	`PUT /carts/123/items`

Update	PATCH resource instance `PATCH /carts/123`
Delete All, Remove All, Clear, Reset	DELETE resource collection `DELETE /carts/123/items`
Delete	DELETE resource instance `DELETE /carts/123/items/456`
Search, Secure Search	POST custom search action on the resource collection `POST /carts/search`
<other verbs>	POST as a custom action on a resource collection or instance `POST /books/123/deactivate`

Step 3: Assign Response Codes

The API design is starting to emerge. The next step is to assign the expected response codes for each operation. HTTP response status codes belong to three primary response code families:

- **200 codes** indicate success, some with more clarity (e.g., 201 CREATED vs. 200 OK).

- **400 codes** indicate a failure in the request that the client may wish to fix and resubmit.

- **500 codes** indicate a failure on the server that is not the fault of the client. The client may attempt a retry at a future time, if appropriate.

Be sure to use the right code for the right reason. When in doubt, refer to the most current RFC that details the intended usage for the code. If a specific code isn't available within the response code family, then use the default 200, 400, or 500 code as appropriate.

Resource Path	Operation Name	HTTP Method	Description	Request	Response
/books	listBooks()	GET	List books by category or release date	categoryId/releaseDate	Book[]
/books/search	searchBooks()	POST	Search for books by author, title	searchQuery	Book[]
/books/{bookId}	viewBook()	GET	View book details	bookId	Book
/carts/{cartId}	viewCart()	GET	View the current cart and total	cartId	Cart
/carts/{cartId}	clearCart()	DELETE	Remove all books from the customer's cart	cartId	Cart
/carts/{cartId}/items	addItemToCart()	POST	Add a book to the customer's cart	cartId	Cart
/carts/{cartId}/items/{cartItemId}	removeItemFromCart()	DELETE	Remove a book from the customer's cart	cartId/cartItemId	Cart
/authors	getAuthorDetails()	GET	Retrieve the details of an author	authorId	BookAuthor

Figure 7.6 *Using the list of paths identified earlier, assign the appropriate path and HTTP method to each operation based on the intended usage.*

Don't Invent Your Own Response Codes

Over the years, some strange decisions have been made by API designers. One is the decision to use UNIX-style codes, where 0 indicates success and 1 through 127 indicate an error, for HTTP response code. Please do not invent your own response codes. HTTP is designed to be layered, which means that middleware servers that you don't own might be involved between the client and server. Creating your own codes will only cause problems with these intermediary layers.

While the list of HTTP response codes is quite large, there are several that are commonly used in API design. These are detailed in Table 7.3.

API clients should be prepared for any kind of response code, but it is not necessary to capture every possible response code. Start by identifying at least one success response code for each operation, along with any error codes that the API may explicitly return. While the list of errors may not be comprehensive, start by identifying the typical error codes that may be returned. Figure 7.7 shows the possible success and error codes for the Shopping API.

Step 4: Documenting the REST API Design

Upon the completion of step 3, the high-level API design work is finished. Using the work done so far, it is now time to capture the API design using an API description format. This will allow for sharing the API design within and across teams for feedback.

Table 7.3 *Common HTTP Response Codes Used in API Design*

HTTP Response Code	Description
200 OK	The request has succeeded.
201 Created	The request has been fulfilled and resulted in a new resource being created.
202 Accepted	The request has been accepted for processing, but the processing has not been completed.
204 No Content	The server has fulfilled the request but does not need to return a body. This is common for delete operations.
400 Bad Request	The request could not be understood by the server due to malformed syntax or invalid input.
401 Unauthorized	The request requires user authentication.
403 Forbidden	The server understood the request but is refusing to fulfill it.
404 Not Found	The server has not found anything matching the requested URL/URI.
500 Internal Server Error	The server encountered an unexpected condition which prevented it from fulfilling the request.

Resource Path	Operation Name	HTTP Method	Description	Request	Response
/books	listBooks()	GET	List books by category or release date	categoryIdreleaseDate	Book[] 200
/books/search	searchBooks()	POST	Search for books by author, title	searchQuery	Book[] 200
/books/{bookId}	viewBook()	GET	View book details	bookId	Book 200, 404
/carts/{cartId}	viewCart()	GET	View the current cart and total	cartId	Cart 200, 404
/carts/{cartId}	clearCart()	DELETE	Remove all books from the customer's cart	cartId	Cart 204, 404
/carts/{cartId}/items	addItemToCart()	POST	Add a book to the customer's cart	cartId	Cart 201, 400
/carts/{cartId}/items/{cartItemId}	removeItemFromCart()	DELETE	Remove a book from the customer's cart	cartIdcartItemId	Cart 204, 404
/authors	getAuthorDetails()	GET	Retrieve the details of an author	authorId	BookAuthor 200, 404

Figure 7.7 *Expanding the Shopping API design with success and error response codes captured in the Response column of the table.*

Organizations typically have a preferred API description format, such as the OpenAPI Specification (OAS) or API Blueprint. If a format hasn't been selected or standardized, refer to Chapter 13, "Documenting APIs," to learn more about the various formats available. No matter what format is selected, the result is to have a machine-readable version of the API design for review, rendering API reference documentation and tooling support.

For the purposes of demonstrating the key areas of documentation during the API design phase, the examples in this chapter use the OpenAPI Specification v3 (OAS v3). Screenshots show the OAS v3 description file using the Swagger Editor[3] to render the result side by side for illustrative purposes.

Start the documentation process by leveraging details about the API captured throughout the API modeling and design process. Includes an API name, description, and other details about the API. The description should reference any other APIs that may be used in collaboration with this one. Summarize the purpose of the API and the kinds of operations offered. Avoid referencing internal details of how the API is implemented, as those details can be stored outside the API description in a wiki or similar collaboration tool for future developer reference. Figure 7.8 shows the result of capturing these details in OAS v3.

```
1   openapi: 3.0.0
2   info:
3     title: Bookstore Shopping API - REST Example
4     description: |
5       Supports the shopping experience of an online bookstore, including browsing and searching
          for available books and shopping cart management.
6
7       The Order Creation API is used to convert the shopping cart into an order that is prepared
          to accept shipping details, payment, and fulfillment tracking.
8
9       The API includes the following shopping operations by capability:
10
11      | Capability          | Operation                                           |
12      |---------------------|-----------------------------------------------------|
13      | List Recent Books   | List Recent Books In Store                          |
14      | List Recent Books   | Search for a book by topic or keyword               |
15      | List Recent Books   | View Book Details                                   |
16      | Place an Order      | Create Cart                                         |
17      | Place an Order      | Add Book to Cart                                    |
18      | Place an Order      | Remove Book from the Cart                           |
19      | Place an Order      | Modify Book in Cart                                 |
20      | Place an Order      | View Cart with Totals                               |
21
22      contact: {}
23      version: '1.0'
24   servers:
25   - url: https://{defaultHost}
26     variables:
27       defaultHost:
28         default: www.example.com/shop
```

Figure 7.8 *Capturing the Shopping API design into the OpenAPI Specification v3, starting with the name, description, and other important details.*

---

3. https://swagger.io

Next, capture the details of each operation. For OAS v3, this begins with the path, followed by each HTTP method supported at the path. It is also recommended to add an operationId property to each operation. Use the operation name from the API profile, defined in Chapter 6. This makes the documentation process effortless and helps to map the OAS description back to the API profile.

Using the details captured in the associated job stories created in Chapter 3, "Identify Digital Capabilities," write a short summary of the API to help readers understand its purpose. Expand the details in the description field using the information captured in the API profile in Chapter 6. Also, ensure all path parameters and query arguments are captured. This is shown in Figure 7.9.

```
29  paths:
30    /books:
31      get:
32        tags:
33        - Books
34        summary: Returns a paginated list of available books
35        description: "Returns a paginated list of available books based on the
            search criteria provided. If no search criteria is provided, books are
            returned in alphabetical order. \n"
36        operationId: ListBooks
37        parameters:
38        - name: q
39          in: query
40          description: A query string to use for filtering books by title and
              description. If not provided, all available books will be listed.
              Note that the query argument 'q' is a common standard for general
              search queries
41          style: form
42          explode: true
43          schema:
44            type: string
45        - name: daysSinceBookReleased
46          in: query
47          description: A query string to use for filtering books released within
              the last number of days, e.g. 7 means in the last 7 days. The
              default value of null indicates no time filtering is applied.
              Maximum number of days to filter is 30 days since today
48          style: form
49          explode: true
50          schema:
51            type: integer
52            format: int32
53        - name: offset
54          in: query
55          description: A offset from which the list of books are retrieved,
              where an offset of 0 means the first page of results. Default is an
              offset of 0
56          style: form
```

Figure 7.9 *Expanding the Shopping API design documentation to include each operation.*

Finally, capture all schema elements for resource representations in the schema definitions section of the OAS v3 description. Use the resource models created during API modeling, as described in Chapter 6. This is shown in Figure 7.10, where a ListBooksResponse captures the response of the ListBooks operation.

Note in Figure 7.10 that the ListBooks operation returns an array of Book Summary instances that contain the basic details of each book in a search result. Adding schema definitions that wrap an array response or that limit the acceptable properties for each operation's request/response payload is often necessary. Operations that

```
344   components:
345     schemas:
346       ListBooksResponse:
347         title: ListBooksResponse
348         type: object
349         properties:
350           books:
351             type: array
352             items:
353               $ref: '#/components/schemas/BookSummary'
354             description: ''
355         description: "A list of book summaries as a result of a list or filter
                request. The following hypermedia links are offered:\n \n  - next:
                (optional) indicates the next page of results is available\n  -
                previous: (optional) indicates a previous page of results is
                available\n  - self: a link to the current page of results\n  - first:
                a link to the first page of results\n  - last: a link to the last page
                of results"
356       BookSummary:
357         title: BookSummary
358         type: object
359         properties:
360           bookId:
361             type: string
362             description: An internal identifier, separate from the ISBN, that
                  identifies the book within the inventory
363           isbn:
364             type: string
365             description: The ISBN of the book
366           title:
367             type: string
368             description: The book title, e.g. A Practical Approach to API Design
369           authors:
370             type: array
371             items:
372               $ref: '#/components/schemas/BookAuthor'
373             description: ''
374         description: "Summarizes a book that is stocked by the book store. The
                following hypermedia links are offered:\n \n  - bookDetails: link to
                fetch the book details"
```

Figure 7.10 *Finalizing the Shopping API design documentation to include schema definitions.*

```
427     NewCart:
428       title: NewCart
429       required:
430       - bookId
431       - quantity
432       type: object
433       properties:
434         bookId:
435           type: string
436           description: The book that is being added to the cart
437         quantity:
438           minimum: 1
439           type: integer
440           description: The number of copies of the book to be added to the
                 cart
441           format: int32
442       description: Creates a new cart with the initial cart item added
443     NewCartItem:
444       title: NewCartItem
445       required:
446       - bookId
447       - quantity
448       type: object
449       properties:
450         bookId:
451           type: string
452           description: The book that is being added to the cart
453         quantity:
454           minimum: 1
455           type: integer
456           description: The number of copies of the book to be added to the
                 cart
457           format: int32
458       description: Specifies a book and quantity to add to a cart
459     ModifyCartItem:
460       title: ModifyCartItem
```

Figure 7.11 *Keep in mind that some operations may require custom schema definitions to exclude specific fields not permitted for specific operations or to wrap search responses that contain only summary details.*

create or update a resource may also require separate schema definitions to prevent read-only fields from being submitted. This is shown in Figure 7.11.

Use sequence diagrams to validate that the API design meets the needs captured during the creation of job stories, EventStorming, and API modeling. Figure 7.12 shows a sequence diagram with a simplified form of HTTP for demonstrating typical interaction patterns to produce the desired outcomes.

Once the API design has been captured in an API description format, the generated documentation and sequence diagrams can be shared with others to obtain feedback on the design. This is the final step in the API design process.

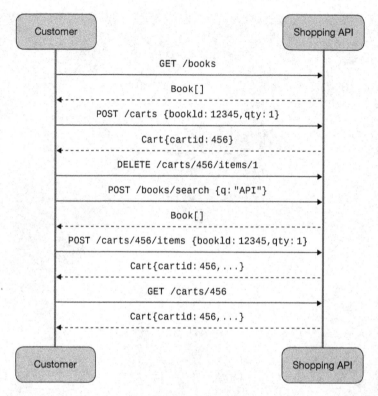

Figure 7.12 *Use sequence diagramming to validate that the API design meets the needs previously modeled.*

Step 5: Share and Gather Feedback

The final step is to share the API design for feedback from the immediate team, API architects from the organization, and internal/external teams planning to immediately integrate the API once ready.

Once the API has been officially released and integrated, the API design is locked, and only nonbreaking changes may be made. New endpoints may be added, and perhaps new fields added to existing resource representations, but renaming or modifying existing endpoints will break existing API consumers, leading to upset customers and perhaps customer churn. Getting it right the first time is important. Sharing the API design early for feedback helps to avoid significant design changes post release.

Mock implementations of an API are also helpful to explore API designs. Because reading API documentation provides only a basic understanding of an API, mock implementations offer a chance for developers to experience how the API may work using mock data. Tools are beginning to emerge that accept an API description format, such as OAS, and generate a mock API implementation without writing a single line of code.

Refer to Chapter 16, "Continuing the API Design Journey," regarding other API lifecycle techniques that help to gain feedback on an API, even after it has been developed and deployed.

Selecting a Representation Format

So far, the discussion of resource design has been centered on the resource names and properties. However, the representation format of an API's resources needs to be determined as well. Selecting a representation format is an important step.

For some organizations, the preferred representation format has already been determined as part of the API style guide and standards. In that case, the decision has been made already and no further action is required. However, if this is a new API product or one of the first APIs of a new API program or API platform, then there is more work to be done to complete the design effort.

Whenever possible, select a single format as the default representation format that will be offered across all APIs. Using a single format ensures consistency when a developer integrates with this and other existing and future APIs from the organization.

Additional formats may be added for operations over time, allowing an existing API to slowly migrate to a new format without disrupting existing integrations. A multiformat approach requires the use of content negotiation, a technique offered in HTTP to allow clients to specify the preferred representation format desired. Content negotiation is discussed further in the HTTP primer offered in Appendix I.

Table 7.4 summarizes the four categories of representation formats available.

Each category builds upon the previous one, adding more options for representing resource and messaging formats. However, with more options often comes more complexity. Each category is explained, and an example presented to inform the selection process. The examples provided in this chapter are available in the API workshop examples[4] GitHub repository.

---

4. https://bit.ly/align-define-design-examples

Table 7.4 *Categories of API Representation Formats*

Category	Overview
Resource Serialization	The representation reflects the serialization of a resource into various formats, e.g., JSON, XML, Protocol Buffers, and Apache Avro
Hypermedia Serialization	A serialized representation with support for embedded hypermedia controls
Hypermedia Messaging	A general message format that supports resource properties with hypermedia controls
Semantic Hypermedia Messaging	A general message format that supports semantic field mapping with hypermedia controls

Resource Serialization

The resource serialization category of representation formats is the most commonly encountered. They directly map each property of the resource and its value into the desired format, often in JSON, XML, or YAML. Binary formats such as Protocol Buffers[5] and Apache Avro[6] are gaining acceptance as well.

These representation formats require explicit code that handles the serialization between the resource and the target format. This mapping logic may be created through code generators or hand coded. Formatter and representer libraries often help to manage some of the mapping between the target format and an object or struct that represents the resource in code.

No matter how serialization is handled, the parsing and mapping code is unique to the resource, as it must be aware of the expected fields and any nested structures. Listing 7.1 provides an example of a Book resource using a serialized representation in JSON.

Listing 7.1 *Serialized Representation Using JSON*

```
{
    "bookId": "12345",
    "isbn": "978-0321834577",
    "title": "Implementing Domain-Driven Design",
    "description": "With Implementing Domain-Driven Design, Vaughn has made an
important contribution not only to the literature of the Domain-Driven Design
community, but also to the literature of the broader enterprise application
architecture field.",
    "authors": [
      { "authorId": "765", "fullName": "Vaughn Vernon" }
    ]
}
```

---

5. https://developers.google.com/protocol-buffers/docs/proto3
6. https://avro.apache.org/docs/current

Resource serialization–based formats offer only the properties of the resource using key-value pairs.

Hypermedia Serialization

The hypermedia serialization category is similar to resource serialization but adds specifications on how hypermedia links are represented. It may also include specifications for including related and/or nested resources, called *embedded resources,* in a uniform way.

Formats such as Hypertext Application Language (HAL)[7] enable resource serialization formats to be extended with hypermedia with few to no changes. This prevents breaking existing API clients while migrating existing serialization-based APIs to include hypermedia controls. This is why HAL tends to be a popular choice when moving to hypermedia APIs. Listing 7.2 shows an example of a HAL-based representation that extends Listing 7.1 with hypermedia links and a related list of author resources.

Listing 7.2 *Hypermedia Serialization Approach Using HAL*

```
{
    "bookId": "12345",
    "isbn": "978-0321834577",
    "title": "Implementing Domain-Driven Design",
    "description": "With Implementing Domain-Driven Design, Vaughn has made
an important contribution not only to the literature of the Domain-Driven
Design community, but also to the literature of the broader enterprise ap-
plication architecture field.",
    "_links": {
        "self": { "href": "/books/12345" }
    },
    "_embedded": {
      "authors": [
        {
          "authorId": "765",
          "fullName": "Vaughn Vernon",
          "_links": {
```

---

7. Mike Kelly, "JSON Hypertext Application Language" (2016), https://tools.ietf.org/html/draft-kelly-json-hal-08.

```
            "self": { "href": "/authors/765" },
            "authoredBooks": { "href": "/books?authorId=765" }
          }
        }
    ]
  }
}
```

Not all hypermedia formats offer the same features. Mike Amundsen has created a list of these factors, called H-Factors,[8] that support reasoning about the level and sophistication of hypermedia support across formats.

Hypermedia Messaging

Hypermedia messaging formats differ from serialization in that they propose a uniform message-based format to capture resource properties, hypermedia controls, and embedded resources. This makes it easy to use a single parser across all resources represented by the message format rather than unique mapping code for each resource type to parse a serialized format such as JSON or XML.

While the differences are nuanced between serialization and message-based formats, consider that teams will no longer need to argue about what the JSON or XML payload should look like. Instead, they focus on the resource representations, relationships, and hypermedia controls within the message format itself. No more meetings to decide if a data wrapper is required around a JSON-based response!

Hypermedia messaging formats include JSON:API[9] and Siren.[10] Both of these formats offer a single structured message that is flexible enough to include simple or complex resource representations and embedded resources, and both offer hypermedia control support.

Siren's messaging capabilities are similar to JSON:API's, but it also adds metadata that is useful for creating Web-based user interfaces with minimal customization effort.

JSON:API is an opinionated specification that removes the need to decide on many design options commonly included in an API style guide. Representation format, when to use different HTTP methods, and how to optimize network connections through response shaping and eager fetching of related resources are just a few of the decisions already provided by JSON:API.

Listing 7.3 provides an example of a JSON:API message-based representation.

---

8. http://amundsen.com/hypermedia/hfactor
9. https://jsonapi.org
10. https://github.com/kevinswiber/siren

Listing 7.3 *A JSON:API Demonstrating Message-Based Representations*

```
{
  "data": {
    "type": "books",
    "id": "12345",
        "attributes": {
        "isbn": "978-0321834577",
        "title": "Implementing Domain-Driven Design",
        "description": "With Implementing Domain-Driven Design, Vaughn has
made an important contribution not only to the literature of the Domain-
Driven Design community, but also to the literature of the broader enterprise
application architecture field."
    },
    "relationships": {
      "authors": {
          "data": [
            {"id": "765", "type": "authors"}
          ]
        }
    },
    "included": [
      {
        "type": "authors",
        "id": "765",
        "fullName": "Vaughn Vernon",
        "links": {
          "self": { "href": "/authors/765" },
          "authoredBooks": { "href": "/books?authorId=765" }
          }
        }
      }
  }
}
```

Semantic Hypermedia Messaging

Semantic hypermedia messaging is the most comprehensive category, as it adds semantic profile and linked data support, making APIs part of the Semantic Web.

By applying semantics of resource properties through linked data, more meaning is assigned to each property without requiring an explicit name to be used. Linked data usually relies on a shared vocabulary from Schema.org or other resources. With the growth of data analytics and machine learning, linking data to shared vocabularies enable automated systems to easily derive value of the data provided from APIs. Common formats that support semantic hypermedia messaging include Hydra,[11] UBER,[12] Hyper,[13] JSON-LD,[14] and OData.[15]

Listing 7.4 provides an example of the UBER representation format.

Listing 7.4 *UBER Semantic Hypermedia Messaging Format*

```
{
  "uber" :
  {
    "version" : "1.0",
    "data" :
      [
        {"rel" : ["self"], "url" : "http://example.org/"},
        {"rel" : ["profile"], "url" : "http://example.org/profiles/books"},
        {
          "name" : "searchBooks",
          "rel" : ["search","collection"],
          "url" : "http://example.org/books/search?q={query}",
          "templated" : "true"
        },
        {
          "id" : "book-12345",
          "rel" : ["collection","http://example.org/rels/books"],
          "url" : "http://example.org/books/12345",
          "data" : [
            {
              "name" : "bookId",
              "value" : "12345",
              "label" : "Book ID"
            },
            {
```

11. Markus Lanthaler, "Hydra Core Vocabulary: A Vocabulary for Hypermedia-Driven Web APIs" (Hydra W3C Community Group, 2021), http://www.hydra-cg.com/spec/latest.
12. Mike Amundsen and Irakli Nadareishvili, "Uniform Basis for Exchanging Representations (UBER)" (2021), https://rawgit.com/uber-hypermedia/specification/master/uber-hypermedia.html.
13. Irakli Nadareishvili and Randall Randall, "Hyper - Foundational Hypermedia Type" (2017), http://hyperjson.io/spec.html.
14. https://json-ld.org
15. https://www.odata.org

```
                    "name" : "isbn",
                    "value" : "978-0321834577",
                    "label" : "ISBN",
                    "rel" : ["https://schema.org/isbn"]
                 },
                 {
                    "name" : "title",
                    "value" : "Example Book",
                    "label" : "Book Title",
                    "rel" : ["https://schema.org/name"]
                 },
                 {
                    "name" : "description",
                    "value" : "With Implementing Domain-Driven Design, Vaughn
 has made an important contribution not only to the literature of the Domain-
 Driven Design community, but also to the literature of the broader enterprise
 application architecture field.",
                    "label" : "Book Description",
                    "rel" : ["https://schema.org/description"]
                 },
                 {
                    "name" : "authors",
                    "rel" : ["collection","http://example.org/rels/authors"],
                    "data" : [
                      {
                        "id" : "author-765",
                        "rel" : ["http://schema.org/Person"],
                        "url" : "http://example.org/authors/765",
                        "data" : [
                          {
                            "name" : "authorId",
                            "value" : "765",
                            "label" : "Author ID"
                          },
                          {
                            "name" : "fullName",
                            "value" : "Vaughn Vernon",
                            "label" : "Full Name",
                            "rel" : "https://schema.org/name"
                          }]}]},
          ]}]}}
```

Notice how the size of the representations grows compared to the more compact resource serialization formats. With the increased size comes the addition of linked data and more powerful interactions with API clients. These representation formats offer more insight into how to navigate related resources and tap into new operations, including operations that were not available when the client was built.

The goal is to enable generic clients to interact with APIs without the need for custom code or user interfaces. Instead, a client can interact with an API it has never seen before, all using the details provided in a semantic, message-based resource representation.

Remember that is always better to include additional details in the message than to force clients to write more code that infers behavior. This is the essence of why HTML works so well, as browsers are not required to implement custom code for every Web site that exists. Instead, the browser implements rendering logic, and the HTML message is crafted to deliver the desired result. While this may result in a more verbose message, the result is a more resilient API client that avoids hardcoded behavior.

Common REST Design Patterns

While covering REST API design patterns is the subject of a separate book, this section provides some basic patterns commonly encountered in REST-based API designs. Each of the following patterns offers an overview of when they should be applied to help API designers address commonly encountered design requirements.

Create-Read-Update-Delete

CRUD-based APIs are APIs that offer resource collections that contain instances. The resources instances will offer some or all of the create, read, update, and delete lifecycle pattern.

The CRUD pattern may offer a complete or partial CRUD lifecycle around a resource collection and its instances in a consistent way. The CRUD pattern follows this familiar pattern:

- `GET /articles`—List/paginate/filter the list of available articles

- `POST /articles`—Create a new article

- `GET /articles/{articleId}`—Retrieve the representation of an article instance

- `PUT /articles/{articleId}`—Replace an existing article instance

- `PATCH /articles/{articleId}`—Update specific fields (i.e., a selective update) for an article instance

- `DELETE /articles/{articleId}`—Delete a specific article instance

It is recommended to avoid fine-grained CRUD-based APIs, which result in multiple API calls that cross transactional boundaries. Not only does it force the client to orchestrate multiple API requests across fine-grained resources, but clients will be unable to rollback previously successful requests when encountering failures in subsequent API requests. Instead, design resources around digital capabilities rather than based on backend data models.

Extended Resource Lifecycle Support

It is not uncommon to identify a state transition that goes beyond the typical CRUD interaction model. With the limited selection of HTTP methods, designers must find new ways to offer the extended lifecycle while honoring the HTTP specification.

For example, consider a content management system that manages a resource collection, Articles, that now needs to add basic review and approval workflows beyond the standard CRUD-based lifecycle. Additional operations may be provided to facilitate the workflow, such as

- `POST /articles/{articleId}/submit`

- `POST /articles/{articleId}/approve`

- `POST /articles/{articleId}/decline`

- `POST /articles/{articleId}/publish`

Using this functional operation approach, article resource instances are able to support the workflow necessary. In addition, it offers a few advantages:

- Fine-grained access control can be enforced at the API management layer because each specific action is a unique URL that can be assigned different authorization requirements. This avoids coding specific authorization logic into a single update operation, such as a PUT or PATCH, when the state of a field is changed

- Hypermedia controls are used to signal to clients the possible action(s) available based on the user's authorization scope, as discussed earlier in this chapter.

- The workflow supported by the API is more explicit, as clients don't have to look at the PATCH endpoint documentation to understand the valid status values available, along with re-creating the state machine rules for every API client.

For teams that prefer to avoid this style of functional operations for a resource instance or collection, an alternative approach is to support hypermedia controls that reference the same PUT or PATCH operation but support different message structures based on the type of action being taken.

Singleton Resources

Singleton resources represent a single resource instance outside of a resource collection. Singleton resources may represent a virtual resource for direct interaction of an existing resource instance within a collection (e.g., a user's one and only profile).

APIs may also offer nested singleton resources when there is a one and only one instance in the relationship between the parent resource and its child resource (e.g., a user's configuration). The following examples illustrate possible uses of a singleton resource:

- `GET /me`—Used in place of `GET /users/{userId}`, avoiding the need for consumers to know their own user identifier or risk accessing another user's data due to an insecure security configuration

- `PUT /users/5678/configuration`—Used to manage a single configuration resource instance for a specific account

Singleton resources should already exist and therefore should not require a client to create them ahead of time. While singleton resources may not offer the full spectrum of CRUD-style lifecycles like their collection-based brethren, they may still offer `GET`, `PUT`, and/or `PATCH` HTTP methods.

Background (Queued) Jobs

HTTP is a request/response protocol, requiring that a response be returned for any submitted request. For operations that take a long time to complete, it may not be optimal for applications to block with an open connection waiting for a response. HTTP provides the `202 Accepted` response code for this purpose.

For example, suppose an API operation exists to support bulk importing user accounts. The API client could submit the following valid request:

```
POST /bulk-import-accounts
Content-Type: application/json

{
    "items": [
        { ... },
        { ... },
        { ... },
        { ... }
    ]
}
```

The server could return the following response to indicate that the request was valid but that that it could not be processed fully:

```
HTTP/1.1 202 Accepted
Location: https://api.example.com/import-jobs/7937
```

The client could then follow up to determine the status by submitting a request to the URL provided in the `Location` header:

```
HTTP/1.1 200 OK

{
    "jobId": "7937",
    "importStatus": "InProgress",
    "percentComplete": "25",
    "suggestedNextPollTimestamp": "2018-10-02T11:00:00.00Z",
    "estimatedCompletionTimestamp": "2018-10-02T14:00:00.00Z"
}
```

This is called a *fire-and-follow-up pattern*. If the client doesn't need to monitor the job status, then it can ignore the URL provided and move on to other tasks. This is known as the *fire-and-forget pattern*.

Long-Running Transaction Support in REST

There may be times when a transaction requires more than one API operation to complete. During the days of SOAP, the WS-Transaction specification was provided to manage transactions across one or more requests. This often required a transaction manager that was costly in terms of both licensing and integration effort. To avoid this requirement with REST-based APIs, the builder design pattern can be applied to support similar semantics.

For example, imagine an API that is meant to support reserving seats for a music or sporting event. Perhaps the API must require payment within a specific time frame before the seats are placed back into the pool of available seats. A Seats resource may be used for searching for that favorite group of four seats together in a premium area:

```
GET /seats?section=premium&numberOfSeats=4
```

Perhaps a group of four seats is available. Yet, we cannot use the Seats resource to reserve the seats, as it would require four separate API calls that are not able to be wrapped in a transaction:

```
PUT /seats/seat1 to reserve seat #1
PUT /seats/seat2 to reserve seat #2
```

```
PUT /seats/seat3 to reserve seat #3 <-- this one failed. What now?
PUT /seats/seat4 to reserve seat #4
```

Instead, consider creating a Reservation resource that represents the transaction:

```
POST /reservations
{
  "seatIds": [ "seat1","seat2", "seat3", "seat4"]
}
```

If successful, a new Reservation is created and can be used to complete the payment process. It may also be used to further customize the reservations with add-ons, group meal plans, and so on. Alternatively, if the time limit is exceeded, the reservation is invalidated or deleted from the system and the API client begins again.

Looking for More Patterns?

These are only a few of the many design patterns useful for REST and other API styles. Refer to the API workshop examples[16] GitHub repository for more pattern resources.

Summary

When speaking about REST-based APIs, many conflate the idea of CRUD-based APIs that use JSON with the REST architectural style. However, REST defines a set of architectural constraints that help APIs mimic the best aspects of the Web. Of course, REST APIs may apply various design patterns, including CRUD, to produce an approachable interaction model for resources.

By applying a five-step design process, a resource-based API design is created that applies the REST constraints to the API profiles created during the API modeling process. Mapping the design into machine-readable API description allows tools to generate documentation for review by the team and the initial set of developers that will consume the API.

What if REST isn't the right API style for some or all the APIs identified during API modeling? Chapter 8 examines how GraphQL and gRPC are two additional API styles available when REST may not be the best choice or needs to be expanded with new interaction styles.

---

16. https://bit.ly/align-define-design-examples

Chapter 8

RPC and Query-Based API Design

Choosing the right architectural style for a network-based application requires an understanding of the problem domain and thereby the communication needs of the application, an awareness of the variety of architectural styles and the particular concerns they address.

— Roy Fielding

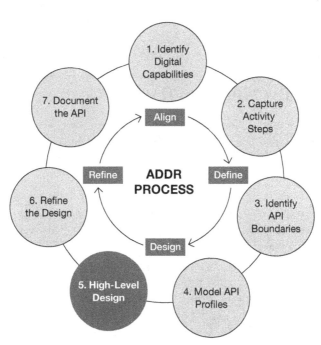

Figure 8.1 *The Design phase offers several options for API styles. Alternatives to REST-based APIs are detailed in this chapter.*

While the REST-based API style comprises most API products available in the market today, that may not always be the case. Nor is a REST-based API style always the best option for every API. As an API designer, it is important to understand the options available and the tradeoffs of each API style to determine the best fit for the target developers that will consume the API.

Remote procedure call (RPC)–based and query-based API styles are two additional API styles beyond REST. RPC-based APIs have been available for decades but have begun to experience a resurgence through the introduction of gRPC. Query-based APIs are gaining popularity owing to the introduction of GraphQL, making it the choice for many frontend developers who wish to have greater control over the shape of API responses.

With multiple API styles available, it is important to understand the advantages and challenges of each API style. For some API products and platforms, a single API style may be sufficient. For others, a mixture of intended uses and preferences for the developers tasked with integrating the API may require a mixture of API styles.

This chapter explores RPC- and query-based API styles and how they may be used as an alternative or supplement to REST-based (Figure 8.1). The chapter also defines a design process for RPC- and query-based API styles based on the API profiles captured during the Define phase outlined in Chapter 6, "API Modeling."

What Is an RPC-Based API?

RPC-based APIs execute a unit of code, the procedure, over the network as if it were being executed locally. The client is given a list of available procedures that may be invoked on the server. Each procedure defines a typed and ordered parameter list and the structure of a response structure.

It is important to recognize that the client is tightly coupled to the server's procedure. If the procedure on the server is modified or removed, it then becomes the responsibility of developers to accommodate the changes. This includes modifying the client code so that the client and server are in sync and communicating properly once more. However, with this tight coupling often comes better performance.

RPC-based APIs must agree to a specification that supports the marshaling of the procedure invocation for the target programming language(s). In the early days of Java, the use of the remote method invocation (RMI) libraries supported Java-to-Java communication, with Java's object serialization capabilities used as the binary format exchanged between Java processes. Other popular RPC standards include CORBA, XML-RPC, SOAP RPC, XML-RPC, JSON-RPC, and gRPC.

Following is an example of a JSON-RPC call over HTTP. Notice the explicit mention of the method (the procedure) and the ordered parameter list that results in a tight coupling between client and server:

```
POST https://rpc.example.com/calculator-service HTTP/1.1
Content-Type: application/json
Content-Length: ...Accept: application/json

{"jsonrpc": "2.0", "method": "subtract", "params": [42, 23], "id": 1}
```

Most RPC-based systems take advantage of a helper library and code generation tooling to generate the client and server stubs that are responsible for network communications. Those familiar with the fallacies of distributed computing[1] recognize that failures can occur whenever code is executed remotely. While one of RPC's goals is to make remote invocation behave as if it is calling a local procedure, network outages and other failure-handling support is often incorporated into the client and server stubs and raised as an error.

The remote procedures are defined using an interface definition language (IDL). Code generators use the IDL to generate the client stub and a server stub skeleton that is ready for implementation. RPC-based APIs are generally faster to design and implement for this reason but are less resilient to method renaming and reordering of parameters.

The gRPC Protocol

gRPC was created by Google in 2015 to speed the development of services through the use of RPC and code generation. Initially started as an internal initiative, it has since been released and adopted by many organizations and open-source initiatives, including Kubernetes.

gRPC is built upon HTTP/2 for transport and Protocol Buffers[2] for serialization. It also leverages the bidirectional streaming offered by HTTP/2, allowing the client to stream data to the server and the server to stream data back to the client. Figure 8.2 shows how multiple programming languages communicate using generated client stubs with a gRPC server within a GoLang-based service.

---

1. Wikipedia, s.v. "Fallacies of Distributed Computing," last modified July 24, 2021, 20:52, https://en.wikipedia.org/wiki/Fallacies_of_distributed_computing.

2. https://developers.google.com/protocol-buffers.

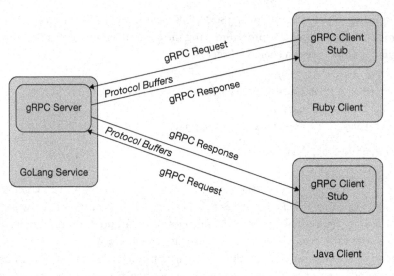

Figure 8.2 *An overview of how gRPC server and client stubs, generated for each programming language, work together.*

By default, gRPC uses the proto file format used by Protocol Buffers to define each service, the service methods offered, and the messages exchanged. Listing 8.1 shows an example IDL file for a calculate service that offers a subtract operation.

Listing 8.1 *gRPC-Based IDL That Defines a Subtract Operation*

```
// calculator-service.proto3
service Calculator {
  // Subtracts two integers
  rpc Subtract(SubtractRequest) returns (CalcResult) {}
}


// The request message containing the values to subtract
message SubtractRequest {
    // number being subtracted from
  int64 minuend = 1;
    // number being subtracted
  int64 subtrahend = 2;
}
```

```
// The response message containing the calculation result
message CalcResult {
  int64 result = 1;
}
```

Factors When Considering RPC

RPC-based APIs often trade performance for tighter coupling. Code generation offered by many RPC protocols, such as gRPC, speed the development process by autogenerating client stubs and producing skeleton code for server implementation purposes. These factors result in teams selecting RPC-based APIs when they own both API client and server sides, allowing for development-time and runtime performance improvements.

However, there are several disadvantages to using an RPC-based API style that should be considering before proceeding:

- The integration between client and server are tightly coupled. Once in production, the order of the fields cannot be changed without breaking API clients.

- The serialization format for marshaling and unmarshaling of procedure calls is fixed. Unlike REST-based APIs, multiple media types cannot be used, and HTTP-based content negotiation is therefore not possible.

- Some RPC protocols, such as gRPC, require custom middleware to work with browsers and to enforce authorization and role-based access when operations are tunneled through a single URL.

Finally, keep in mind that gRPC depends on HTTP/2 and requires overriding default security restrictions to perform considerable customization of HTTP request headers; browsers cannot support gRPC natively. Instead, projects such as grpc-web[3] offer a library and gateway to transform HTTP/1 requests into gRPC-based procedure calls.

In summary, RPC-based APIs are best used when the organization owns both the API client and server. The API team exposes an RPC-based service or API for other teams within the organization to consume as needed but must strive to keep their client code up to date with the latest changes.

---

3. https://github.com/grpc/grpc-web

RPC API Design Process

The RPC design process leverages the API profiles created during API modeling, as described in Chapter 6. Because the API profiles already identified operations and basic input/output details, the RPC API design process is a rapid three-step process. While the examples provided use gRPC and Protocol Buffers 3, the process may be adapted with little or no modification for other RPC-based protocols.

Step 1: Identify RPC Operations

Migrate the list of operations, including their descriptions and request/response details, into a new tabular format designed to capture the high-level design. This is shown in Figure 8.3.

Though not necessary, following a verb-resource operation naming pattern, such as listBooks(), helps the RPC-based API to be more resource-centric and therefore more familiar to those who have used REST-based APIs.

Step 2: Detail RPC Operations

Expand each operation's request and response details using the resource definitions and fields captured during API modeling. Most RPC protocols support a parameter list of fields, much like a local method invocation. In this case, list the input parameters that will be part of the request and the value(s) that will be returned in the response.

For gRPC-based APIs that use Protocol Buffers, the parameter list must be wrapped within the definition of a message. Ensure each request has an associated message type defined that includes each input parameter. Likewise, each response will return a message, an array of messages, or an error status response. Figure 8.4 shows the Shopping Cart API design for a gRPC-based API.

It is important to standardize on an error response type so that clients are able to process server-side errors consistently. For gRPC, it is recommended to use the google.rpc.Status message type, which supports an embedded details object with any additional details that the client may need to process.

Operation Name	Description	Request	Response
listBooks()	List books by category or release date		
searchBooks()	Search for books by author, title		
viewBook()	View book details		
viewCart()	View the current cart and total		
clearCart()	Remove all books from the customer's cart		
addItemToCart()	Add a book to the customer's cart		
removeItemFromCart()	Remove a book from the customer's cart		
getAuthorDetails()	Retrieve the details of an author		

Figure 8.3 *A table that captures the initial RPC operations based on the previous API profile examples from Chapter 6.*

Operation Name	Description	Request	Response
listBooks()	List books by category or release date	ListBookRequest -categoryId -releaseDate	ListBookResponse -Book[] or google.rpc.Status + ProblemDetails
searchBooks()	Search for books by author, title	SearchQuery -query	SearchQueryResponse -Book[] or google.rpc.Status + ProblemDetails
viewBook()	View book details	ViewBookRequest -bookId	Book or google.rpc.Status + ProblemDetails
viewCart()	View the current cart and total	ViewCartRequest -cartId	Cart or google.rpc.Status + ProblemDetails
clearCart()	Remove all books from the customer's cart	ClearCartRequest -cartId	Cart or google.rpc.Status + ProblemDetails
addItemToCart()	Add a book to the customer's cart	AddCartItemRequest -cartId -quantity	Cart or google.rpc.Status + ProblemDetails
removeItemFromCart()	Remove a book from the customer's cart	RemoveCartItemRequest -cartId -cartItemId	Cart or google.rpc.Status + ProblemDetails
getAuthorDetails()	Retrieve the details of an author	GetAuthorRequest: -authorId	BookAuthor or google.rpc.Status + ProblemDetails

Figure 8.4 *The gRPC design complete with request and response basic message details.*

Step 3: Document the API Design

Use the design details from the previous two steps to compose the IDL file for the RPC-based API. In the case of gRPC, the IDL file is in the Protocol Buffers format. Listing 8.2 provides a skeleton of a gRPC-based Shopping Cart API to demonstrate the documentation process.

Listing 8.2 *IDL File for the gRPC Version of the Shopping Cart API*

```protobuf
// Shopping-Cart-API.proto3

service ShoppingCart {
  rpc ListBooks(ListBooksRequest) returns (ListBooksResponse) {}
  rpc SearchBooks(SearchBooksRequest) returns (SearchBooksResponse) {}
  rpc ViewBook(ViewBookRequest) returns (Book) {}
  rpc ViewCart(ViewCartRequest) returns (Cart) {}
  rpc ClearCart(ClearCartRequest) returns (Cart) {}
  rpc AddItemToCart(AddCartItemRequest) returns (Cart) {}
  rpc RemoveItemFromCart(RemoveCartItemRequest) returns (Cart) {}
  rpc GetAuthorDetails() returns (Author) {}
}
message ListBooksRequest {
  string category_id = 1;
  string release_date = 2;
}
message SearchBooksRequest {
  string query = 1;
}
message SearchBooksResponse {
  int32 page_number = 1;
  int32 result_per_page = 2 [default = 10];
  repeated Book books = 3;
}
message ViewBookRequest {
  string book_id = 1; }
message ViewCartRequest {
  string cart_id = 1;
}
message ClearCartRequest {
  string cart_id = 1;
}
```

```
message AddCartItemRequest {
  string cart_id = 1;
  string book_id = 2;
  int32 quantity = 3;
}
message RemoveCartItemRequest {
  string cart_id = 1;
  string cart_item_id = 2;
}
message CartItem {
  string cart_item_id = 1;
  Book book = 2;
  int32 quantity = 3;
}
message Cart {
  string cart_id = 1;
  repeated CartItem cart_items = 2;
}
```

That's it! The RPC-based API now has a high-level design. Details can now be added to complete the API and code generators used to jumpstart the development and integration work. Generating human-readable documentation is also recommended using a tool such as protoc-gen-doc.[4]

Keep in mind that owing to RPC's tight coupling with code, many code changes will have a direct impact on the design of an RPC-based API. Put another way, RPC-based API designs are replaced, not modified, when code changes are applied.

Notice how most of the effort took place in the API modeling step. By using the API modeling technique as the foundation of the design effort, the work of bridging the desired outcomes of the customer is easily mapped into an RPC-based design. Should additional API styles be required, such as REST, the same API modeling work can be reapplied to the design effort for the API style of choice.

What Is a Query-Based API?

Query-based APIs offer robust query capabilities and response shaping. They support fetching a complete resource representation by identifier, paginated listing of resource collections, and resource collection filtering using simple and advanced

---

4. https://github.com/pseudomuto/protoc-gen-doc

filter expressions. Most query-based styles support mutating data as well, supporting a full create-read-update-delete (CRUD)-based lifecycle along with custom actions.

Most query-based API styles also offer response shaping, allowing API clients to specify the fields to include in the response. Response shaping also supports deep and shallow fetches of resource graphs. Deep fetches allow nested resources to be retrieved at the same time as the parent, avoiding multiple API calls to recreate a large graph on the client. Shallow fetches prevent this from happening to avoid sending unnecessary data in the response. Response shaping is often used for mobile apps, when a smaller amount of data is required compared to a Web application that can render more information in a single screen.

Understanding OData

Two of the most popular query-based API styles are OData and GraphQL. OData[5] is a query-based API protocol that is standardized and managed by OASIS. It is built upon HTTP and JSON and uses a resource-based approach familiar to those already familiar with REST.

OData queries are made through specific resource-based URLs via GET. It also supports hypermedia controls for following related resources and data linking for expressing resource relationships using hypermedia links rather than identifiers during a create or an update operation. OData supports custom actions, which may mutate data in ways beyond the standard CRUD pattern. Functions are also supported to support calculations. Listing 8.3 demonstrates the use of a filtered GET to retrieve any airports located in San Francisco, California, using an OData query.

Listing 8.3 *OData Using a Filter to Find Airports in San Francisco*

```
GET /OData/Airports?$filter=contains(Location/Address, 'San Francisco')

{
    "@odata.context": "/OData/$metadata#Airports",
    "value": [
        {
            "@odata.id": "/OData/Airports('KSFO')",
            "@odata.editLink": "/OData/Airports('KSFO')",
            "IcaoCode": "KSFO",
            "Name": "San Francisco International Airport",
```

---

5. https://www.odata.org/documentation

```
            "IataCode": "SFO",
            "Location": {
                "Address": "South McDonnell Road, San Francisco, CA 94128",
                "City": {
                    "CountryRegion": "United States",
                    "Name": "San Francisco",
                    "Region": "California"
                },
                "Loc": {
                    "type": "Point",
                    "coordinates": [
                        -122.374722222222,
                        37.6188888888889
                    ],
                    "crs": {
                        "type": "name",
                        "properties": {
                            "name": "EPSG:4326"
                        }
                    }
                }
            }
        }
    ]
}
```

Some developers find the complexity of adopting the OData specification too much for simple APIs. However, the mixture of REST-based API design with robust query options makes OData a popular choice for larger API products and platforms.

OData has considerable support and investment from companies such as Microsoft, SAP, and Dell. The Microsoft Graph API,[6] which unifies the Office 365 platform under a single API, is built on OData and is an excellent example of constructing data-centric REST-based APIs with advanced query support.

---

6. Microsoft, "Overview of Microsoft Graph," June 22, 2021, https://docs.microsoft.com/en-us/graph/overview.

Exploring GraphQL

GraphQL[7] is an RPC-based API style that supports the querying and mutation of data. It is a specification that was developed internally by Facebook in 2012 before being publicly released in 2015. It was originally designed to overcome the challenges of supporting Web and mobile clients that need to obtain data via APIs at different levels of granularity and with the option of retrieving deeply nested graph structures. Over time, it has become a popular choice by frontend developers who need to bridge backend data stores with single-page applications (SPAs) and mobile apps.

All GraphQL operations are tunneled through a single HTTP POST- or GET-based URL. Requests use the GraphQL query language to shape the response of desired fields and any nested resources in a single request. Mutations support modifying data or performing calculation logic and use a similar language to queries to express the data input for a modification or calculation request. All resource structures are defined in one or more schema files, ensuring that clients may introspect resources at design time or runtime. Listing 8.4 provides an example of a GraphQL query.

Listing 8.4 *GraphQL Query to Fetch the San Francisco Airport by IATA code*

```
POST /graphql

{
  airports(iataCode : "SFO")
}

{
  "data" : {
    {
      "Name": "San Francisco International Airport",
      "iataCode": "SFO",
      "Location": {
        "Address": "South McDonnell Road, San Francisco, CA 94128",
        "City": {
          "CountryRegion": "United States",
          "Name": "San Francisco",
          "Region": "California"
        },
```

---

7. https://graphql.org

```
       "Loc": {
         "type": "Point",
         "coordinates": [
           -122.374722222222,
           37.6188888888889
         ]
       }
     }
   }
  }
 }
}
```

While GraphQL is popular with frontend developers, it has also gained significant traction across enterprises as a means to stitch multiple REST APIs together into a single query-based API. It is also useful for producing query-only reporting APIs alongside existing REST-based APIs, offering a best-of-breed approach to API platforms.

Many of the challenges around GraphQL are centered on its choice to tunnel through a single endpoint rather than take advantage of the full capabilities of HTTP. This prevents the use of HTTP content negotiation for the support of multiple media types beyond JSON. It also prevents the use of concurrency controls and optimistic locking offered by HTTP conditional headers. Similar challenges were experienced with SOAP-based services, which was designed to work across multiple protocols including HTTP, SMTP, and JMS-based message brokers.

Enforcing authorization is also a challenge because traditional API gateways that expect to enforce access control by URL are limited to the single GraphQL operation. However, some API gateways are extending their capabilities to include authorization enforcement around GraphQL-based queries and mutations. Likewise, rate limiting, often associated to a combination of path and HTTP method, must be rethought to accommodate this new interaction style.

Query-Based API Design Process

The process used to design a query-based API is similar to that of other API design styles, such as RPC and REST. The primary difference is that the steps require the creation of a resource graph prior to designing the operations. To demonstrate the process, a GraphQL-based API is designed based on the API modeling effort shown in Chapter 6.

Step 1: Designing Resource and Graph Structures

The first and most important step for query-based APIs is to design the graph structure of all resources. If the API modeling work outlined in Chapter 6 has been done, then this step is already complete. If the API modeling work hasn't been completed, go back to Chapter 6 and complete those steps before proceeding. Figures 8.5 and 8.6 revisit the resources and relationships identified in Chapter 6 for the bookstore example.

Once all top-level resources, along with related resources, have been identified, proceed to the next step to design the query and mutation operations.

Step 2: Design Query and Mutation Operations

The next step is to migrate all operations captured in the API profile during API modeling in Chapter 6. The API profiles capture each operation and include a safety classification of *safe, idempotent,* or *unsafe.* Classify each operation marked as safe as a query. Operations marked as idempotent or unsafe will be mutations. For the Shopping Cart API, there are both query and mutation operations, as shown in Figure 8.7.

Book Resource	
Property Name	**Description**
title	The book title
isbn	The unique ISBN of the book
authors	List of Book Author resources

Book Author Resource	
Property Name	**Description**
fullName	The full name of the author

Figure 8.5 *The Book resource is the first top-level resource that needs to be supported for the Shopping Cart API modeled in Chapter 6.*

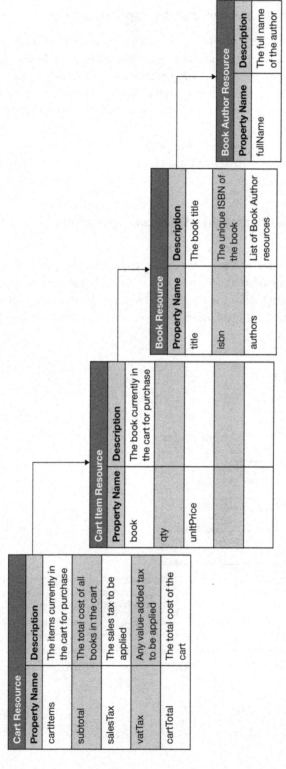

Figure 8.6 *The Cart resource is the second top-level resource that needs to be supported for the Shopping Cart API modeled in Chapter 6.*

Operation Type	Operation Name	Description	Request	Response
Query	listBooks()	List books by category or release date		
Query	searchBooks()	Search for books by author, title		
Query	viewBook()	View book details		
Query	viewCart()	View the current cart and total		
Mutation	clearCart()	Remove all books from the customer's cart		
Mutation	addItemToCart()	Add a book to the customer's cart		
Mutation	removeItemFromCart()	Remove a book from the customer's cart		
Query	getAuthorDetails()	Retrieve the details of an author		

Figure 8.7 *The Shopping Cart API profile, modeled in Chapter 6, is migrated to a tabular format that helps with query-based API design.*

If the chosen protocol supports only query operations, then mutations must be handled using a different API style. GraphQL supports both, so the design can include both query and mutations within the same API definition.

Once the basic operation details have been captured, expand the request and response columns with further details about the input and output values. These input and output values were already determined during the API modeling in Chapter 6. Migrate these values into the new API design table. The Shopping Cart API operations are expanded in Figure 8.8.

Step 3: Document the API Design

Finally, document the resulting API using the preferred format for the chosen protocol. In the case of GraphQL, a schema is used to define the queries and mutations available, as shown in Listing 8.5.

Listing 8.5 *Shopping Cart API Captured as a GraphQL Schema*

```
# API Name: "Bookstore Shopping API Example"
#
# The Bookstore Example REST-based API supports the shopping experience of
an online bookstore. The API includes the following capabilities and opera-
tions...
#

type Query {
    listBooks(input: ListBooksInput!): BooksResponse!
    searchBooks(input: SearchBooksInput!): BooksResponse!
    viewBook(input: GetBookInput!): BookSummary!
    getCart(input: GetCartInput!): Cart!
    getAuthorDetails(input: GetAuthorDetailsInput!): BookAuthor!
}
type Mutation {
    clearCart(): Cart
    addItemToCart(input: AddCartItemInput!): Cart
    removeItemFromCart(input: RemoveCartItemInput!): Cart
}
type BooksResponse {
    books: [BookSummary!]
}
type BookSummary {
    bookId: String!
```

```
        isbn: String!
        title: String!
        authors: [BookAuthor!]
    }
    type BookAuthor {
        authorId: String!
        fullName: String!
    }
    type Cart {
        cartId: String!
        cartItems: [CartItem!]
    }
    type CartItem {
        cartItemId: String!
        bookId: String!
        quantity: Int!
    }
    input ListBooksInput {
        offset: Int!
        limit: Int!
    }
    input SearchBooksInput {
        q: String!
        offset: Int!
        limit: Int!
    }
    input GetAuthorDetailsInput {
        authorId: String!
    }
    input AddCartItemInput {
        cartId: String!
        bookId: String!
        quantity: Int!
    }
    input RemoveCartItemInput {
        cartId: String!
        cartItemId: String!
    }
```

Operation Type	Operation Name	Description	Request	Response

Query	listBooks()	List books by category or release date	query {
			　Book (categoryId, releaseDate) {
			　　.....
			　}
			}
				Book[]

Query	searchBooks()	Search for books by author, title	query {
			　Book (searchQuery) {
			　　.....
			　}
			}
				Book[]

Query	viewBook()	View book details	query {
			　book(bookId) {
			　　.....
			　}
			}
				Book

Query	viewCart()	View the current cart and total	query {
			　cart(cartId) {
			　　.....
			　}
			}
				Cart

Mutation	clearCart()	Remove all books from the customer's cart	mutation clearCart {
			　cartId
			}
				Cart

Mutation	addItemToCart()	Add a book to the customer's cart	mutation addItemToCart {
			　cartId
			　bookId
			　quantity
			}
				Cart

Mutation	removeItemFromCart()	Remove a book from the customer's cart	mutation removeItemFromCart {
			　cartId
			　cartItemId
			}
				Cart

Query	getAuthorDetails()	Retrieve the details of an author	query {
			　BookAuthor (authorId) {
			　　.....
			　}
			}
				BookAuthor

Figure 8.8 The Shopping Cart GraphQL API design is now expanded with additional details about queries and mutations.

It is recommended to generate human-readable documentation using a tool such as graphql-docs.[8] Be sure to offer an interactive interface using GraphQL Playground[9] to enable developers to craft requests directly in the browser before writing their integration code.

All examples provided in this chapter are based on the API workshop examples[10] available on GitHub.

Summary

REST is not the only API style available. RPC- and query-based APIs provide additional interaction styles that help developers integrate with an API product or platform quickly. They may also be combined with REST-based APIs to provide robust query operations for reporting and fast code generation options.

While the design process is slightly different for each API style, all styles build upon the investment of aligning the needs of business, customers, and developers. The next step in the design process is to determine if one or more asynchronous APIs would benefit the API consumer. This topic is discussed in detail in Chapter 9, "Messaging, Streaming, and Event-Based Async APIs."

8. https://www.npmjs.com/package/graphql-docs
9. https://github.com/graphql/graphql-playground
10. https://bit.ly/align-define-design-examples

Chapter 9

Async APIs for Eventing and Streaming

The key to safety lies in the encapsulation. The key to scalability lies in how messaging is actually done.

— Alan Kay

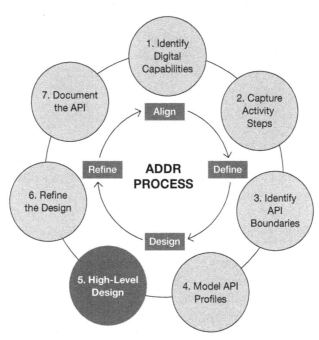

Figure 9.1 *The Design phase offers several options for API styles. This chapter covers asynchronous API design.*

Most discussions that surround Web-based APIs center on synchronous request/response interaction styles common with REST-based, query-based, and remote procedure call (RPC)–based APIs. They are easy to understand and approachable for developers and non-developers with minimal experience working with HTTP.

Yet, synchronous APIs have their limitations. The API server is unable to inform interested parties about changes in the representation of a resource or notify when a workflow between multiple parties have completed. Instead, they require the client to initiate the interaction with an API server before receiving any notifications.

Asynchronous APIs, or async APIs, unlock the full potential of a digital product or platform. They extend the API conversation from client-originated to server-originated, allowing clients to react to an event rather than start a conversation. New capabilities may be built based on a single type of event notification. And all of this may be done without the involvement of the team that owns an API.

Including async API design as part of an overall API design effort empowers teams to craft new solutions based on notifications or data streams. But it takes a few considerations to unlock the full potential of an async API. This chapter presents some of the challenges and design patterns around designing async APIs. It also demonstrates how to design and document an async API by building on the previous API modeling steps outlined in Chapter 6.

The Problem with API Polling

If an API client wishes to know when new data is available, it must periodically check with the server to see if any new resources have been added or existing resources have been modified. This pattern is known as *API polling* and is a common solution for clients that need to become aware of new resources or modifications to existing resources.

API polling is flexible and may be implemented by the client on top of just about any API that uses a request/response style. However, API polling isn't an ideal solution. Coding the logic necessary to detect and track modifications is complex, wasteful, and can result a poor user experience. The API client must send a GET request to a resource collection to fetch the latest list of resources, compare the list to the last list retrieved by the API client, and determine if anything new has been added. Some APIs offer an operation to provide recent changes based on a timestamp since the last request, but it is up to the API client to continue to perform API polling to determine when changes have been made.

Yet, many developers are forced to build API polling code to constantly check for changes in server-side state. Building polling code includes additional challenges to the developer:

- The API sends responses back with default, nonoptimal sorting (e.g., oldest-to-newest). The consumer must then request all entries to find out if anything new is available, often keeping a list of the IDs already seen to determine what is new.

- Rate limiting may prevent making requests at the desired intervals to detect change in a timely fashion.

- The data offered by the API doesn't provide enough details for the client to determine if a specific event has occurred, such as a resource modification.

The ideal situation is to have servers inform any interested API consumers about new data or recent events. However, this isn't possible with traditional request/response API styles common with HTTP, as API clients are required to submit a request before the API server can communicate any changes.

Async APIs help address this need. Rather than constantly polling and implementing change detection rules on the API client, API servers send asynchronous push notifications to interested API clients when something on the server has changed. This opens a whole new series of possibilities compared to traditional, synchronous Web-based APIs that are rooted in HTTP request/response.

Async APIs Create New Possibilities

As discussed in Chapter 1, "The Principles of API Design," APIs provide interfaces to data and behavior to deliver digital capabilities, typically over HTTP. Digital capability examples include a customer profile search, customer registration, and attaching a customer profile to an account. These digital capabilities are combined to create API products and API platforms that empower business units within an organization and among partners and customers to create new outcomes.

Async APIs are digital capabilities as well. They go beyond traditional REST-based Web APIs to open new possibilities for digital business:

- **Reacting to business events in real-time:** Solutions can react to internal state changes and critical business events when they happen.

- **Extending the value of solutions with message streams:** Additional value is unlocked from existing solutions and APIs. New opportunities emerge to take advantage of internal events by surfacing them alongside the capabilities offered by their APIs. New solutions are built on top of existing APIs through an event-driven interaction style.

- **Improving API efficiency:** Constant API polling is no longer needed to check for state changes. This reduces the resources required to support an API by pushing state change events to those interested, thereby reducing infrastructure costs.

CASE STUDY
GitHub Webhooks Created a New CI/CD Marketplace

GitHub Webhooks have been around for some time, allowing teams to be notified when new code has been pushed to a GitHub-hosted repository. While Git supports writing scripts to react to these kinds of events within a source code repository, GitHub was one of the first vendors to turn these script-based hooks into Webhooks. Any individual or organization hosting their code with GitHub could be notified, via an HTTP-based POST, when new code was available and trigger a new build process.

Over time, continuous integration and delivery (CI/CD) tools that were previously restricted to on-premises installation could now be offered via a software-as-a-service (SaaS) model. These solutions would be granted permission to receive the Webhook-based notification and start a new build process.

This one async API notification ultimately created an entire SaaS market of hosted CI/CD tools. That is the power of async APIs.

Before the full potential of async APIs can be unlocked, it is important to understand messaging fundamentals.

A Review of Messaging Fundamentals

Messages contain data that are published by a message producer to a message receiver. Receivers may be a local function or method, another process on the same host, a process on a remote server, or middleware such as a message broker.

There are three common types of messages: commands, replies, and events:

- A **command message** requests that work be done immediately or in the future. Command messages are often imperative: `CreateOrder`, `RegisterPayment`, and so on. Command messages are sometimes referred to as *request messages*.

- A **reply message** provides the result, or outcome, of a command message. Reply messages often add the suffix `Result` or `Reply` to differentiate them from their command counterparts: `CreateOrderReply`, `RegisterPaymentResult`, and so on. Reply messages are also referred to as *response messages*. Not all command messages result in a reply message.

- **Event messages** tell the receiver about something that happened in the past. A good event name uses past tense to indicate that an action has taken place: `OrderCreated`, `PaymentSubmitted`, and so on. Event messages are typically used when a business event has occurred, a workflow state has changed, or data has been created or modified.

Messages Are Immutable

It is important to note that messages are immutable. Once they are published, they may not be modified. Therefore, a message that requires modification must be republished as a new message. If necessary, include a correlation identifier to map the new message to the original message.

Figure 9.2 shows an example of each kind of message and the context that it provides.

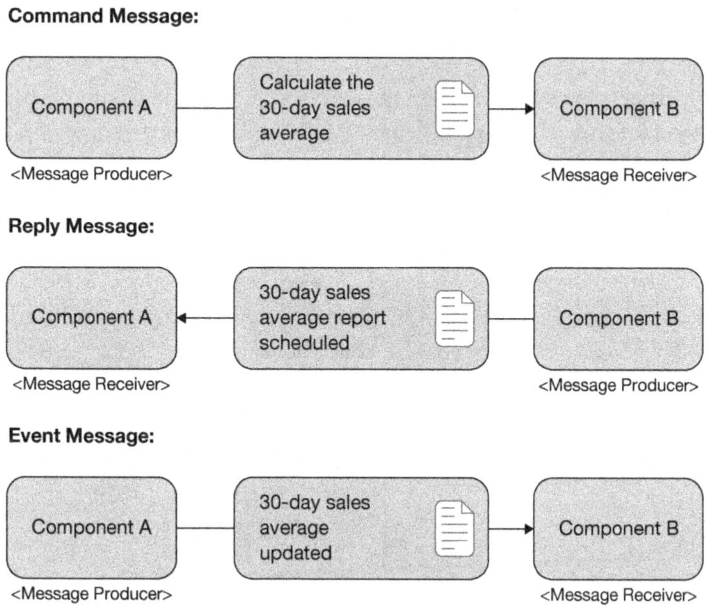

Command Message:

Reply Message:

Event Message:

Figure 9.2 *Examples of the three primary types of messages.*

Messaging Styles and Locality

An application or service may choose from one or more styles of messaging:

- **Synchronous messaging** involves the message producer sending a message and waiting while the receiver processes it and returns a reply.

- **Asynchronous messaging** allows the message producer and receiver to operate in their own time rather than waiting upon one another. The message producer sends the message to the receiver, but the receiver may not be able to process it immediately. The message producer is free to perform other tasks while waiting for a reply from the message receiver.

In addition, messages may be exchanged across different localities:

- **Local messaging** assumes that messages are sent and received within the same process. As such, the programming language and host will be the same as well. The Smalltalk programming language was built to support sending and receiving messages between objects. Actor-based frameworks, such as Vlingo,[1] also support this kind of messaging. A "mailbox" sits between the code that produces the message and the code that will process the message. The consumer code processes each message as soon as possible, sometimes using threads or dedicated CPU cores to process multiple messages in parallel.

- **Interprocess messaging** exchanges messages between separate processes but on the same host. Examples include UNIX sockets and dynamic data exchange (DDE).

- **Distributed messaging** involves two or more hosts for messaging. Messages are transmitted over a network using the desired protocol. Examples of distributed messaging include message brokers using Advanced Message Queuing Protocol (AMQP), Message Queuing Telemetry Transport (MQTT), SOAP-based Web services, REST-based APIs, and so on.

The combination of synchronous and asynchronous messaging styles, along with the locality of the messaging, determines the possibilities of a message-based solution.

---

1. https://vlingo.io

The Elements of a Message

When a discussion around message design emerges, most of the focus is on the message body. The message body is usually in a structured format, such as JSON or XML, though binary or plain text are also valid. Some organizations choose to wrap the message body within a message envelope that contains useful metadata about the message contents and the message publisher.

There is more to a message than just the message body, however. Messages may also include transport protocol semantics. Network protocols such as HTTP, MQTT, and AMQP include message headers with details such as creation timestamps, time-to-live (TTL), priority/quality of service, and so on. A message is not fully described unless it includes all necessary information to process the message over the protocol. Figure 9.2 demonstrates the elements of each message exchanged between an API client and API server for a REST-based API.

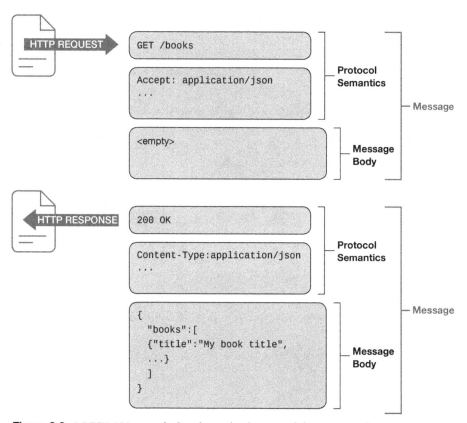

Figure 9.3 *A REST API example that shows the elements of the request and response messages exchanged between the API client and the API server.*

Understanding Messaging Brokers

Message brokers act as an intermediary between message producers and message receivers. The result is a more loosely coupled design, as producers are only aware of the message broker but not the components ultimately receiving the messages. Examples of message brokers include RabbitMQ,[2] ActiveMQ,[3] and Jmqtt.[4]

Message brokers also offer additional features such as the following:

- **Transactional boundaries** ensure that messages are published or marked as delivered only if the transaction is committed.

- **Durable subscriptions** store messages prior to dispatching to message receivers. Undeliverable messages, perhaps because the message receiver is offline, are stored on the client's behalf until they reconnect (i.e., the store and forward pattern).

- **Client acknowledgement mode** specifies how a message is considered acknowledged by the client to provide flexibility in balancing performance with failure recovery. A message is considered dispatched successfully either (1) automatically upon delivery or (2) upon client acknowledgment that the message was processed successfully.

- **Message processing failures** are handled by dispatching messages to a different receiver in the event of a failure or outage of the original message receiver. This behavior is controlled by the client acknowledgment mode established by the client upon connecting to the broker.

- A **dead letter queue (DLQ)** stores messages that could not be processed because of unrecoverable errors by message receivers. Allows automated or manual review and processing of failed message delivery.

- **Message priority and TTL** assist the message broker in prioritizing the delivery of messages and removing unprocessed messages if they exceed a specific period of time without being processed.

- **Standards-based connectivity** is achieved through the AMQP protocol, along with optimized protocols for Java via Java Message Service (JMS) and other language bindings.

---

2. https://www.rabbitmq.com
3. http://activemq.apache.org/index.html
4. https://github.com/Cicizz/jmqtt

Message brokers offer two methods of message distribution: point-to-point and fanout.

Point-to-Point Message Distribution (Queues)

Point-to-point messaging allows a publisher to send a message to a single subscriber selected from a pool of registered subscribers. The broker is responsible for selecting the subscriber that will receive the published message for processing via a round robin or similar selection process. Only one subscriber will receive a message published to the queue. If the subscriber fails to process the message within a given timeout period, the broker selects a new subscriber for message processing. Figure 9.4 demonstrates an example of a point-to-point queue.

Point-to-point queues are useful for publishing command messages that should have only one consumer processing a message at a time to ensure consistency and predictability and to avoid duplicate message processing. This is a common pattern for background job processing, where each job should be processed only once by a pool of workers.

Fanout Message Distribution (Topics)

Fanout messaging allows every message published to a topic to be distributed to every subscriber currently registered (see Figure 9.5). The broker doesn't care if the message was processed by all subscribers or just a subset of them. Unlike point-to-point queues, a message will be processed by all subscribers.

All topic subscribers will receive a copy of each published message. This distribution method supports independent, parallel processing logic for each published event message. Subscribers are not aware of each other or the publisher, only that a new message has been sent to them for processing.

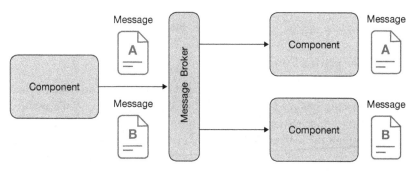

Figure 9.4 *A point-to-point queue that dispatches each message to a single message receiver subscribed to the queue.*

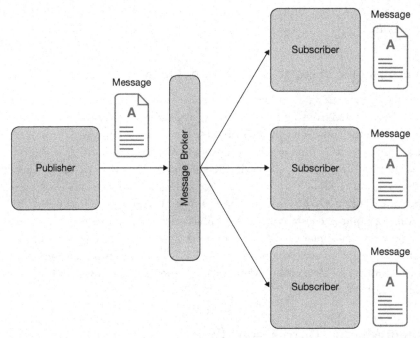

Figure 9.5 *A fanout topic that dispatches each message to all subscribed message receivers.*

A Note about Message Broker Terminology

The terms *queues* and *topics,* as used in this chapter, are commonly found in resources about distributed messaging. Keep in mind that some vendors, such as RabbitMQ, offer more distinct options for topics. Options range from general broadcasting of messages, termed *fanout,* to selective broadcasting, which they term *topics*. Be sure to read the vendor documentation carefully to understand the terminology vendors prefer to achieve the desired goals.

Message Streaming Fundamentals

Message brokers are most often transactional and are designed to manage the state of durable subscriptions for failure recovery of offline receivers. While useful for a number of application and integration solutions, transactional support and other characteristics limit the scalability of traditional message brokers.

Message streaming builds on the decades of message broker expertise but shifts some responsibilities away from the server while adding new capabilities to address today's complex data and messaging needs. It uses a fanout pattern for push notification of new messages to one or more subscribers, much like message broker topics. Examples of streaming servers include Apache Kafka,[5] Apache Pulsar,[6] and Amazon Kinesis.[7]

Unlike message brokers, subscribers may request messages at any point from the topic's available message history. This allows for the replay messages or for simply picking up where processing previously left off. Unlike message brokers, most streaming servers shift state management from the server to the client. The client is now responsible for tracking the last message seen. Error recovery is also pushed to the client, forcing the client to resume processing messages at the last known message.

Support for this style of interaction is accomplished by shifting message management from a traditional queue or topic to an append-only log. These logs may store all messages or limit the history of messages for specified retention period. A topic using a distributed log with two consumers is shown in Figure 9.6.

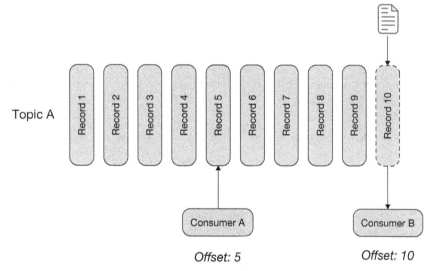

Figure 9.6 *A streaming topic comprising a distributed log of recorded messages, consumed by two separate consumers who have two separate offsets to reflect their current message.*

---

5. https://kafka.apache.org

6. https://pulsar.apache.org

7. https://aws.amazon.com/kinesis

With the ability to specify the offset of where they wish to start, clients are able to solve new kinds of problems using solutions that were not possible with message brokers:

- Achieve near real-time data processing and data analytics as soon as incoming data is received from other systems or third parties due to the highly scalable and low-latency design of message streaming servers.

- Use historical messages to verify the results of code changes prior to pushing new code to production.

- Execute experimental data analytics against historical messages.

- Remove the need to subscribe to all message broker queues and topics in an effort to store all messages processed by a message broker for auditing purposes.

- Push data into a data warehouse or data lake for consumption by other systems, without the need for traditional extract-transform-load (ETL) processes.

The higher scalability of message streaming lends itself to a shift in the way data is managed and shared. Rather than sharing access to a data store or replicating the data store, each new or modified data event message is pushed to a topic stream. Any consumers are then able to process the data change, including storing it locally for caching or for further analysis.

Message Streaming Considerations

In certain circumstances, message streaming may not be the best option:

- **Duplicate message processing:** Subscribers must keep track of their current location in the stream. Therefore, duplicate message processing must be expected and handled. This may be the case if the current location was not able to be stored prior to a failure.

- **No message filtering:** Message brokers support filtering messages on a queue or topic based on specific values. Message streaming does not support this filtering out of the box. Instead, it requires receivers to process all messages from a given offset or to apply a third-party solution, such as Apache Spark.

- **Authorization is limited:** Because message streaming is relatively new, fine-grained authorization control and filtering is limited or nonexistent for today's solutions. Be sure to verify authorization needs are satisfied by the chosen vendor before proceeding. There are solutions beginning to emerge that bridge streams with REST, which may allow API gateways to apply more rigorous authorization strategies.

Async API Styles

Async APIs are an API interaction style that allows the server to inform the consumer when something has changed. There are a variety of API styles that support asynchronous APIs: webhooks, Server-Sent Events (SSE), and WebSocket are the most common.

Server Notification Using Webhooks

Webhooks allow API servers to publish notifications to other interested servers when an event has occurred. Unlike traditional callbacks, which occur within the same codebase, webhooks occur over the Web, using an HTTP POST. The term *webhooks* was coined by Jeff Lindsay[8] in 2007. Since then, the REST Hooks patterns[9] have been developed to offer a standard way to manage and secure webhook subscriptions and notifications.

Webhooks are dispatched when the API server sends a POST request to a URL that is provided by the system wishing to receive the callbacks. For example, an interested subscriber may register to receive new task event notifications on a specific URL they provide, such as https://myapp/callbacks/new-tasks. The API server then sends a POST request to each subscriber's callback URL with a message containing the event details. The full sequence is shown in Figure 9.6.

Webhooks must be network accessible by the API server and must be able to host an API server of its own to receive the POST requests. As such, webhooks are a good fit for server-to-server communication between systems but not useful for browser and mobile applications.

Implementing Webhooks Effectively

Webhooks require a variety of considerations, including handling delivery failures, securing communications between client and server, and callbacks that take too long to acknowledge the notification. Refer to the REST Hooks documentation[10] for tips on implementing webhook servers effectively.

---

8. Jeff Lindsay, "Webhooks to Revolutionize the Web" (blog), Wayback Machine, May 3, 2007, https://web.archive.org/web/20180630220036/http:/progrium.com/blog/2007/05/03/web-hooks-to-revolutionize-the-web.

9. https://resthooks.org

10. https://resthooks.org/docs

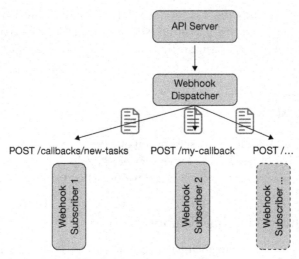

Figure 9.7 *An API server's webhook dispatcher that sends a message to each registered URL that wishes to receive the callback using HTTP POST.*

Server Push Using Server-Sent Events

SSE is based on the EventSource browser interface,[11] standardized as part of HTML5 by the W3C. It defines the use of HTTP to support longer-lived connections to allow servers to push data back to the client. These incoming messages contain event details that are useful to the client.

SSE is a simple solution that supports server-push notification while avoiding the challenges of API polling. While SSE was originally designed to support pushing data to a browser, it is becoming a more popular way to push data to a mixture of browsers and server-side subscribers.

SSE uses a standard HTTP connection but holds onto the connection for a longer period of time rather than disconnecting immediately. This connection allows API servers to push data back to the client when it becomes available.

The specification outlines a few options for the format of the data coming back, allowing for event names, comments, single- or multiline text-based data, and event identifiers.

Subscribers submit a request to the SSE operation using a GET with the media type of text/event-stream (see Figure 9.8). Existing operations are therefore able to support both standard request/response interactions using JSON, XML, and other

---

11. https://developer.mozilla.org/en-US/docs/Web/API/EventSource

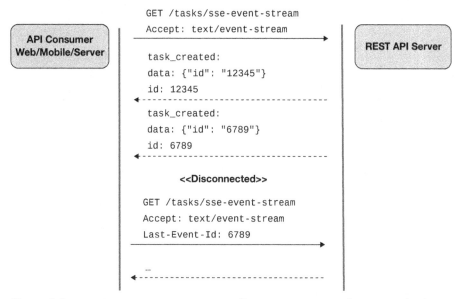

Figure 9.8 *Using Server-Sent Events (SSE) to allow API servers to push events to the client over a long-lived connection. Connections may be resumed using the* Last-Event-Id *request header.*

supported media types using content negotiation. Clients interested in using SSE may do so by specifying the SSE media type instead of JSON or XML in the Accept request header.

Once connected, the server then pushes new events, separated by a newline. If the connection is lost for any reason, the client is able to reconnect to start receiving new events. Clients may provide the Last-Event-ID HTTP header to recover any missed events since the last event ID seen by the client. This is useful for failure recovery.

The format for the data field may be any text-based content, from simple data points to single-line JSON payloads. Multiple lines may be provided using multiple data-prefixed lines.

SSE supports several use cases:

- State change notifications to a frontend application, such as a browser or mobile app, to keep a user interface in sync with the latest server-side state

- Receiving business events over HTTP, without requiring access to an internal message broker or streaming platform such as RabbitMQ or Kafka

- Enabling clients to process data incrementally, rather than all at once, by streaming long-running queries or complex aggregations results as they become available

SSE does have a few cases where it may not be a fit:

- The API gateway isn't capable of handling long-running connections or has a brief timeout period (e.g., less than 30 seconds). While this isn't a showstopper, it will require the client to reconnect more often.

- Some browsers do not support SSE. Refer to Mozilla's list of compatible browsers[12] for more information.

- Bidirectional communication between client and server is required. In this case, the WebSocket protocol may be a better option, as SSE is server push only.

The W3C SSE specification is easy to read and offers additional specifications and examples.

Bidirectional Notification via WebSocket

WebSocket supports the tunneling of a full-duplex protocol, called a *subprotocol*, within a single TCP connection that is initiated using HTTP. Because they are full-duplex, bidirectional communication becomes possible between API clients and servers. Clients are able to push requests to the server over a WebSocket connection, all while the server is able to push events and responses back to the client.

WebSocket is a standardized protocol maintained by the Internet Engineering Task Force as RFC 6455.[13] Most browsers support WebSocket, making it easy to use for browser-to-server, server-to-browser, and server-to-server scenarios. Because WebSocket connections are tunneled through HTTP connections, they can also overcome proxy restrictions found in some organizations.

An important factor to keep in mind is that WebSocket doesn't behave like HTTP, even though it uses HTTP to initiate the connection. Instead, a subprotocol must be selected. There are many subprotocols officially registered with IANA.[14] WebSocket supports both text and binary format subprotocols. Figure 9.9 shows an example WebSocket interaction using a plain text subprotocol.

WebSocket is more complex to implement but supports bidirectional communication. This means that they allow clients to send data to the server as well as receive data pushed from the server using the same connection. While SSE is easier

---

12. MDN Web Docs, "Server-Sent Events," last modified August 10, 2021, https://developer.mozilla.org/en-US/docs/Web/API/Server-sent_events.

13. Internet Engineering Task Force (IETF), *The WebSocket Protocol* (Request for Comments 6455, December 2011), https://tools.ietf.org/html/rfc6455.

14. Internet Assigned Numbers Authority (IANA), WebSocket Protocol Registries, last modified July 19, 2021, https://www.iana.org/assignments/websocket/websocket.xhtml.

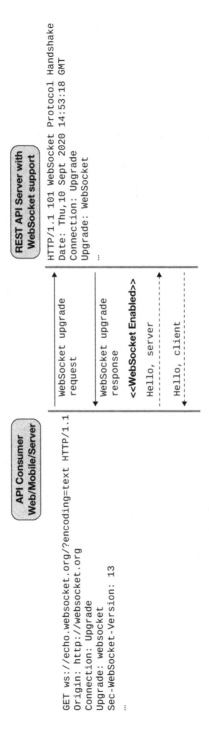

Figure 9.9 *An example interaction between an API client and server using WebSocket and a plain text subprotocol to create a chat application.*

to implement, clients are not able to send requests on the same connection, making WebSocket a better option when full duplex communication is necessary. Keep this in mind when choosing an async API style.

gRPC Streaming

TCP protocol is optimized for long-lived bidirectional communications. HTTP/1.1 was built on top of TCP but required multiple connections to allow clients to achieve concurrency. While this multiconnection requirement is easy to load balance and therefore scale, it has a considerable performance impact, as each connection requires establishing a new TCP socket connection and protocol negotiation.

HTTP/2 is a new standard built on the work of the SPDY protocol by Google to optimize portions of HTTP/1.1. Part of the optimization includes request and response multiplexing. In response multiplexing, a single HTTP/2 connection is used for one or more simultaneous requests. This avoids the overhead of creating new connections for each request, similar to how HTTP/1.1 supports keep-alive connections. However, HTTP/2 multiplexing allows all requests to be sent at once rather than sequentially using a keep-alive connection.

In addition, HTTP/2 servers may push resources to the client rather than require the client to initiate the request. This is a considerable shift from the traditional Web-based request/response interaction style of HTTP/1.1.

gRPC takes advantage of HTTP/2's bidirectional communication support, removing the need to separately support request/response alongside WebSocket, SSE, or other push-based approaches on top of HTTP/1.1. Because gRPC supports bidirectional communication, async APIs can be designed and integrated alongside traditional request/response RPC methods using the same gRPC-based protocol.

There are three options for gRPC streaming: client-to-server, server-to-client, and bidirectional, illustrated in Figure 9.10.

Like WebSocket, gRPC can send and receive messages and events across a single, full-duplex connection. Unlike WebSocket, there are no subprotocol decisions to be made and supported, as gRPC uses Protocol Buffers by default. However, browsers have no built-in gRPC support. The grpc-web project[15] is working on bridging gRPC to browsers, but with limitations. Therefore, gRPC streaming is often limited to service-to-service interactions.

---

15. https://github.com/grpc/grpc-web

gRPC Async Option 1: Client Streams to Server

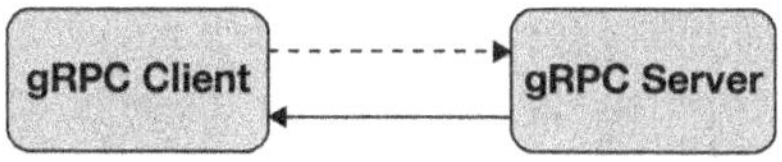

```
service Main {
 rpc GetLatestOrders(stream OrderQuery)
  returns (OrderResults) {}
}
```

gRPC Option 2: Server Streams to Client

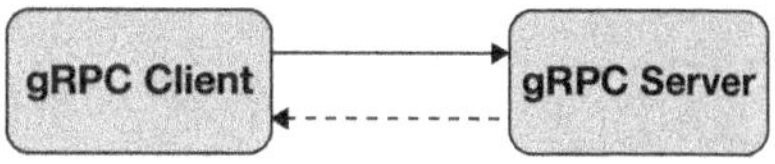

```
service Main {
 rpc GetLatestOrders(OrderQuery)
  returns (stream Order) {}
}
```

gRPC Async Option 3: Bidirectional Streaming

```
service Main {
 rpc GetLatestOrders(stream OrderQuery)
  returns (stream Order) {}
}
```

Figure 9.10 *The three gRPC-based streaming options available: client-to-server, server-to-client, and bidirectional.*

Selecting an Async API Style

While there are several choices available for async APIs, it is important to note that some choices may be a better option than others, depending on the circumstances and constraints of the solution. Following are some considerations for each async API style to help teams determine which style(s) may be the best options for an API:

- **Webhooks:** Webhooks are the only async API style that may be server-originated—that is, they don't require the client to initiate a connection first. Because subscriptions require being able to receive a POST-based callback, use Webhooks when server-to-server notification is needed. Web browsers and mobile apps are unable to take advantage of Webhooks, as they cannot establish an HTTP server to receive the callback. Subscribers that have inbound communication restricted by a firewall will not be able to receive the callback, as there won't be a network path to the callback server.

- **Server-Sent Events:** SSE is typically the easiest to implement on the server and client sides but has limited browser support. It also lacks bidirectional communication between client and server. Use SSE when there is a need for the server-push of events that follows RESTful API design.

- **WebSocket protocol:** WebSocket is more complex to implement due to the need to support one or more subprotocols, but it supports bidirectional communication. WebSocket is more broadly supported across browsers as well.

- **gRPC streaming:** gRPC takes full advantage of HTTP/2, so all infrastructure and subscribers must be able to support this newer protocol to take full advantage of gRPC streaming. Like WebSocket, it offers bidirectional communication. gRPC isn't supported fully by browsers, so gRPC streaming is best suited for service-to-service communication or for APIs that manage and configure infrastructure.

Designing Async APIs

Designing async APIs is similar to the process used to design traditional request/ response APIs using a REST-, RPC-, or query-based style. Begin with the resources identified during the API modeling step, as outlined in Chapter 6, "API Modeling." Revisit the events identified while capturing the operation details of each API profile. Then, determine what commands and events would be beneficial for API consumers.

Command Messages

Command messages incorporate all of the details necessary to request another component to perform a unit of work. When designing commands for async APIs, it is important to design the command message with sufficient details to process the request. It may also include a target location where the result message may be published. This target location may be a URL to POST the results, a URI to a message broker topic, or perhaps a URL to a shared object store such as Amazon S3.

When designing commands, it may be easy to use built-in language mechanisms such as object serialization to simplify the development of the command producer and consumer. However, this will limit the systems that will be able to consume and process these commands. Instead, seek to use a language-agnostic message format, such as the UBER hypermedia format, Apache Avro, Protocol Buffers, JSON, or XML.

The following is an example JSON-based command message to request a customer's billing address to be updated asynchronously:

```
{
  "messageType": "customerAddress.update",
  "requestId": "123f4567",
  "updatedAt": "2020-01-14T02:56:45Z",
```

```
    "customerId": "330001003",
    "newBillingAddress": {
        "addressLine1": "...",
        "addressLine2": "...",
        "addressCity": "...",
        "addressState": "...",
        "addressRegionProvince": "...",
        "addressPostalCode": "..."
    }
}
```

An additional `replyTo` field could be provided with the URL for callback, or other subscribers could listen for a `customerAddress.updated` event to react to the change, perhaps updating the billing address in a third-party system.

Event Notifications

Event notifications, sometimes referred to as *thin events,* notify subscribers that a state change or business event has occurred. They seek to provide only the necessary information sufficient for the subscriber to determine if the event is of interest.

The event subscriber is responsible for fetching the latest representation of the details via an API to avoid using stale data. Providing hypermedia links as part of a thin event helps to integrate API operations for retrieving the latest resource representation(s) with async APIs such as events. This is shown in the following example event payload:

```
{
  "eventType": "customerAddress.updated",
  "eventId": "123e4567",
  "updatedAt": "2020-01-14T03:56:45Z",
  "customerId": "330001003",
  "_links": [
    { "rel": "self", "href":"/events/123e4567" },
    { "rel": "customer", "href":"/customers/330001003" }
  ]
}
```

Thin events are used for events related to resources that change frequently, forcing the event subscriber to retrieve the latest resource representation to avoid working with stale data. While not necessary, thin events may also include details about the specific properties that changed when an update occurred to help consumers determine if the event is of interest.

Event-Carried State Transfer Events

Event-carried state transfer events contain all available information at the time of the event. This avoids the need to contact an API for the complete resource representation, although additional APIs may be used to augment the data required by the subscriber to perform any processing.

There are a few reasons why event-carried state transfer may be preferred over thin events:

- Subscribers want a snapshot of the resource associated with the event rather than the few details and associated hypermedia links offered by thin events.

- Data state changes are using message streaming to support replaying message history, requiring a complete point-in-time snapshot of a resource.

- Messaging via async APIs is used for interservice communication, requiring the publication of a full resource representation to avoid increased API traffic and tighter coupling between services.

It is common for this style of message design to mimic API representation structures whenever possible. Deviation is common when the event must offer the old and new values of any modified properties on an update event.

Finally, use nested rather than flat structures to group related properties for medium-to-large payloads. This helps drive evolvability, as property names are scoped to the parent property, avoiding property name collisions or long property names to clarify relationships. The following is a demonstration of a flat structure to event-carried state transfer message styles:

```
{
  "eventType": "customerAddress.updated",
  "eventId": "123e4567",
  "updatedAt": "2020-01-14T03:56:45Z",
  "customerId": "330001003",
  "previousBillingAddressLine1": "...",
  "previousBillingAddressLine2": "...",
  "previousBillingAddressCity": "...",
  "previousBillingAddressState": "...",
```

```
  "previousBillingAddressRegionProvince": "...",
  "previousBillingAddressPostalCode": "...",
  "newBillingAddressLine1": "...",
  "newBillingAddressLine2": "...",
  "newBillingAddressCity": "...",
  "newBillingAddressState": "...",
  "newBillingAddressRegionProvince": "...",
  "newBillingAddressPostalCode": "...",
  ...
}
```

A more structured approach is demonstrated in the following example:

```
{
  "eventType": "customerAddress.updated",
  "eventId": "123e4567",
  "updatedAt": "2020-01-14T03:56:45Z",
  "customerId": "330001003",
  "previousBillingAddress": {
      "addressLine1": "...",
      "addressLine2": "...",
      "addressCity": "...",
      "addressState": "...",
      "addressRegionProvince": "...",
      "addressPostalCode": "..."
  },
  "newBillingAddress": {
      "addressLine1": "...",
      "addressLine2": "...",
      "addressCity": "...",
      "addressState": "...",
      "addressRegionProvince": "...",
      "addressPostalCode": "..."
        },
  ...
}
```

When applying structured composition to the event-carried state transfer style, the consumer is able to reuse value objects to contain the details of each nested object and easily detect differences in fields or visualize the changes within a user interface at a later date. Without the pattern, a large value object plus additional coding effort are required to associate the flattened fields for performing things such as detecting a difference between the previous and new address.

Event Batching

While most async APIs are designed to notify a subscriber when each message is available, some designs may benefit from grouping events into a batch. Event batching requires that subscribers handle one or more messages within each notification. A simple example is to wrap the notification with an array and enclose each message within the response, even if there is only one event message at the time:

```
[
  {
    "eventType": "customerAddress.updated",
    "eventId": "123e4567",
    "updatedAt": "2020-01-14T03:56:45Z",
    "customerId": "330001003",
    "_links": [
      { "rel": "self", "href":"/events/123e4567" },
      { "rel": "customer", "href":"/customers/330001003" }
    ]
  },
  ...,
  ...
]
```

Another design option is to provide an envelope that wraps each batch of events along with additional metadata about the batch:

```
{
  "meta": {
    "app-id-1234",
    ...
  },
  "events": [
    {
      "eventType": "customerAddress.updated",
```

```
    "eventId": "123e4567",
    "updatedAt": "2020-01-14T03:56:45Z",
    "customerId": "330001003",
    "_links": [
      { "rel": "self", "href":"/events/123e4567" },
      { "rel": "customer", "href":"/customers/330001003" }
    ]
  },
  ...,
  ...
  ]
}
```

Keep in mind that batching messages or events allows for grouping based on a specific timeframe, number of events per batch, or through other grouping factors.

Event Ordering

Most event-based systems offer delivery of messages in order when possible. However, this may not always be the case. Event receivers may go offline and must restore missing messages while also accepting new inbound messages as they arrive. Or the message broker is unable to provide the guarantee of ordered message delivery. In complex distributed systems, multiple brokers and/or message styles may be used in combination, making it difficult to keep messages in order.

When event ordering is necessary, considerations must be made regarding message design. For a single message broker, the broker may offer message sequence numbering or timestamp-based ordering using the timestamp of when the message was received. In distributed architectures, the timestamp cannot be trusted, as each host may have slight variations in system time, called *clock skew*. This requires a centralized sequence-generation technique to be used and assigned to each message.

Be sure to factor order needs into the message design and across various architectural decisions. It may be necessary to research and understand distributed synchronization using techniques such as a Lamport Clock[16] to overcome clock skew across distributed nodes while ensuring proper ordering of messages across hosts.

---

16. Wikipedia, s.v. "Lamport Timestamp," last modified March 22, 2021, 00:201 https://en.wikipedia.org/wiki/Lamport_timestamp.

Documenting Async APIs

The AsyncAPI specification[17] is a standard for capturing definitions of async messaging channels. AsyncAPI supports traditional message brokers, SSE, Kafka and other message streams, and Internet of Things (IoT) messaging such as MQTT. This standard is becoming popular as a single solution to define message schemas and the protocol binding specifics of message-driven protocols. It is important to note that this specification isn't related to the OpenAPI Specification (OAS) but has been inspired by it and strives to follow a similar format to make adoption easier.

Listing 9.1 demonstrates an Async API description file with message definitions for the Shopping API's notification events, modeled in Chapter 6.

Listing 9.1 *AsyncAPI Definition of Shopping API Events*

```
#
# Shopping-API-events-v1.asyncapi.yaml
#
asyncapi: 2.0.0
info:
  title: Shopping API Events
  version: 1.0.0
  description: |
    An example of some of the events published during the bookstore's shop-
ping cart experience...
channels:
  books.searched:
    subscribe:
      message:
        $ref: '#/components/messages/BooksSearched'
  carts.itemAdded:
    subscribe:
      message:
        $ref: '#/components/messages/CartItemAdded'
components:
  messages:
    BooksSearched:
```

---

17. https://www.asyncapi.com

```
  payload:
    type: object
    properties:
      queryStringFilter:
        type: string
        description: The query string used in the search filter
      categoryIdFilter:
        type: string
        description: The category ID used in the search filter
      releaseDateFilter:
        type: string
        description: The release date used in the search filter
CartItemAdded:
  payload:
    type: object
    properties:
      cartId:
        type: string
        description: The cartId where the book was added
      bookId:
        type: string
        description: The book ID that was added to the cart
      quantity:
        type: integer
        description: The quantity of books added
```

Keep in mind that the AsyncAPI specification also supports the addition of protocol bindings for each channel's publish and subscribe messages. This flexibility allows the same message definition to be used across multiple messaging protocols, including message brokers, SSE, message brokers, and message streams. Visit the AsyncAPI Web page[18] for more information on the specification and additional resources to help get started using this async API description format. For example asynchronous API descriptions, refer to the API workshop examples[19] available on GitHub.

---

18. https://asyncapi.com
19. https://bit.ly/align-define-design-examples

Summary

Teams can benefit from shifting the API design approach from strictly request/response APIs to thinking in terms of how APIs can offer both synchronous request/response operations and asynchronous events. These events enable the API to push notifications to other teams that can build entirely new capabilities and perhaps product offerings on top of the original API. The result will be increased innovation and more transformative APIs as part of an API product or API platform initiative.

Part V

Refining the API Design

Following the Align-Define-Design-Refine (ADDR) process so far, the outcomes are identified and digital capabilities captured during the Align phase. The Define phase then elaborates on these details, forming API profiles with bounded scope and responsibilities. The Design phase applies one or more API styles to the API profile, producing a high-level design of the APIs needed to deliver the desired outcomes.

The Refine phase seeks to improve the developer experience and prepare for delivery of the API. Topics addressed in Part V include decomposing an API into services to shift complexity, applying proper API testing strategies, and strategies for offering robust API documentation. Offering helper libraries and command-line interfaces is also explored. Finally, tips are provided for scaling the ADDR process for larger organizations.

Chapter 10

From APIs to Microservices

The biggest fallacy about monoliths is you can have only one.

— Kelsey Hightower

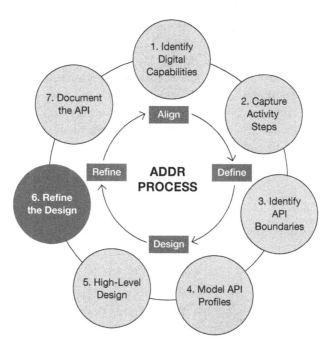

Figure 10.1 *Refining the API design may include decomposing it into smaller services to reduce the overall complexity of the solution.*

All organizations want to deliver business value as fast as possible. At the same time, they must ensure their software consistently works as expected. Increasing the speed of development risks an increase in bugs and decrease in reliability. The larger a software solution becomes, the greater this risk.

To mitigate these risks, organizations are required to reduce velocity in software delivery by coordinating through meetings. These meetings seek to optimize delivery while addressing any risks along the way. The larger the software solution, the more meetings that are required to mitigate associated risks. Yet, every meeting slows down the delivery process. Therefore, the balance between speed and delivering quality software is important.

Decomposing APIs into microservices (Figure 10.1) is one option for teams to address this need for balance. This chapter explores the topic of microservices, including benefits, challenges, and alternatives to microservices.

What Are Microservices?

Microservices are small, independently deployed components that deliver one or a small number of bounded digital capabilities. Each service offers one of the many digital capabilities required, ensuring that each service has a limited scope. When combined, microservices deliver a highly complex solution using smaller building blocks than the traditional service-oriented approach, as shown in Figure 10.2.

Microservice adoption has typically been used to decompose highly complex systems into independently deployed components rather than containing the complexity within a single codebase. The cognitive load required to understand a single microservice is lowered compared to that of understanding a single codebase.

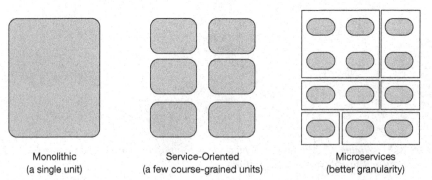

| Monolithic | Service-Oriented | Microservices |
| (a single unit) | (a few course-grained units) | (better granularity) |

Figure 10.2 *The traditional way of thinking about monolithic, service-oriented, and microservice architectures. Dashed lines represent traditional course-grained boundaries that are further decomposed to reduce the complexity of more course-grained services.*

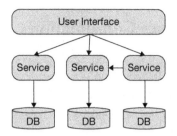

Figure 10.3 *Microservices decompose high complexity into smaller, independently deployable components.*

Testing becomes more approachable, and automated test suites become more focused on the single component (see Figure 10.3).

The idea of microservices has been around for more than a decade but only recently have microservices gained widespread use by the late majority. In the early days of microservices, teams had to weigh the effort required to establish and maintain the infrastructure necessary for a microservices architecture. Over time, many of these factors were addressed through cloud-native infrastructure, the growth of the DevOps culture, better delivery pipeline automation, and the use of containerization for producing self-contained deployment packages.

A Warning about the Term Microservices

It is important to recognize that there are a variety of definitions and scope assigned to microservices. Some organizations or individuals may define microservices as individual entities that offer a Web API, resulting in many network calls between services unnecessarily. Other definitions exist as well. Use caution when the organization makes a broad declaration that it is moving to microservices.

First, be sure to understand what is meant by the term. Be specific in the definition and intent. Next, seek a reference architecture and one or more reference applications to demonstrate the desired target state. Ask questions as necessary to ensure a shared understanding of the purpose and outcomes desired when shifting to microservices. Otherwise, everyone will assign their own definition of a microservice, and chaos will reign across the organization.

Finally, recognize that organizations may be using the term microservices in a specific way, while others may simply use the term to indicate that teams should "think smaller" than large, siloed systems that exist today. Do not assume understanding without following these recommended steps to align on a mutual definition and goals when shifting to microservices.

Microservices Reduce Coordination Costs

With many of these factors addressed today, organizations are now taking a microservice-based approach by default. However, it is important to understand both the benefits and the challenges of architectural decisions around microservices. Both technical and nontechnical factors that can have a positive or negative impact on the people behind the services and must be considered in the decision making.

The cost of coordinating many teams working within the same codebase is extremely high. Meeting after meeting is required to ensure that developers don't introduce bugs and that merge conflicts are avoided. For large organizations, the introduction of additional middle managers is required to coordinate the coordination.

The single greatest benefit of microservices is to reduce team coordination. A team operating independently to maintain one or a few microservices can coordinate within their team with limited coordination points outside their team.

Based on Metcalfe's law,[1] smaller teams result in fewer communication paths. The benefit is that it takes fewer meetings to communicate intent and resolve issues across the organization. The result is a team with more time to design, code, test, and deliver their services.

Coordination across teams is not eliminated with microservices, however. Integration must be coordinated to ensure that all the microservices fit the solution needs. Timelines must still be coordinated between product managers, business, and service teams. Therefore, the number of smaller team meetings may increase, whereas the number of attendees and the scope of discussion is greatly reduced for each meeting. Teams are given more independence and meetings are more efficient as coordination efforts are limited to the scope of the team's deliverables.

To achieve the goal of reduced team coordination, several factors are required:

- Self-service, automated infrastructure resources that ensure rapid onboarding of new services. These resources are commonly associated with a DevOps culture of automation tooling combined with continuous delivery processes.

- Team ownership of services throughout the software development lifecycle, including enhancements and support services. Team ownership across the lifecycle results in a culture of "you own it, you manage it" rather than siloed delivery to operations teams but may also include software reliability engineers and other roles to augment the team.

- Removal of centralized data ownership, allowing each service to own and manage the data associated with their services.

---

1. Wikipedia, s.v. "Metcalfe's Law," last modified April 13, 2021, 13:48, https://en.wikipedia.org/wiki/Metcalfe%27s_law.

Without incorporating these important factors, any shift to microservices will be met with challenges, including bloated microservices, slower velocity of delivery, and even project failure. This topic is discussed further in Chapter 6 of *Strategic Monoliths and Microservices*[2] in the section "Open-Host Service."

The benefits of moving to microservices have less to do with technology choices and more to do with the impact they have on the organization. The shift to microservices must be considered thoughtfully, as they may have a positive or negative impact on day-to-day development and operations.

The Difference between APIs and Microservices

While API products and microservices each offer network-based APIs, the differences between them are vast:

- API products target stability and evolvability, whereas microservices enable experimentation. Consumers of an API expect the contract to never break unless migrating to a new version of an API. Microservices are designed for experimentation and constant change. As such, microservices may be split, combined, or removed at any time.

- API products offer a set of digital capabilities for integration into solutions. Microservices decompose a solution into distributed components. They are not an external contract with the developer beyond the immediate boundary. If an external contract becomes a requirement, the service must be transitioned to an API product with a stable interface.

Just because the codebase is small doesn't make it a microservice. A microservice is an internal component and shouldn't be shared directly with external consumers. API products may be shared within a specific team, across teams, across the organization, and/or with partners/public developers.

Weighing the Complexity of Microservices

The most important factor when considering microservices is the complexity of the solution. Complexity cannot be fully removed from a software solution. However, it may be distributed across the solution. Microservices allow the complexity to be

---

2. Vaughn Vernon and Tomasz Jaskula, *Strategic Monoliths and Microservices: Driving Innovation Using Purposeful Architecture* (Boston: Addison-Wesley, 2021).

spread across components, making each individual component easier to build and manage. However, separating the problem into distributed components introduces other complexity.

Each team and organization must consider both the complexity of a solution and the complexities that microservices introduce to determine if a shift to microservices will help or hinder the organization's ability to deliver solutions with both speed and safety. While a single microservice may offer lower complexity, the infrastructure and automation requirements to deliver, monitor, and protect the service at runtime increases.

If the solution has a low factor of complexity, then microservices are often unnecessary and may even be detrimental to solution success. If the complexity of the solution is unknown, weigh the factors that follow and then consider starting with a minimal solution that balances these factors, migrating to microservices when and if the complexity increases.

Self-Service Infrastructure

Microservices require a self-service, fully automated infrastructure. Teams must be able to design a microservice, build it, and deploy code without any manual processes or approvals. Organizations that have not fully automated their provisioning and deployment pipeline will encounter considerable friction. Without full automation support, new code will be added to existing microservices to avoid manual processes, resulting in a few very large, siloed services.

Independent Release Cycles

Microservices must have their own release cycle. Some organizations opt to use their existing release processes, such as a two-week sprint and release, rather than allowing microservices to be released when they are ready. This coordinated deployment of all microservices at once results in a large release process rather than independent teams that may deploy their microservices as needed.

Shift to Single-Team Ownership

Each microservice should be owned, monitored, and managed by a single team. Teams should own only one or a few microservices to focus their efforts. They must own the service from definition to design and delivery. They must support the service, much like a product that seeks to incorporate improvements as feedback is received from other teams.

Smaller organizations find it challenging to assign single-team ownership, instead sharing the ownership of all services across a small number of developers. Developers spend more time moving between codebases and dealing with the challenges of distributed computing than they spend delivering solutions to market.

Organizational Structure and Cultural Impacts

Microservices require proper organizational support and structure. Organizational structure and culture may be at odds with the ownership and independence of microservices teams. Reporting structures may be optimized for larger delivery teams. Challenges may arise in trying to coordinate service integrations across teams that span managers. Organizations that prefer centralized oversight may encounter difficulties shifting control to individual teams.

These organizational challenges may create an unhealthy tension that makes it difficult to move to microservices while achieving the speed and safety often promised with microservices. Keep the organization's structure in mind before shifting to microservices by ensuring that buy-in exists from the executive team and managers who oversee service teams.

> **Tip**
>
> Don't discount the organizational and cultural impacts of adopting microservices. The shift from product- or project-based ownership to the ownership of one or a few microservices within a bounded area will have an impact on reporting structures and team alignment. Count the cost before proceeding. Otherwise, the organization may be trading code complexity for organizational complexity.

Shift in Data Ownership

Microservices must own their own data. This can be a challenging item, as rarely do teams think beyond the source code when it comes to shifting to microservices. When services do not own their data, the coordination cost of underlying schema changes can ripple across multiple microservices that share the data. It can require large, coordinated release efforts to bring every service in line with a breaking schema change within a shared data source.

Distributed Data Management and Governance

Microservices require considerable data management and governance. Because microservices own their own data, investment must be made to ensure that proper data management policies exist for reporting and analytics. Today data management is typically handled through extract-transform-load (ETL)–based processes that migrate data into an online analytical processing (OLAP)–based data store for optimized queries and decision support.

Shifting to microservices requires shifting to data streaming rather than ETL processes to bring together data from multiple services for the purposes of data aggregation and reporting. More emphasis needs to be placed on managing glossaries that create a strong ontology and taxonomy to unify distributed data models. Organizations with centralized data model governance and large shared databases must use caution when migrating to a microservices architecture. Finally, don't underestimate the effort required to separate a monolithic data store into a data store per service.

Distributed Systems Challenges

The journey toward microservices requires a deep understanding of distributed systems. Those not as familiar with the concepts of distributed tracing, observability, eventual consistency, fault tolerance, and failover will encounter a more difficult time with microservices. The eight fallacies of distributed computing,[3] written by L. Peter Deutsch and others at Sun Microsystems in 1994 and still applicable today, must be understood by every developer.

In addition, many find that architectural oversight is required to initially decompose and subsequently integrate services into solutions. Teams unable to have architectural support may suffer from lack of architectural consideration in the design of their microservices, resulting in poor boundaries and overlapping team responsibilities that produce increased cross-team coordination. The Align phase of the ADDR process seeks to address this concern early.

Finally, layered architectures are common within a monolithic codebase but are frowned upon with microservices. If microservices are layered incorrectly, a change to a single microservice may ripple to other services and require additional coordination efforts to synchronize the changes. Microservices that apply a layered approach must ensure that the impact of a service change is limited. Revisit the layered principle of REST to see how layers may be used to add independence between components.

---

3. Wikipedia, s.v. "Fallacies of Distributed Computing," last modified July 24, 2021, 20:52, https://en.wikipedia.org/wiki/Fallacies_of_distributed_computing.

Resiliency, Failover, and Distributed Transactions

With more microservices comes greater complexity when calls between services are required. Synchronous microservices require call chaining across a network and are therefore susceptible to network failure.

Resilience must be built into each microservice to ensure retries and failover occur in the event of a temporary network outage. The concept of a service mesh, discussed further in Chapter 15, "Protecting APIs," was introduced to address these crosscutting concerns, but a service mesh introduces further deployment and operational complexity that may be unnecessary for simple solutions.

Another side effect of synchronous call chaining is that failures beyond the first call require previous service calls to roll back transactions. During the height of service-oriented architecture (SOA), transaction managers were used to create distributed transactions, usually through the use of two-phase commit (2PC) transactions. This isn't an option with a highly distributed microservice architecture.

Instead, distributed transactions are often implemented using the Saga pattern.[4] A transactional context is applied within each service call, with compensating transactions used to apply the opposite operation when a rollback is required. State machines are required for each resource involved. Event sourcing is often used alongside the Saga pattern to ensure that all operations are atomic transactions backed by a ledger for auditing and troubleshooting purposes.

Refactoring and Code Sharing Challenges

Refactoring code is more challenging with microservices, as integrated development environments (IDEs) and other refactoring tools can only refactor within a single codebase. Refactoring code across multiple microservice codebases becomes more error prone.

When microservices use the same programming language, the tendency is to utilize a shared codebase for common code. Sharing code between services can create coordination coupling, requiring more meetings to ensure a change to code shared across microservices doesn't negatively impact others. When sharing code between services, all changes must be optional to avoid forcing other teams to be in lockstep.

---

4. Chris Richardson, "Pattern: Saga," Microservice Architecture, accessed August 19, 2021, https://microservices.io/patterns/data/saga.html.

Do You Really Need Microservices?

After weighing the challenges of microservices and the underlying operational complexity, it may be determined that an API boundary doesn't need to be decomposed into microservices. Instead of microservices, perhaps all that is needed is one or more monolithic APIs that are designed to be modular, known as *modular monoliths*.

Modular monoliths apply loose coupling and high cohesion within a single codebase to avoid the complexity of distributed computing. Over time, the monolith may be decomposed into microservices if the solution becomes too complex for a single codebase. However, only apply this approach once all paths to refactoring and reorganizing the modules of a single codebase have been exhausted.

Remember that organizations aren't limited to a single monolith. Multiple modular monoliths may be sufficient for the needs of the team. Each monolith offers one or a few APIs that support the operations within the bounded contexts contained within the monolith.

Synchronous and Asynchronous Microservices

Microservices may be designed to be synchronous or asynchronous. Synchronous microservices apply a more traditional request/response model, typically via HTTP using REST, RPC, or a query API style.

While synchronous, request/response–based APIs are more familiar to developers, the result can be the creation of fragile integrations. Services that orchestrate API calls between services may fail midstream if a problem occurs with a single service, requiring a reversal of previously successful API calls. Services that call other services, termed call *chaining*, may also fail midstream but are unable to reverse the previous API calls themselves. Figure 10.4 illustrates this concern, as the service client only called Service A, which results in more service calls that can fail in the event of a downstream error.

Alternatively, an asynchronous access pattern may be used for microservice integration. In this style, messages are submitted to a message queue or topic hosted on a message broker or streaming server. One or more microservices listen for messages, process them in turn, and then emit messages containing business events as the result.

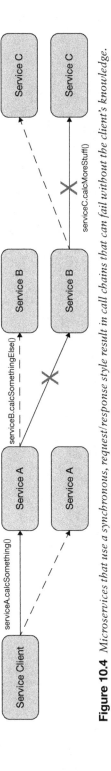

Figure 10.4 *Microservices that use a synchronous, request/response style result in call chains that can fail without the client's knowledge.*

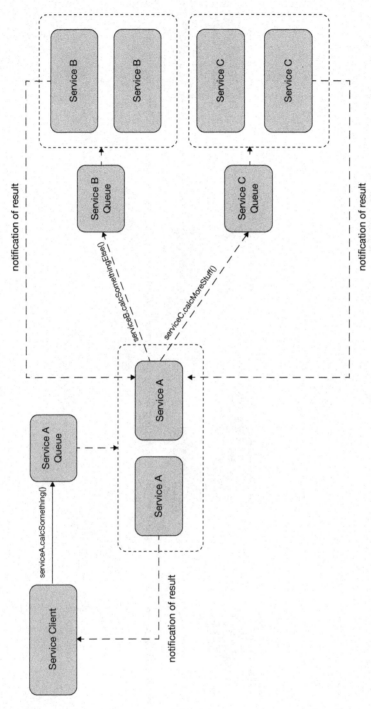

Figure 10.5 *Asynchronous microservices are able to receive command messages and respond with results without the need for fragile call chaining.*

Asynchronous microservices offer several advantages. The greatest advantage is that new microservices can be brought online to replace older ones without the knowledge of the consumer. The new microservice subscribes to the same topic or queue and begins processing messages.

In addition, consumers have the flexibility to use one or more of the following interaction patterns, as needed: fire-and-forget, fire-and-listen for events, or fire-and-follow-up using the provided response URL.

Finally, asynchronous error handling and recovery is built in to message brokers and streaming solutions. Avoiding the need for synchronous call chaining error recovery greatly simplifies the infrastructure requirements, reducing or eliminating the need for a service mesh.

Of course, asynchronous integration is a more complex interaction than a standard request/response approach. Developers must learn to integrate with asynchronous services and handle failures by checking for error response messages and process unprocessed messages using dead letter queues (DLQs).

Microservice Architecture Styles

A microservice-based architecture is not limited to a single style or approach. There are three common styles of applying microservices. Each one offers a slight variation on how microservices may be used to reduce coordination between teams. Some have chosen to apply one or more of these styles in combination to support the needs and culture of the organization.

Direct Service Communication

In this style, each service communicates with other services directly using a synchronous or asynchronous model. This approach is the most common style found during the early days of microservices. Those using a synchronous model encounter challenges such as service communication failure and call chain fragility. The introduction of a service mesh helps to overcome these challenges, as does the shift to a more asynchronous model that is message driven. Figure 10.6 depicts this more traditional microservice architecture style.

API-Based Orchestration

This style starts with the design of an API that is further decomposed into microservices as appropriate. The API becomes the stable orchestration layer across one or more microservices, offering a more stable contract externally while

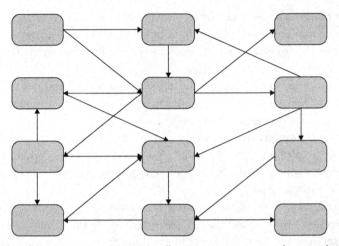

Figure 10.6 *Direct service communication allows any service to invoke any other service.*

supporting experimentation and splitting of microservices internally. This is a style chosen by organizations that have struggled with some of the challenges of the direct service communication model. Many of the organizations that were early adopters of microservices are moving to this model. This model is shown in Figure 10.7.

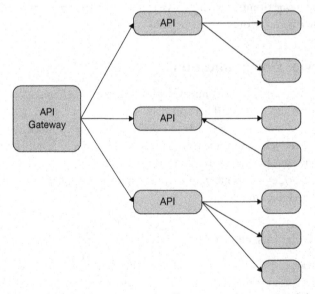

Figure 10.7 *The API-based orchestration style offers increased contract stability while hiding the internal microservices.*

Cell-Based Architecture

A cell-based architecture (see Figure 10.8) blends the previous two styles to bring a more modular approach to microservices. Each cell offers one or more digital capabilities, provided through a synchronous or asynchronous API. The API is externalized via a gateway, hiding the internal details of service decomposition through encapsulation. Cells are combined to create larger solutions. Because of the modular composability of this style, it is often found in large organizations, as it offers better management for their evolving systems.

Uber Engineering recently shifted from the integration of many small services to this cell-based architecture model. It discovered that complexity increases are far outweighed by the value that microservices provided. Uber refers to this approach as Domain-Oriented Microservice Architecture (DOMA) and offers a helpful article[5] that summarizes the approach. It resembles many of the elements of a cell-based architecture by reducing the complexity of a large-scale microservice architecture while maintaining the flexibility and benefits that it provides.

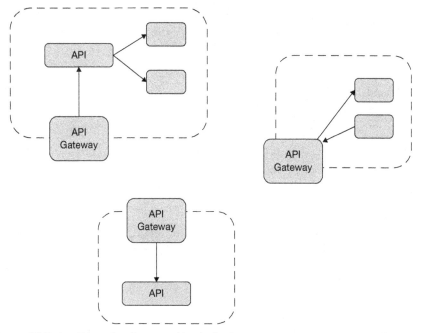

Figure 10.8 *A cell-based architecture blends the direct service communication and API-based orchestration styles into a more modular approach for large organizations or complex systems.*

---

5. Adam Gluck, "Introducing Domain-Oriented Microservice Architecture," Uber Engineering, July 23, 2020, https://eng.uber.com/microservice-architecture.

Right-Sizing Microservices

Organizations on the path to microservices often struggle with finding the right size for microservices. Teams often ask, "What is the maximum allowable size for a microservice?" A better question would be, "What is the right size for this microservice based on what is needed today?"

Microservices aren't frozen in time. Instead, they grow and become more complex. Over time, a microservice may need to be split. At other times, two microservices may become codependent and benefit from being combined into a single service. Therefore, the size of a microservice will change over time.

It is also important to note that services tend to grow over time, requiring that the boundaries of a microservice be reevaluated often. This can only be done efficiently if service ownership resides with a single team. Services shared across teams require further coordination meetings.

Right-sizing microservices requires a continuous process of design and reevaluation:

1. Identify where transactional boundaries exist to find candidate service boundaries. Defining boundaries helps to reduce the chances of spreading transactions across services.

2. Design two or a few course-grained microservices based on the identified boundaries. This step ensures your microservice operations retain integrity within a transactional boundary and avoids the challenges of rolling back transactions across multiple microservice calls over the network.

3. Keep splitting services as they grow, being guided by the needs of transactional boundaries while keeping team coordination costs low.

> **Tip**
>
> It is best to focus less on the size of the microservice and more on the purpose of the service. Microservices should seek to make future change easier, even if that means the service is more course-grained at the start.

Decomposing APIs into Microservices

If the team has determined that decomposing the API into two or more microservices would be beneficial, then there are a few additional steps needed when starting the delivery phase: extending previously created API sequence diagrams with more detail, identifying candidate services, and capturing the service design details.

Step 1: Identify Candidate Microservices

The first step in decomposing APIs is to identify candidate microservices. Start by expanding the web sequence diagrams, created during the API modeling and design phases, to include external systems and data stores. The diagrams help to identify natural boundaries between services. Figure 10.9 expands the Shopping API with the inclusion of an external search engine that will support basic and advanced query support.

Because the search engine integration is read-only within the Search Books operation of the Shopping API, this is a good candidate for decomposing into a separate service. The team that will own this candidate microservice will be responsible for

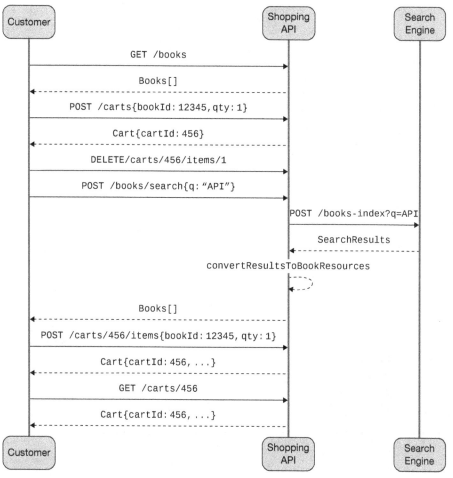

Figure 10.9 *Expanded Shopping API web sequence diagram that now includes any external system.*

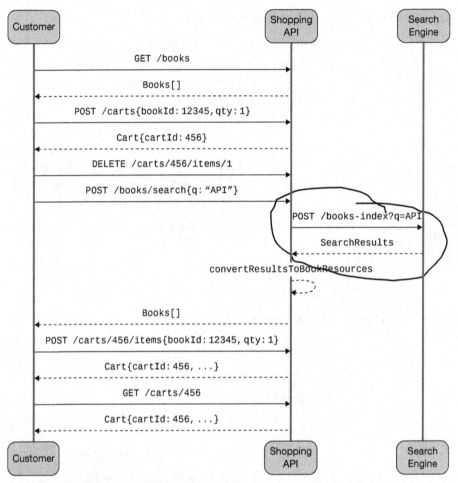

Figure 10.10 *The search engine integration will require specialized knowledge of how to properly index and search entities, so the Search Books operation is a good candidate for a separate microservice.*

ensuring the search engine indexes are both performant and deliver the search capabilities required by customers. Figure 10.10 show the boundary for the candidate microservice that will support book searches.

Step 2: Add Microservices into API Sequence Diagrams

Next, revise the sequence diagram to show the introduction of the candidate microservice. Determine if the integration should use a synchronous API, such as REST, or if an asynchronous service would be better. An updated sequence diagram for the Shopping API is shown in Figure 10.11.

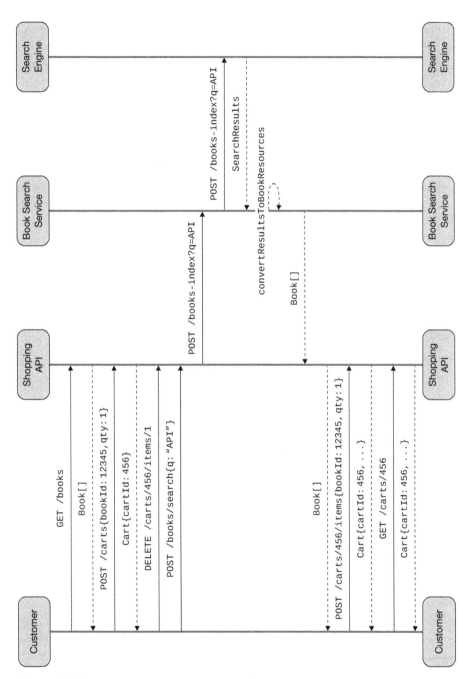

Figure 10.11 *Updated sequence diagram with the candidate microservice involved, which allows for identifying possible network or transaction challenges.*

Review the updates and determine if the candidate microservice is doing too much and should be further decomposed. Or, perhaps the service is doing too little, introducing too many network calls and therefore should be combined into a slightly larger service.

Step 3: Capture Using the Microservice Design Canvas

Finally, capture the design details of the candidate microservice. The use of the Microservice Design Canvas (MDC)[6] is recommended, as it helps to focus on the commands, queries, and events that the service will support. If the details of the service cannot fit into a single-page MDC, it may be responsible for too much. In this case, revisit the design to see if it should be further decomposed or if it is right-sized for supporting the needs of the API. Figure 10.12 shows an example MDC for the Book Search Service.

At this point, the MDC provides sufficient details to proceed with building and integrating the service with one or more APIs. However, there are some additional design considerations to address before proceeding.

Additional Microservice Design Considerations

Note that not all APIs will benefit from service decomposition. Anytime there is a new microservice involved, there is an opportunity for increased network latency that could negatively impact API clients.

Increased network latency is of particular importance when service call chaining occurs as a result of a synchronous service calling another, which may call another, and so on. The total time for a client to receive a response is the sum of the time required to execute each service call sequentially. For highly efficient service implementations that are less than 10 milliseconds each, latency may not be too much of a concern. Services that integrate with legacy systems that may suffer from degraded performance during peak usage, resulting in several seconds of wait time for an end user. Finally, for some microservice ecosystems, it may not be possible to know how many services are involved or to predict the total time required for execution.

When possible, keep a transaction within a single service boundary. Transaction boundaries that span multiple service calls require additional design considerations. If a service call fails, any previous service calls must be rolled back. Because each service manages its own transactional boundary, a compensating transaction may be required to reverse the transaction—this is the Saga pattern in action. Whenever possible, seek to decompose microservices such that transaction integrity is maintained.

---

6. https://launchany.com/canvas

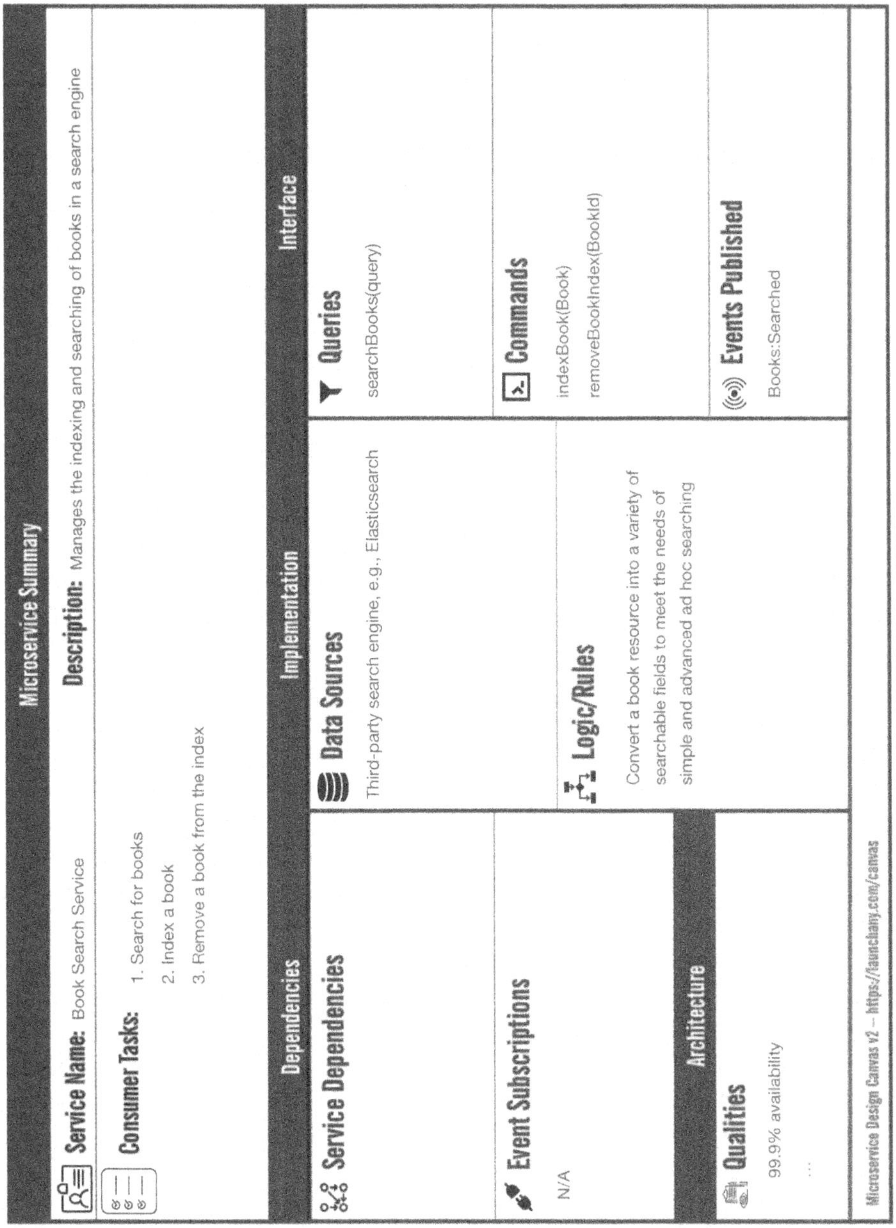

Microservice Summary

Service Name: Book Search Service

Description: Manages the indexing and searching of books in a search engine

Consumer Tasks:

1. Search for books
2. Index a book
3. Remove a book from the index

Dependencies

Service Dependencies

Event Subscriptions

N/A

Architecture

Qualities

99.9% availability

...

Implementation

Data Sources

Third-party search engine, e.g., Elasticsearch

Logic/Rules

Convert a book resource into a variety of searchable fields to meet the needs of simple and advanced ad hoc searching

Interface

Queries

searchBooks(query)

Commands

indexBook(Book)

removeBookIndex(BookId)

Events Published

Books:Searched

Microservice Design Canvas v2 — https://launchany.com/canvas

Figure 10.12 *A Microservice Design Canvas that captures the candidate microservice, including design considerations, prior to implementation.*

In addition, consider whether a dedicated team will own the microservice. If so, does the introduction of the candidate microservice reduce or increase cross-team coordination? Not all decisions about service decomposition are about reducing code size.

Finally, avoid splitting services based on the CRUD lifecycle, creating one service per operation (e.g., Create Project Service, Update Project Service, Read Project Service, List Projects Service, Delete Project Service). This pattern creates more coordination requirements between each service team. A change to the resource representation for a project requires coordinating with each of the teams that own the service. The exception is when complexity dictates the need to split one part of a CRUD lifecycle due to increased complexity. For example, the complexity of payment processing integration may merit shifting this behavior to a separate microservice.

Considerations When Transitioning to Microservices

While there are many benefits to moving to microservices, the transition shouldn't be taken lightly. After some time and reflection, some organizations choose to simplify their microservice journey, others decide to abandon their journey in favor of thinking smaller but without microservices, and the rest continue to move forward with microservices.

First, verify that a microservices-based approach is being applied to the correct context. Some microservices initiatives are dictated from the executive team without proper context. It usually starts with an executive who mandates microservices so that teams can increase the velocity of delivery. However, context isn't provided to inform teams to avoid microservices complexity when the solution is simple (e.g., an application that offers CRUD-based forms to manage a dataset). The result is wasted time and effort to decompose a simple solution into microservices that introduce unnecessary complexity around runtime management, troubleshooting complexity, and distributed transaction management.

Next, be sure that the organization's reporting structure and culture are ready to shift alongside the move to microservices. Some organizations are not prepared for teams to own services for the long term. Instead, they treat microservices as projects that are delivered but never owned beyond delivery. The team that built the service moves on to other projects and higher priority initiatives. Teams that could benefit from a minor change to an existing service are required to build their own service as a result.

Finally, find ways to build smaller. Modularize code within a single codebase. Design clear APIs for consumers to use. Decompose APIs into microservices only when high complexity makes it necessary.

Summary

Microservices are independently deployable units of code that are combined to create distributed systems. Moving to microservices requires a combination of new technologies and top-down organizational support. After an organization reflects carefully on the decision factors, its shift to microservices may result in the primary benefit of reduced coordination costs across multiple teams.

Be wary of technology trends that do not inject more benefit than the complexity they require. Microservices have offered benefits to some organizations, but not without their challenges. Organizations must count the cost of moving to microservices to determine if the complexity of designing, building, and operating microservices outweighs the complexity of a single, monolithic codebase.

Alternatives, such as modular monoliths and cell-based architectures, support many of the goals of microservices but with varying support for reduced coordination and local decision optimization. When in doubt, apply the "you ain't gonna need it" (YAGNI) principle of agile software by starting with a modular monolith API and decomposing it into microservices when the need arises.

Chapter 11

Improving the Developer Experience

Every useful API that delivers value will typically have multiple consumers.
This is a natural asymmetry, which will only increase over time.

— Mark O'Neill

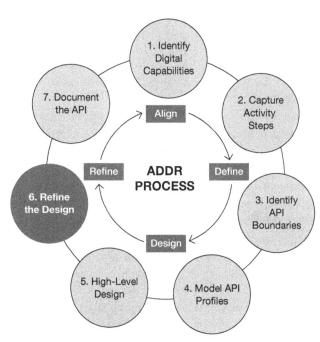

Figure 11.1 *Refining the API design includes improving the developer experience through helper libraries and command-line interfaces.*

When teams think about delivering an API, the primary focus is on the code that must be built. They focus on considerations such as the target programming language, frameworks that aid in building the API, continuous integration and delivery (CI/CD) pipelines, and other factors. While all of these decisions are important, they involve the API provider only. They do not directly empower the tens, hundreds, or thousands of future API consumers that will use the API.

As an API provider, it is important to keep the API consumers first in everything that is designed and delivered. This responsibility includes creating mock APIs to help early adopters provide feedback early on the API design (Figure 11.1). It also requires consideration of whether to offer helper libraries and command-line interfaces to reduce the integration time by developers across all skill levels consuming the API. This chapter addresses these concerns in an effort to multiply the impact across the many current and future API consumers that will integrate the API.

Creating a Mock API Implementation

API design is a mixture of patterns and subjective design decisions. What makes sense during the API design phase may not make sense to developers once they integrate the API. API mocking is the creation of a simulated version of an API design. Generating a mock version of an API design helps to verify that the API design will meet the needs of target developers.

Mock implementations are quick to deliver, as they lack production-ready code. They also bypass backend database servers and legacy systems. Mock APIs implement the API design while returning static responses or responses based on synthesized data sets.

With mock implementations, developers are able to integrate portions of an API before the implementation has begun. Consequently, API teams can see if the API design is missing critical functionality. Mock implementations also help teams to identify important data elements that may be missing from the API design.

API design includes making compromises. Once developers start to integrate with an API, they will provide feedback on how it should be changed. If the API design is frozen, this change must wait until a new version of the API is released. Integrating with a mock implementation identifies these problem areas early, when the cost of change is much lower.

An added benefit is that mock implementations help accelerate the delivery process. Rather than waiting until the entire API has been coded, mock implementations may be used to produce API integration code for frontend development. They may also be used to drive automated test creation. Over time, the mock integration is replaced with the actual API until the mock is no longer needed and is removed completely. The interface remains constant, but the implementation is replaced over time. Meanwhile, teams are able to proceed in parallel.

There are three primary types of API mock implementations: static mocking, prototyping, and README-based mocking. Each may be used independently or in combination to explore an API design prior to delivery. Mocks may also be used for standing up a local or cloud-based learning environment that is separate from production.

Static API Mocking

One of the easiest ways to explore an API design before writing code is to write a static version of some or all of the expected API requests and responses. Static mocks capture API interactions through JSON- or XML-based files that may be shared with developers and API design reviewers. They offer examples to view and to improve upon before coding.

The following mock response demonstrates a Book resource instance for the Shopping API example using the JSON:API specification:

```
{
  "data": {
    "type": "books",
    "id": "12345",
        "attributes": {
        "isbn": "978-0321834577",
        "title": "Implementing Domain-Driven Design",
        "description": "With Implementing Domain-Driven Design, Vaughn has
made an important contribution not only to the literature of the Domain-
Driven Design community, but also to the literature of the broader enterprise
application architecture field."
    },
    "relationships": {
      "authors": {
          "data": [
          {"id": "765", "type": "authors"}
          ]
      }
    },
```

```
  "included": [
    {
      "type": "authors",
      "id": "765",
      "fullName": "Vaughn Vernon",
      "links": {
        "self": { "href": "/authors/765" },
        "authoredBooks": { "href": "/books?authorId=765" }
      }
    }
  }
}
```

Static mocks may be provided using a Web server, such as Apache or nginx, to allow frontend developers to integrate the mock API responses into the user interface. They will then be able to provide feedback early and often as they start to parse and integrate the static mocks into their code.

It is important to note that static mocks lack any implementation, so mock integration will be limited to GET-based operations only. However, creating a static mock of an API operation that retrieves a resource representation is quite useful, easy to build, and provides opportunities for plenty of feedback.

API Prototype Mocking

A throwaway prototype provides greater validation of an API design than a static mock. Unlike a static mock, which is often limited to GET-based operations, an API prototype is able to support all types of operations, including those that create or modify resource state.

However, API prototypes take more effort to produce manually. Typically, teams select a preferred programming language and framework that is optimized for rapid delivery. Ruby, Python, PHP, and Node.js are popular choices because of their fast development and abundant libraries for producing APIs and synthesized data sets.

> **Note**
>
> Teams may wish to select a language and framework that isn't supported for production by the organization. Doing so will ensure that prototypes intended to be throwaway don't suddenly become production code.

The use of an API mocking tool, often based on an API description format such as the OpenAPI Specification (OAS), allows teams to skip most or all development efforts. These tools produce simple mock implementations that store data temporarily for common create-read-update-delete (CRUD)–based operations. Some tools generate code for the mock implementation, and others create the mock API on the fly.

It is recommended to keep API prototypes simple at first. Expand the prototype as needed to deep-dive into any contentious areas that need further exploration or areas that can encourage parallel development.

README-Based Mocking

README-based mocking provides an alternative prototyping style without the need to write code. A README file is created to demonstrate how to use an API to accomplish one or more desired outcomes. README-based mocks help to validate the API design before implementation starts by sharing the intent of API usage to produce desired outcomes.

Most README-based mocks use Markdown, enabling the combination of text and code examples to be easily produced and rendered in a browser. Tools such as GitHub and GitLab have built-in Markdown support, although static site generation tools such as Jekyll or Hugo may also be used.

Following is a README-based mock that demonstrates how to retrieve book details, then add the book to a cart using the JSON:API media format:

```
1. Retrieve Book Details

GET /books/12345 HTTP/1.1
Accept: application/vnd.api+json


HTTP/1.1 200 OK
Content-Type: application/vnd.api+json
...


{
  "data": {
    "type": "books",
    "id": "12345",
      "attributes": {
      "isbn": "978-0321834577",
```

```
      "title": "Implementing Domain-Driven Design",
      "description": "With Implementing Domain-Driven Design, Vaughn has
made an important contribution not only to the literature of the Domain-
Driven Design community, but also to the literature of the broader enterprise
application architecture field."
    },
    "relationships": {
      "authors": {
        "data": [
          {"id": "765", "type": "authors"}
        ]
      }
    },
    "included": [
      {
        "type": "authors",
        "id": "765",
        "fullName": "Vaughn Vernon",
        "links": {
          "self": { "href": "/authors/765" },
          "authoredBooks": { "href": "/books?authorId=765" }
        }
      }
    ]
  }
}
```

2. Add Book to Cart

```
POST /carts/6789/items HTTP/1.1
Accept: application/vnd.api+json

HTTP/1.1 201 Created
Content-Type: application/vnd.api+json
...

{
  "data": {
    "type": "carts",
    "id": "6789",
      "attributes": {
```

```
        ... truncated for space ...
      }
  }
}


3. Remove a Book from a Cart


...
```

Using this approach gives teams time to think through the API design and how it will be used to produce outcomes—without the overhead of writing or changing code. It also increases the quality of documentation and the surrounding conversations about the design. README-driven design can be thought of as the hand-written version of an acceptance test using behavior-driven development (BDD) frameworks such as Cucumber.[1]

Providing Helper Libraries and SDKs

Client-side helper libraries wrap all of the HTTP connection management, error detection, JSON marshaling, and other concerns for a single programming language. Some developers prefer helper libraries, as they help speed development by avoiding the need to deal with low-level HTTP concerns. They also enable code completion within popular integrated development environments (IDEs) that isn't possible when working directly with HTTP.

A software development kit, or SDK, is a packaged solution that includes helper libraries, documentation, example code, reference applications, and other resources for developers. While SDKs may be distributed by API providers, the growth of API developer portals have replaced the need to package a complete SDK.

Many developers tend to use the terms interchangeably, but there is a distinct difference between an SDK and helper library. The important thing is to be clear about what is provided in the distribution to set proper expectations with the developer.

Don't expect all developers to take advantage of helper libraries, however. Those familiar with HTTP generally prefer working with it directly rather than with a helper library. This preference is centered on the inflexibility of some helper libraries that, because of missing features within the library, may prevent developers from being able to fit the exact needs of the use case.

---

1. https://cucumber.io

Options for Offering Helper Libraries

There are three options for offering helper libraries:

- **Provider supported:** Provider-supported helper libraries are built and maintained by the API provider. The provider owns them, manages them, and keeps them in sync as API operations are added or enhanced through manual coding or code generation.

- **Community contributed:** Instead of the vendor offering the helper library, the community contributes the SDK. This may be the case for all programming languages or just for currently unsupported programming languages. Vendors may choose to allow the community-contributed helper libraries to thrive on their own, work with the authors to make them better, or eventually offer to take over maintenance. Be aware that community-contributed SDKs have a tendency to lose the interest of contributors or available maintainers over time and may be abandoned. Communication with community supporters is critical, as many developers may assume that they are vendor-backed and complain if they are no longer maintained.

- **Consumer generated:** With the growth of API definition formats such as Swagger, RAML, Blueprint, and others, it is becoming easier for API consumers to generate their own client library from any of these formats. Consumer-generated helper libraries give consumers the most flexibility, as they may opt to create a lightweight wrapper around the HTTP layer or perhaps generate a robust library with objects/structures that mimic API resources.

API teams must determine how they plan to provide helper libraries, which programming languages they plan to support, and how community- or consumer-generated helper libraries may impact their developer support program.

Versioning Helper Libraries

Helper libraries will have their own version numbering scheme, which may confuse developers. Versioning is common when helper libraries make breaking changes to how they surface the API as objects.

For example, version 1 of a helper library may return a hash of name/value pairs containing resource properties, eventually choosing to abandon this approach in favor of returning objects. The API may still be version 1, but the helper library may be on version 2.1.5 for Ruby, and the Python module may be on version 1.8.5.

Including SDK language and version number in the `User-Agent` header for all requests can help. However, the most important factor is to ensure that everything is logged on the client side and server side.

Support emails will become more confusing when trying to determine the language, helper library version, and API version being used. Add community-contributed helper libraries into the process, and more confusion will occur. This confusion can exist for even the most experienced developer.

The addition of a request identifier or correlation identifier is a common solution to this problem. These identifiers help to correlate client requests with server-side logs as developers correspond with API support team. Application performance management (APM) tools may be useful for diagnosing issues as well.

Helper Library Documentation and Testing

Developers integrating an API will not want to move between API documentation and an undocumented helper library while trying to figure out how to code up their idea. To overcome this poor developer experience, thorough helper library documentation is required for every programming language. In addition, example code in the developer portal should include examples for each supported programming language.

For each release, API teams need to factor in sufficient time to keep helper library documentation updates across all supported programming languages. Automated tests for each helper library must also be maintained to ensure that libraries are in sync with the latest API operation enhancements as they are released.

Offering CLIs for APIs

While most APIs target developers who will integrate it into a larger application, it is important not to overlook command-line interfaces (CLIs) as another developer use case. It is not uncommon to encounter CLIs that wrap an API, much like helper libraries offer programming language–specific wrappers around a Web-based API.

Unlike helper libraries, CLIs offer a human-friendly method of interacting with remote systems without requiring coding skills. The CLI is both an API consumer and an automation tool. It may be used for many purposes, including the following:

- Providing quick, one-off scripting for automation engineers
- Extracting data locally for proofs of concept (POCs)
- Automating infrastructure using tooling such as Kubernetes, Heroku, Amazon Web Services (AWS), Google Cloud (gcloud)

Offering a CLI tool expands the reach of an API beyond full-time developers to automation engineers who are better equipped to write shell scripts rather than applications to integrate with APIs. CLI tools may offer human-friendly output, in addition to JSON, CSV, or other output formats that support better automation and tool chaining.

Designing a CLI tool that wraps an API is no different than designing the API itself. It requires understanding the desired outcomes, activities, and steps required to accomplish the jobs to be done (JTBD). Then, design the CLI interface to meet these outcomes. The following code block shows how a CLI interface could be designed to support the Shopping API designed in previous chapters:

```
$> bookcli books search "DDD"


| Title                        | Authors        | Book ID         |
|------------------------------|----------------|----------------|
| Implementing Domain-Driven ... | Vaughn Vernon | 12345          |


$> bookcli cart add 40321834577


Success!


$> bookcli cart show


Cart Summary:


| Total         | Estimated Sales Tax |
|---------------|---------------------|
| $42.99 USD    | $3.44 USD           |


Cart Items:


| Title                        | Price       | Qty | Book ID         |
|------------------------------|-------------|-----|----------------|
| Implementing Domain-Driven ... | $42.99 USD | 1   | 12345          |


$> ...
```

To offer a great CLI experience, API teams need to become students of human-first CLI design. The excellent *Command Line Interface Guidelines*[2] site offers in-depth details on how to design a human-first CLI based on 40 years of patterns and practices across tooling and operating systems.

Also, teams should seek to understand the pipe and filter design pattern commonly seen across *nix tools such as sed, awk, and grep to better understand how tool chaining works. Finally, carefully examining popular CLIs from Kubernetes, Heroku, and others help teams to see how to design a user-friendly CLI that wraps remote APIs.

Using Code Generators for Helper Library and CLI Generation

Whether a small team is tasked with delivering multiple APIs in quick succession or an organization is scaling its API program, leveraging code-generation tools is essential. Code generation ensures APIs are delivered consistently and at scale by incorporating boilerplate code and common patterns. While some API styles such as gRPC rely heavily on code generation, other API styles consider code-generation support as optional. Code generators are helpful to generate SDKs and helper libraries consistently across a variety of target programming languages.

For REST-based APIs, the Swagger Codegen[3] project is the most popular. This project offers open-source client-side code generators for a variety of programming languages. Another popular option for REST-based APIs is APIMatic,[4] which is a freemium tool that offers code-generation support. All of these tools generate client code based on an OAS description file. The resulting code may be packaged up and distributed by the API team.

Some organizations have found that creating their own client-side code generators is a better option. While doing so requires more investment, the generated code may be customized as needed. For example, code can be customized to track rate limiting, detect special error response codes, and incorporate retry loops where appropriate.

---

2. Aanand Prasad, Ben Firshman, Carl Tashian, and Eva Parish, *Command Line Interface Guidelines,* accessed August 20, 2021, https://clig.dev.
3. https://swagger.io/tools/swagger-codegen
4. https://www.apimatic.io

Summary

API design doesn't stop with the details of API operations and protocol semantics. It requires thoughtful consideration regarding how the API will be integrated by developers. While some code decisions are important for the API provider, these are internal concerns that do not have a direct impact on the many API consumers that will use the API. The more complex the API, the more tooling (e.g., API mocks, helper libraries, CLIs) is required to support the design and delivery process.

API teams must consider how their decisions may have a positive or negative impact on future API consumers. Avoid making decisions that provide local optimizations for a few developers, instead opting to make global optimizations for the many current and future consumers of the API.

Chapter 12

API Testing Strategies

Software defect removal is the most expensive and time-consuming form of work for software.

— Caspers Jones

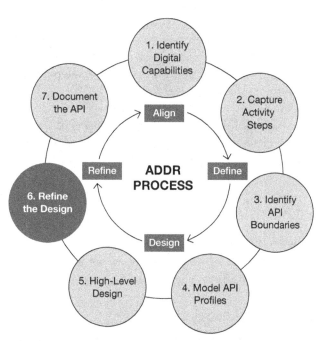

Figure 12.1 *API testing refines the API design by identifying API quality issues early.*

When building an API product or platform, it is important to have an API testing strategy established. Selecting the right approach for API testing contributes to the success of an API program's supportability. It also contributes to faster delivery while avoiding one of the costliest aspects of software development: defect removal. Finally, it offers another perspective on the developer experience of an API because of the consumer-oriented nature of automated testing.

Acceptance Testing

Acceptance testing, also called *solution-oriented testing,* ensures that the API supports the captured job stories. It seeks to answer the following questions:

- Does the API solve real problems that our customers have?
- Does it produce the desired outcomes for the jobs to be done?

Acceptance testing verifies the collaboration of API operations required to achieve a desired outcome. Composing acceptance tests entails using only the API interface to verify that the system meets all expected end-to-end functionality. The internals of the API can and likely will change over the course of development, but this should not affect the results of the acceptance tests.

Acceptance testing is the most valuable style of testing for an API. The process of writing acceptance tests helps identify poor developer experience for a single API operation or across the end-to-end integration. It is where the most testing effort should be spent, after code testing, when limited time is available.

Automated Security Testing

Each week, a new headline appears that indicates a company has been hacked and private information exposed. Security is a process, not a product, and a continual one at that. Security testing aims to answer the following questions:

- Is the API protected against attacks?
- Does the API offer opportunities for sensitive data to be leaked?
- Is someone scraping my API and compromising business intelligence through data?

While not typically associated with automated testing, security testing is an active process that includes design-time review processes, development-time static and dynamic code analysis, and runtime monitoring.

Design-time and development-time security testing often comprise policies and tools that are designed to prevent leaking sensitive data through design reviews that identify potential concerns. It also includes authorization policies for each API operation to ensure proper access is enforced.

An API management layer may be employed to apply runtime monitoring and enforcement. Authorization enforcement is managed through configuration, avoiding the need to implement access restrictions within the API implementation. Log analysis may be used to detect and block malicious attacks. More details on security protection are offered in Chapter 15, "Protecting APIs."

Operational Monitoring

APIs can and often do provide the primary interface for applications to interact with a system. Because the API service plays the role of a dependency, it is critical for the service to be available, whether to other services that are internal to an organization or to external partners and customers. In addition, there may be service-level agreements (SLAs) that the company has agreed to undertake with customers and partners regarding the performance and uptime of an API. Failing to meet an SLA could yield a negative financial result as well as angry or upset customers.

Operational monitoring answers the following questions:

- Is the API available and performing as expected?

- Is the API staying within expected SLAs?

- Is there a need to provision more infrastructure to meet performance goals?

Monitoring and analytics solutions are an important component to API operational monitoring. Analytics verify that real-world usage matches what was seen in testing for both correctness and performance. Analytics measurements can be as simple as logging of performance counters or as complex as integrating third-party libraries with extensive monitoring and visualization support.

API Contract Testing

API contract testing, sometimes referred to as *functional testing,* is used to verify that each API operation meets the expected behavior and honors the API's defined contract for the consumer.

Contract testing answers the following questions:

- Is each operation working to the specification for all success cases?
- Are input parameters being followed? How are bad inputs handled?
- Are the expected outputs received?
- Is response formatting correct? Are the proper data types used?
- Are errors being handled correctly? Are they reported back to the consumer?

In the Align-Define-Design-Refine (ADDR) process, API descriptions are defined during the design process, prior to implementation. These description files may be used to verify the API contract as part of the contract testing process. Some common contract specification formats for REST APIs include OpenAPI (Swagger), API Blueprint, and RESTful API Modeling Language (RAML). GraphQL APIs have a schema defined, which helps drive contract testing. gRPC APIs define service contracts using an interface definition language (IDL) file. This topic is discussed further in Chapter 13, "Documenting the API."

API contract testing must first ensure the correctness of each API operation. Handling thousands of clients per minute does no good if the information that the API is providing or acting on does not meet the API's specification. Identifying and eliminating bugs, hunting out inconsistencies, and verifying that an API meets the specification against which it has been designed all fall under the umbrella of testing for correctness.

Next, API contract testing must focus on reliability. The API should provide the correct information every time an operation is called. Executing the same action repeatedly for an API operation designed to be idempotent should produce the same results. API operations that support pagination should page through results in a predictable way.

Finally, API contract testing should submit invalid and missing data and verify that the expected error response is received. String values may be submitted in place of numeric values, along with values outside the range of acceptable values. Date formats should be incorrect or result in dates outside an expected range of acceptable dates.

User Interface Testing versus API Testing

Some team members may suggest that building dedicated tests for an API is wasteful. They may attempt to make the case that user interface (UI) tests cover the API sufficiently, given that the UI calls the API. However, this is not the case. Instead, the UI tests the API only as far as the UI exercises the API. This means that if the UI is performing client-side validation of user input, then UI tests would never verify the API's ability to handle bad data.

While some may say that this level of testing is sufficient, they may be forgetting the recommendation of the Open Web Application Security Project (OWASP): do not trust user input. A user or client will not always submit data in a way that an API expects. Always validate the data that comes from forms as well as from HTTP request headers.

One of the goals of API testing is to ensure that the API is able to handle a multitude of good and bad values that may be submitted outside of a specific UI. If we depend only on UI tests, then the API should not be considered sufficiently tested.

Another goal of API testing is to ensure that the API cannot be deployed into production without passing tests. This requires that API tests become part of the continuous integration and delivery pipeline, just like all other types of automated testing.

Selecting Tools to Accelerate Testing

Some organizations may have an established quality assurance (QA) group that specializes in automated testing and manual exploratory testing. QA teams may be comprised of those who write code and others who use testing tools that help compose test automation suites without the need to write code. Other organizations may not have dedicated QA teams at all, instead relying on developers to write and maintain API test code. These factors must be considered when selecting API testing tools.

A number of open source and commercial testing tools are available today that support the creation of API testing using API specification formats to help jumpstart the testing process. Some are designed to support the creation of tests through a UI to reduce or eliminate the need to write test code. Others are designed to offer a scripting environment or test libraries that require coding. Be sure to select the right solutions that match the testing preferences and skills found in the organization.

Performance and monitoring solutions, offered as third-party API monitoring-as-a-service solutions, are available from a range of companies and often start as a freemium service for a small number of tests. Open-source monitoring tools are available that can be run on on-premises or cloud-hosted infrastructure. Custom tools built to perform load and performance testing can be modified to run less frequently and at a smaller scale for the purpose of monitoring or soak testing.

API testing is often automated through code or test scripts and executed in a dedicated test environment. Automating these tests has a higher infrastructure cost because of the need for additional nonproduction environments that contain infrastructure resources. Be sure to take into consideration how tests will be automated and the infrastructure cost required to support them.

Finally, consider how test-driven development (TDD) may be extended through the strategic selection of API testing tools. Dedicated QA teams may build automated test suites that can be executed by developers as they implement the API. Developers who are tasked with writing the API tests themselves may wish to take a similar approach, much like they apply TDD to their day-to-day development process. This approach helps to demonstrate progress and validate that an API implementation handles all success, invalid, and error cases.

The Challenges of API Testing

One of the challenges that must not be overlooked when establishing an API test strategy is the need for test data sets. While unit testing may not require complex data sets, API testing has the exact opposite demands. API testing often involves a tremendous amount of effort to build a cohesive set of data that will support the necessary test cases.

There are two common approaches to creating test data sets for APIs: snapshot of existing data sets and cleanroom data set creation. Taking a snapshot of a production system and cleansing the data set of sensitive data is often the most direct path. It requires less effort to try to separate the necessary data, instead opting to accept an entire data store snapshot as a starting point. The snapshot may be used to restore the test data back to a known state. This is a great approach when existing production data exists.

Cleanroom data set creation is a bit more challenging and takes considerable time, but once completed, it enables more robust test cases. Cleanroom data involves the creation of cohesive data sets from the ground up to support the API testing process. Tools such as Mockaroo[1] may be used to synthesize some of the data while providing more real-world values than simply using random values. However, handcrafting data elements is often required to construct deeply nested data sets that represent entire scenarios rather than just a single table of data.

For example, JSON's Bookstore would require books, carts, orders, and customers that are not easily generated randomly. Instead, it is often necessary for domain

---

1. https://mockaroo.com

experts to construct these elements manually, perhaps using a spreadsheet. A script then loads this data into the appropriate data stores, ensuring the elements are properly connected through shared identifiers, foreign keys, and link tables. Tests could then use the API to retrieve a customer, examine their orders, execute a new shopping experience, and verify that the API functions as expected.

Some API testing may depend on third-party services that do not offer their own sandbox or test environments. In this case, techniques such as API mocking may be used to isolate external dependencies and prevent the need to involve production systems as part of an API test suite. Rather than directly connecting to the system, a mock response may be created to take the place of the system. Of course, this often requires additional data preparation work to ensure that the mock data properly satisfies the use cases that are to be supported.

Make API Testing Essential

Too often, teams choose to take shortcuts when time is short, and this typically involves poor or no API testing. Like documentation, testing is often seen as a nice-to-have in the development process. However, we should view testing and documentation as essential steps to truly calling the API done and ready to deploy. Otherwise, we are creating opportunities for bugs to creep into partner and customer interactions. Worse, it could open the organization up to malicious attacks through one or more APIs.

Summary

A robust API testing strategy is an important step to API delivery and is a formidable foe against regressions sneaking into an API. A proper API testing strategy helps to ensure API correctness and reliability while ensuring the desired outcomes are achievable. It should also extend beyond the development phase and into runtime testing to maintain a secure and performance environment. An API should not be considered complete until all tests have been created, executed, and passed.

Chapter 13

Document the API Design

Documentation is the third user interface for APIs, and the most important.

— D. Keith Casey

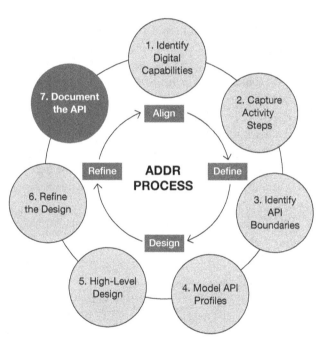

Figure 13.1 *The final step in the Refine phase is to produce robust documentation, incorporating learnings back into the API design.*

Documentation is a very important element of the developer experience. Most API teams assume that reference documentation for each operation is sufficient. However, that is only the beginning of the API documentation effort.

Establishing an API documentation strategy is part of API design. Developer portals must support a variety of personas that all contribute to the success of an API. This chapter outlines the essentials of any API documentation effort and provides insights from the field on how to establish and improve an API developer portal.

The Importance of API Documentation

API documentation is the most important user interface for developers who will integrate the API. It is the primary communication medium between the API provider, tasked with designing and delivering the API, and the many developers who will integrate the API into applications and automation scripts.

Unless the API is part of an open-source product, API consumers will never have access to the source code. Even if access to the source code is possible, reading code to understand an API is unacceptable. It slows down the developer. At best, it causes frustration. At worst, the developers move on to a competitor or build the required functionality themselves.

In addition, organizing the API documentation is important. When API providers create clear areas for getting started guides and reference documentation, developers can locate exactly what they need when they need it. Even the most well-written API documentation suffers if it isn't organized properly into a developer portal.

> **Principle 4: API documentation is the most important user interface for developers**
>
> Documentation is the primary communication medium between the API provider, tasked with designing and delivering the API, and the many developers who will integrate the API into applications and automation scripts. Therefore, API documentation should be first class and not left as a last-minute task.

API Description Formats

Traditionally, technical documentation was captured and shared in PDF, Microsoft Word documents, or plain HTML. While these formats are better than no documentation at all, they limit the usefulness of the documentation to human consumption.

API description formats provide the details of an API in machine-readable format. Tools may convert the description into human-readable documentation, generate client-side libraries, and produce a skeleton of server-side code with common patterns and practices already established.

Some API description formats support adding vendor-specific extensions. These may be used to further define authorization, routing, and configuration rules for use in automating deployment processes and API management layer configuration.

API styles such as GraphQL and gRPC provide their own respective formats. For REST-based or remote procedure call (RPC)–based APIs that are built directly on top of HTTP, a separate description format is needed. This section provides an overview of popular formats to help teams select the format or formats that teams would like to use to drive their API description and documentation efforts.

Documentation examples are available in the API workshop examples[1] repository available on GitHub.

OpenAPI Specification

Formerly known as Swagger, the OpenAPI Specification (OAS) is currently one of the most popular formats for describing the details for an API. It is managed by the Linux Foundation under the stewardship of the OpenAPI Initiative (OAI). The Swagger brand is now owned by SmartBear, which continues to maintain and support various open-source API projects under the Swagger name.

OAS came into popularity owing to the try-it-out feature that is built into the SwaggerUI project. This project was designed to generate HTML-based API reference documentation for developers. The try-it-out feature allows developers and nondevelopers to explore an API against a live server from within the generated documentation. It supports JSON and YAML-based formats.

OAS is currently in version 3 of the specification, although OAS v2 is still encountered in some organizations and open-source projects. The tools ecosystem is vast and continues to grow, making this a popular choice for teams building their first or thirty-first API. An example of OAS v3 is provided in Listing 13.1, based on the API design for the Shopping Cart API created in Chapter 7, "REST-Based API Design."

Listing 13.1 *Example of OpenAPI Specification v3*

```
openapi: 3.0.0
info:
  title: Bookstore Shopping Example
  description: The Bookstore Example REST-based API supports the shopping
```

---

1. https://bit.ly/align-define-design-examples

```
experience of an online bookstore. The API includes the following
capabilities and operations...
  contact: { }
  version: '1.0'
paths:
  /books:
    get:
      tags:
      - Books
      summary: Returns a paginated list of books
      description: Provides a paginated list of books based on the search
criteria provided...
      operationId: ListBooks
      parameters:
      - name: q
        in: query
        description: A query string to use for filtering books by title and
description. If not provided, all available books will be listed...
        schema:
          type: string
      responses:
        200:
          description: Success
          content:
            application/json:
              schema:
                $ref: '#/components/schemas/ListBooksResponse'
        401:
          description: Request failed. Received when a request is made with
invalid API credentials...
        403:
          description: Request failed. Received when a request is made with
valid API credentials towards an API operation or resource you do not have
access to.
components:
  schemas:
    ListBooksResponse:
      title: ListBooksResponse
      type: object
      properties:
```

```
      books:
        type: array
        items:
          $ref: '#/components/schemas/BookSummary'
        description: "A list of book summaries as a result of a list or
filter request..."
    BookSummary:
      title: BookSummary
      type: object
      properties:
        bookId:
          type: string
          description: An internal identifier, separate from the ISBN, that
identifies the book within the inventory
        isbn:
          type: string
          description: The ISBN of the book
        title:
          type: string
          description: "The book title, e.g., A Practical Approach to API
Design"
        authors:
          type: array
          items:
            $ref: '#/components/schemas/BookAuthor'
          description: ''
      description: "Summarizes a book that is stocked by the book store..."
    BookAuthor:
      title: BookAuthor
      type: object
      properties:
        authorId:
          type: string
          description: An internal identifier that references the author
        fullName:
          type: string
          description: "The full name of the author, e.g., D. Keith Casey"
      description: "Represents a single author for a book. Since a book may
have more than one author, ..."
```

API Blueprint

API Blueprint originated from an API tools vendor called Apiary, now a part of Oracle. It combines the idea of easy documentation generation using Markdown with a structure that makes it machine-readable for supporting code generation and other tooling needs.

Because API Blueprint is based on Markdown, any tool capable of rendering and editing files using the Markdown format, including integrated development environments (IDEs), is able to work with this format. While the ecosystem of tooling isn't as vast as that of OAS, it does have considerable community support owing to the preacquisition efforts of Apiary. As Listing 13.2 shows, it is easy to work with and therefore a popular choice for those seeking to combine Markdown-based documentation with a machine-readable API description format.

Listing 13.2 *Example of API Blueprint*

```
FORMAT: 1A
HOST: https://www.example.com


# Bookstore Shopping API Example
The Bookstore Example REST-based API supports the shopping experience of an
online bookstore. The API includes the following capabilities and opera-
tions...


# Group Books


## Books [/books{?q,offset,limit}]


### ListBooks [GET]
Provides a paginated list of books based on the search criteria provided...


+ Parameters
    + q (string, optional)
        A query string to use for filtering books by title and description.
If not provided, all available books will be listed...
    + offset (number, optional) -
        A offset from which the list of books are retrieved, where an offset
of 0 means the first page of results...
        + Default: 0
```

```
    + limit (number, optional) -
        Number of records to be included in API call, defaulting to 25 records
at a time if not provided...
        + Default: 25


+ Response 200 (application/json)
        Success
    + Attributes (ListBooksResponse)
+ Response 401
        Request failed. Received when a request is made with invalid API
credentials...
+ Response 403
        Request failed. Received when a request is made with valid API
credentials towards an API operation or resource you do not have access to.


# Data Structures


## ListBooksResponse (object)
A list of book summaries as a result of a list or filter request...


### Properties


+ 'books' (array[BookSummary], optional)


## BookSummary (object)
Summarizes a book that is stocked by the book store...


### Properties


+ 'bookId' (string, optional) - An internal identifier, separate from the
ISBN, that identifies the book within the inventory
+ 'isbn' (string, optional) - The ISBN of the book
+ 'title' (string, optional) - The book title, e.g., A Practical Approach
to API Design
+ 'authors' (array[BookAuthor], optional)


## BookAuthor (object)
Represents a single author for a book. Since a book may have more than one
author, ...
```

```
### Properties
+ 'authorId' (string, optional) - An internal identifier that references the
author
+ 'fullName' (string, optional) - The full name of the author, e.g., D. Keith
Casey
```

RAML

RAML stands for RESTful API Modeling Language and was designed with the full API design lifecycle in mind. It originated within MuleSoft but included contributors from many other industry leaders. The design of RAML was intended to support design tooling alongside documentation and code-generation tools. RAML is built on the YAML format.

While RAML originated with the help of MuleSoft, the specification and much of the tooling is vendor neutral. RAML focuses on describing resources, methods, parameters, responses, media types, and other HTTP constructs common to REST-based APIs. However, it can be used to describe nearly any HTTP-based API format. Listing 13.3 uses RAML for the Shopping Cart API.

Listing 13.3 *Example of RAML v1.0*

```
#%RAML 1.0
title: Bookstore Shopping API Example
version: 1.0
baseUri: https://www.example.com
baseUriParameters:
  defaultHost:
    required: false
    default: www.example.com
    example:
      value: www.example.com
    displayName: defaultHost
    type: string
protocols:
- HTTPS
documentation:
- title: Bookstore Shopping API Example
  content: The Bookstore Example REST-based API supports the shopping expe-
rience of an online bookstore. The API includes the following capabilities
and operations...
```

```
types:
  ListBooksResponse:
    displayName: ListBooksResponse
    description: A list of book summaries as a result of a list or filter
request...
    type: object
    properties:
      books:
        required: false
        displayName: books
        type: array
        items:
          type: BookSummary
  BookSummary:
    displayName: BookSummary
    description: Summarizes a book that is stocked by the book store...
    type: object
    properties:
      bookId:
        required: false
        displayName: bookId
        description: An internal identifier, separate from the ISBN, that
identifies the book within the inventory
        type: string
      isbn:
        required: false
        displayName: isbn
        description: The ISBN of the book
        type: string
      title:
        required: false
        displayName: title
        description: The book title, e.g., A Practical Approach to API
Design
        type: string
      authors:
        required: false
        displayName: authors
        type: array
```

```
      items:
          type: BookAuthor
  BookAuthor:
    displayName: BookAuthor
    description: Represents a single author for a book. Since a book may
have more than one author, ...
    type: object
    properties:
      authorId:
        required: false
        displayName: authorId
        description: An internal identifier that references the author
        type: string
      fullName:
        required: false
        displayName: fullName
        description: The full name of the author, e.g., D. Keith Casey
        type: string
/books:
  get:
    displayName: ListBooks
    description: Provides a paginated list of books based on the search
criteria provided...
    queryParameters:
      q:
        required: false
        displayName: q
        description: A query string to use for filtering books by title and
description. If not provided, all available books will be listed...
        type: string
      offset:
        required: false
        default: 0
        example:
          value: 0
        displayName: offset
        description: A offset from which the list of books are retrieved,
where an offset of 0 means the first page of results...
        type: integer
        minimum: 0
        format: int32
```

```
    limit:
      required: false
      default: 25
      example:
        value: 25
      displayName: limit
      description: Number of records to be included in API call, defaulting
to 25 records at a time if not provided...
      type: integer
      minimum: 1
      maximum: 100
      format: int32
  headers:
    Authorization:
      required: true
      displayName: Authorization
      description: An OAuth 2.0 access token that authorizes your app
to call this operation...
      type: string
  responses:
    200:
      description: Success
      headers:
        Content-Type:
          default: application/json
          displayName: Content-Type
          type: string
      body:
        application/json:
          displayName: response
          description: Success
          type: ListBooksResponse
    401:
      description: Request failed. Received when a request is made with
invalid API credentials...
      body: {}
    403:
      description: Request failed. Received when a request is made with
valid API credentials towards an API operation or resource you do not have
access to.
      body: {}
```

JSON Schema

The JSON Schema specification offers a machine-readable format for capturing the structure and validation rules for JSON-based structures. The specification is divided into core foundational rules and validation rules, making it a comprehensive solution for defining JSON schemas that require validation. JSON Schema can be thought of as the JSON equivalent to XML Schema.

While independent of any one API style, JSON Schema may be used to describe resource representations for REST-based APIs and other API styles. It is also found in organizations as a single format for defining schema formats for domain objects across the enterprise.

While the schema definition portion of OAS is quite flexible, it lacks some of the robust definition support offered by JSON Schema. Recent efforts with OAS v3.1 have helped to bring JSON Schema and OAS into alignment to allow for the use of both formats. Expect JSON Schema to continue gaining tooling support moving forward given its acceptance within the OAS description format. JSON Schema is demonstrated in Listing 13.4.

Listing 13.4 *Example JSON Schema*

```
{
  "$id": "https://example.com/BookSummary.schema.json",
  "$schema": "http://json-schema.org/draft-07/schema#",
  "description": "Summarizes a book that is stocked by the book store...",
  "type": "object",
  "properties": {
    "bookId": {
      "type": "string"
    },
    "isbn": {
      "type": "string"
    },
    "title": {
      "type": "string"
    },
    "authors": {
      "type": "array",
      "items": {
        "$ref": "#/definitions/BookAuthor"
```

```
      }
    }
  },
  "definitions": {
    "BookAuthor": {
      "type": "object",
      "properties": {
        "authorId": {
          "type": "string"
        },
        "fullName": {
          "type": "string"
        }
      }
    }
  }
}
```

API Profiles Using ALPS

Application-Level Profile Semantics (ALPS) is a description format for defining application-level and domain semantics, independent of the API style(s) and protocol(s) available. It helps to define a profile of the digital capabilities and messages exchanged for an API rather than the specifics of how to interact with the API. ALPS is a machine-readable format that is useful for capturing API profiles produced during API modeling (detailed in Chapter 6, "API Modeling").

ALPS was designed to power API and service discovery, API catalogs, and tooling metadata where an API profile may be implemented using one or multiple API styles, including REST-based, gRPC, and/or GraphQL. The specification provides support for XML, JSON, and YAML formats.

ALPS supports the combination of two fundamental elements: data (the message) and transitions (operations). When combined, these two elements capture the operational and message semantics for an API profile. The default format for ALPS is XML, though a JSON-based specification is planned.

Listing 13.5 provides an example API profile that could be used to describe the operations and messages for any number of API style implementations that are available.

Listing 13.5 *An API Profile in XML Using the ALPS Draft 02 Format*

```xml
<alps version="1.0">
  <doc format="text">A contact list.</doc>
  <link rel="help" href="http://example.org/help/contacts.html" />
  <!-- a hypermedia control for returning BookSummaries -->
  <descriptor id="collection" type="safe" rt="BookSummary">
    <doc>
      Provides a paginated list of books based on the search criteria
provided.
    </doc>
    <descriptor id="q" type="semantic">
      <doc>A query string to use for filtering books by title and
description.</doc>
    </descriptor>
  </descriptor>


  <!-- BookSummary: one or more of these may be returned -->
  <descriptor id="BookSummary" type="semantic">
    <descriptor id="bookId" type="semantic">
      <doc>An internal identifier, separate from the ISBN, that identifies
the book within the inventory</doc>
    </descriptor>
    <descriptor id="isbn" type="semantic">
      <doc>The ISBN of the book</doc>
    </descriptor>
    <descriptor id="title" type="semantic">
      <doc>The book title, e.g., A Practical Approach to API Design</doc>
    </descriptor>
    <descriptor id="authors" type="semantic" rel="collection">
      <doc>Summarizes a book that is stocked by the book store</doc>
      <descriptor id="authorId" type="semantic">
        <doc>An internal identifier that references the author</doc>
      </descriptor>
      <descriptor id="fullName" type="semantic">
        <doc>The full name of the author, e.g., D. Keith Casey</doc>
      </descriptor>
    </descriptor>
  </descriptor>
</alps>
```

Improving API Discovery Using APIs.json

Multiple API description formats may be necessary to help developers consume the API using various tools. APIs.json is a description format that assists in API discovery through a machine-readable index file. It is similar to a site map for a Web site that helps direct search engine indexers to important areas of the Web site.

A single APIs.json file may reference multiple APIs, making this format useful for bundling multiple, separate API description files into a single product or platform view. When combined with other machine-readable formats, APIs may be discovered, indexed, and made available within a public or private API catalog.

As the name indicates, the default format is JSON, although the YAML-based format, shown in Listing 13.6, is also available.

Listing 13.6 *APIs.json Example Offering an Indexed View of an API and Its Various Machine-Readable Description Files*

```
name: Bookstore Example
type: Index
description: The Bookstore API supports the shopping experience of an online
bookstore, along with ...
tags:
  - Application Programming Interface
  - API
created: '2020-12-10'
url: http://example.com/apis.json
specificationVersion: '0.14'
apis:
- name: Bookstore Shopping API
  description: The Bookstore Example REST-based API supports the shopping
experience of an online bookstore
  humanURL: http://example.com
  baseURL: http://api.example.com
  tags:
    - API
    - Application Programming Interface

  properties:
    - type: Documentation
      url: https://example.com/documentation
```

```
    - type: OpenAPI
      url: http://example.com/openapi.json
    - type: JSONSchema
      url: http://example.com/json-schema.json

  contact:
    - FN: APIs.json
      email: info@apisjson.org
      X-twitter: apisjson

specifications:
  - name: OpenAPI
    description: OpenAPI is used as the contract for all of our APIs.
    url: https://openapis.org
  - name: JSON Schema
    description: JSON Schema is used to define all of the underlying objects
used.
    url: https://json-schema.org/

common:
  - type: Signup
    url: https://example.com/signup
  - type: Authentication
    url: http://example.com/authentication
  - type: Login
    url: https://example.com/login
  - type: Blog
    url: http://example.com/blog
  - type: Pricing
    url: http://example.com/pricing
```

Extending Docs with Code Examples

Code examples provide the important guidance necessary for developers to be able to apply the documentation in practice. They help developers to connect the dots between the reference documentation and the actual work of integrating the API.

Code examples come in a variety of forms, from just a few lines that demonstrate how a specific operation works to more complex examples that demonstrate a complete workflow.

Write Getting Started Code Examples First

Initially, the developer must overcome basic understanding of the API and how it will help solve their problem. It is important to remember that during this phase, the developer just wants to see something work.

Time to First Hello World, or TTFHW, is a key metric for determining API complexity. The longer it takes to get developers to their first "win," the more likely they are to struggle with the API and perhaps abandon it or build their own solution.

To help developers get started quickly, provide concise examples that remove the need for explicit coding. Look at the following example from Stripe:

```
require "stripe"
Stripe.api_key = "your_api_token"
Stripe::Token.create(
  :card => {
    :number => "4242424242424242",
    :exp_month => 6,
    :exp_year => 2024,
    :cvc => "314"
})
```

Notice in this example that there is no code to write. The developer only needs to fill in their API key to obtain a credit card token in their sandbox environment.

Example code that requires developers to write lots of code should be avoided at this stage to achieve a lower TTFHW. Never require developers to write code to complete an example when first trying out the API. Instead, make it easy to get started and see the request work successfully.

Expanding Documentation with Workflow Examples

After developers have had time to try the API using some code examples, the next step is to begin to demonstrate common use cases and workflows.

Workflow examples focus on achieving specific outcomes. These examples must offer complete understanding of production-ready coding conventions. The use of inline comments is helpful to explain why each step is necessary. Use hardcoded values to increase understandability. Choose variable and method names that make the code easy to read.

Following is an example of charging a credit card using Stripe's Ruby-based helper library:

```
# Remember to change this to your API key
Stripe.api_key = "my_api_key"

# Token is created using Stripe.js or Checkout!

# Get the payment token submitted by the form:
token = params[:stripeToken]

# Create a Customer:
customer = Stripe::Customer.create(
  :email => "paying.user@example.com",
  :source => token,
)

# Charge the Customer instead of the card:
charge = Stripe::Charge.create(
  :amount => 1000,
  :currency => "usd",
  :customer => customer.id,
)

# YOUR CODE: Save the customer ID and other info
  # in a database for later.

# YOUR CODE (LATER): When it's time to charge the
  # customer again, retrieve the customer ID.

charge = Stripe::Charge.create(
  :amount => 1500, # $15.00 this time
  :currency => "usd",
  :customer => customer_id, # Previously stored, then retrieved
)
```

Note that workflow code examples are more complex than those used to achieve a quick TTFHW. These examples need to be short enough to explain the concepts but not too long that they require considerable time to understand. It is often best to demonstrate scenarios that are easily understood and likely map to customer needs.

Error Case and Production-Ready Examples

While some developers may be more familiar than others with making their code production ready, assistance can smooth the road for developers during the last mile of API integration. Error case and production-ready examples help developers understand how to integrate the API into their production environment.

The examples should help developers properly troubleshoot problems and incorporate retry loops when an API outage occurs. Adding examples that demonstrate how to catch and recover from bad data provided by end users is also important. Finally, show how to obtain the current rate limits for their account and detect when rate limits have been exceeded.

From Reference Docs to a Developer Portal

API documentation is a blanket term for all the work that describes an API and how to use it. Although the term is used as if there is only one kind of documentation, API documentation encompasses more than just the reference docs. It includes having a developer portal that pulls together all of the elements that API consumers need to be successful. It also addresses additional personas, beyond the developer, that participate in the API adoption process.

Increasing API Adoption through Developer Portals

While developers are often the target persona for an API developer portal, other personas also benefit from a developer portal:

- **Executives** involved in the process of discovering, reviewing, and approving a new API

- **Business and product managers** searching for ways to leverage internal and/ or third-party APIs to speed delivery of new solutions

- **Solution architects and tech leads** who are defining a new solution that may leverage existing APIs from an enterprise portfolio

A developer portal helps bring together the different styles of communication needed to ensure that APIs can be found, an understanding of the benefits of using the API, and assistance to developers on how to integrate the API. It also provides the interface on top of the many faceless APIs that exist within an organization's API portfolio for evangelism across the organization.

CASE STUDY
Enterprise Developer Portal Success

An API program initiative for a large enterprise IT group started with just a few key people. After a year of investment, the team had produced several APIs that offered a number of high-value capabilities to the business. However, the team produced only reference documentation—no developer portal. As a result, information about how to start using the API wasn't readily available. With help, the team expanded the reference documentation into a complete developer portal.

Their revised developer portal guides developers through an introduction to the API's structure and capabilities, onboarding in a sandbox environment for integration, and production access through a lightweight certification program.

Influential executives use the developer portal to evangelize the API program throughout the organization, resulting in increased demand for adopting APIs. The developer portal now serves as a central communication tool and a method of promoting the program to both technical and nontechnical teams.

Elements of a Great Developer Portal

A great developer portal consists of the following elements that address the needs of the variety of personas involved in adopting an API:

- **Feature discovery:** An overview of the API addresses concerns such as benefits, capabilities, and pricing to qualify prospects.

- **Case studies:** Case studies highlight applications that have been built using the API. They help readers understand how the API is used within their specific vertical business domain or for specific types of app.

- **Getting started guide:** Sometimes called a *quick start guide,* it introduces developers to common use cases that the API solves and provides a step-by-step guide to getting started for each case.

- **Authentication and authorization:** This element describes how to obtain an API token with the appropriate authorization scopes necessary to use the API as desired.

- **API reference documentation:** Details on each operation, including URL path structures, input and output data structures, and error data structures, are given in the reference documentation.

- **Release notes and changelog:** The changes in each release, including new operations and enhancements to existing operations, are summarized in a historical format.

Beyond these essential elements, developer portals seek to inform and deliver on the following experiences:

- **Easy onboarding:** APIs rarely gain adoption if it is difficult to get started. Easy onboarding, from self-registration to a guided tour and API token creation, helps developers overcome the challenges to adopting a new API. Integration between the developer portal and the API gateway that is responsible for provisioning API tokens is important to effective onboarding.

- **Operational insight:** Is the API available or temporarily down? A simple status page that reflects an API's availability helps to inform developers and operations staff who see increased errors in their applications.

- **Live support:** Including a chat solution, whether embedded into the developer portal or through a communication platform such as Slack, WebEx, or Microsoft Teams, provides direct access to those who can help resolve integration. The team responsible for live support is often called *developer relations,* or DevRel for short. They might be responsible for the developer portal alongside developer support.

Effective API Documentation

To write clear documentation, it is important to answer the questions commonly asked by those considering the adoption of an API. The answers to these questions may be obtained through interviews conducted with developers integrating the API.

It is important to engage in conversations with them whenever possible. Engaging in discussions with API consumers will lead to those critical "aha!" moments that API providers need to improve their documentation.

When discussion with API consumers isn't possible, try to find other developers to review the documentation. Conduct a documentation audit by defining a mythical scenario, then writing some code to call the API to produce a prototype. Along the way, ask questions to identify areas of improvement for the API documentation offered.

Question 1: How Does Your API Solve My Problems?

Ensure that the API documentation has an introduction that covers what the API solves and what it doesn't solve and that it offers example use cases that the API has solved in the past. This information establishes a context for the reader, who may be trying to decide whether the API is the right fit for their need.

Question 2: What Problem Does Each API Operation Support?

Add documentation to clarify what each operation does and when it may be applicable. "Gets all accounts" is not a helpful description of an API operation. Add additional details about what kinds of filters, implied or explicit, are supported.

Offer some example scenarios describing when an API operation may be used or how it may be combined with other operations to achieve particular outcomes. The job stories and API profiles created during the Align-Define-Design-Refine (ADDR) process is a good source for this detail.

Question 3: How Do I Get Started Using the API?

If the API offers self-service onboarding, call out this feature in the documentation as a benefit to getting started faster. For those who require time to go through a partnership program, include details of the program in the documentation as well. This information ensures that the appropriate lead time is factored in prior to developers beginning the first hello world integration.

It is important to offer links to the onboarding process in various locations of the API documentation. Not all developers start from the homepage of the developer portal. Publicly accessible reference documentation will be indexed by search engines, creating organic entry points into a developer portal. Be sure to include a link to the onboarding process somewhere near the top of the reference API documentation.

Finally, don't assume that all developers can figure out how to use an API. Every developer is at a different stage in their career. Some may have the same, more, or less experience than others using Web APIs. Take the time to explain, step by step, how to get started.

The Role of Technical Writer in API Docs

Traditionally, technical writers focused on delivering manuals for software, often in PDF or HTML format. These manuals consisted of screenshots and step-by-step guidance for using software. Extensive knowledge of the user interface, including features that are often overlooked, was required. The role was critical for ensuring end users were able to use the software effectively and efficiently while reducing support costs. Rarely, technical writers were required to have a deep knowledge of one or more programming languages, such as C/C++, Java, or Python.

Over the past decade, the role of technical writers has undergone a transition. In some organizations, technical writers have been replaced by user experience (UX) experts who design user interfaces that require minimal or no documentation. Other organizations have replaced technical writers with marketing and product roles that improve the copy of an app to encourage conversion or increased usage metrics.

With the growth of APIs, technical writers are again in heavy demand. They are required to understand how to use APIs directly via HTTP, along with a variety of programming languages to demonstrate API integration using Java, Python, GoLang, Ruby, JavaScript, Objective-C, Swift, command-line automation, and more. Their target audience spans end users, experienced developers, and developers right out of college. Rather than documentation efforts focused on a few large releases per year, now releases may occur on a weekly or daily basis owing to deployment automation and cloud infrastructure.

The value that technical writers offer to any product is enormous. For APIs, their talent is invaluable. They provide an outside-in perspective on an API's design and documentation to ensure it provides value to the target audience. Questions around the purpose and intended use of each API operation help to hone the API design early.

The challenge for most technical writers is building a sufficient team to handle the vast amount of work before, during, and after every release of every API offered by the organization. A single technical writer for a small API may be able to keep documentation updated. If the organization is large and offers multiple APIs, perhaps even API products, the challenge increases beyond the capabilities of even the most talented technical writer.

Therefore, it is critical that organizations have a team of technical writers. This team should be able to dedicate a few technical writers for emerging APIs while others are focused on maintaining documentation for existing APIs. They must be considered in all API design decisions early and should be part of any API design process from start to finish. All decisions regarding API documentation tools and process should be made by the technical writers, not by developers forcing specific tools upon them. They should be considered first-class team members rather than a siloed team that has API implementations thrown at them at the last minute for a quick-and-dirty documentation effort.

Finally, remember that API documentation is the user interface for developers. Technical writers can make or break an API's success. The same can be said for enterprise API platforms where some APIs are targeting partners, customers, and third-party service integrators.

The Minimum Viable Portal

The minimum viable portal (MVP) builds on the idea of the minimum viable product from lean processes to establish a phased approach to delivering a developer portal. The MVP provides prioritization as three phases, the first being the minimal developer portal needs. As the team matures the API, the developer portal may be enhanced by taking it from minimum documentation to a robust developer portal.

Phase 1: Minimum Viable Portal

The checklist in Table 13.1 lists the five most important modules to provide in an initial API developer portal. Included in the table are questions to answer and information to include in each section to help guide the process.

Table 13.1 *Minimum Viable Portal Checklist*

Section	Questions to Answer	Information to Include
Overview	What type of API do you have?	Type of API (RESTful, SOAP, gRPC, GraphQL, etc.)
	What can users do with your API?	Brief use cases and examples (two or three sentences)
	Are there any access details or restrictions users need to know about?	Base URL, rate limits
Authentication	If your API requires an authentication token or key, how do users get one?	Authentication method
	Do tokens/keys expire?	Expiration intervals (if any)
	What should users do if their token/key expires?	Refreshing expired tokens/keys
	How do users pass authentication to your API?	Example authorization header

Section	Questions to Answer	Information to Include
Workflows	What is the optimal/assumed workflow for the two or three most useful things users can do with your API?	Link to the reference for each operation mentioned in the workflow
Code samples	What does the code look like for a "hello world" and common use cases?	Complete code samples and code snippets that users can copy and paste
Reference	What do users need to know to use each operation?	For each operation: HTTP method (`GET`, `PUT`, `POST`, `DELETE`)
		Complete request URL
		Parameters (path and query): name, type, description, and whether the parameter is required
		Example request (including header and body)
		List of each element in the example request, including the type, description, and whether the element is required
		Example response
		List of each element in the example response, including type and description
		List of error and status codes, including the code, message, and meaning

Once all items on this list are checked off for all sections, the API developer portal is in good shape to support the needs of initial consumers involved in the early stages of API design as well as the needs of future consumers who may discover the API. Depending on available expertise and the number of API operations, the effort required to complete this phase may take between one and three weeks. If necessary, focus on the most common use cases that the API addresses, then incorporate additional documentation in future phases.

Phase 2: Improvement

The best place to spend time improving the portal will depend on the characteristics of the API. If the API has changed, has new operations, or works differently than previously documented, the first priority is updating the docs to incorporate the changes. But if everything is up to date, consider some of the ideas in Table 13.2 as time allows.

Table 13.2 *Improving the Developer Portal*

Type of Improvement	Recommended Improvements
Quick (one or two days)	Add a changelog to list API enhancements and fixes
	Standardize terminology—make sure you always use the same terms to mean the same thing throughout the docs
	Tweak use cases and examples to make sure they're business oriented
	Add chat-based support or public discussion forum for the API
	Add a page that links to users' projects and blog posts about your API (e.g., Sunlight Foundation lists projects that need help and projects that are ready to use)
	Create a shared product roadmap
Not-so-quick (three or more days)	Revise all content with a user-centric rather than developer-centric focus
	Update text to include terms users are likely to search for
	Review the references for missing, incomplete, or confusing information
	Reorganize to improve logical order of sections and content
	Add business-focused content for nontechnical or less-technical users and decision makers
	Implement a new publishing tool
	Extend code examples into complete tutorials
	Create reference apps, available via GitHub, to help developers get started quickly

Phase 3: Focusing on Growth

Once the items from the first two phases that are relevant to team needs have been completed, consider a few additional improvements to shift the portal from supporting customers to generating growth in adoption:

- **Add case studies:** Case studies demonstrate an API's value by describing how clients have used it to solve a problem, expand business, or succeed in some way. They add depth and meaning to API documentation by offering real-world context, which helps readers understand how the API has already benefited others and could benefit them too. Case studies can even inspire new ideas for using an API. If "Case Studies" sounds a little dry or academic, try something like "Success Stories" or "Client Stories" instead.

- **Add getting started guides:** Readers who understand how APIs work might be able to start using an API with authentication details alone, but what about users who are less comfortable? A getting started guide should build users' confidence that they can use the API and inspire them to dig deeper into the rest of the documentation.

- **Incorporate analytics:** Analytics help portal administrators tailor the portal to the needs of the audience based on real data about traffic patterns and help readers move more smoothly through the content.

- **Move to single-page format:** Consider restructuring some portions of the portal on a single page. The benefit of this format is that users can navigate the documentation either with the menu that links to all the section headings or by using Ctrl/Cmd+F to search for text on the page.

- **Translate the documentation:** As the API gains traction, consider whether documentation translation would be helpful. Professional translation is expensive and takes time, so a clear and persuasive business case is necessary before starting this journey. It's rare, but some teams discover that most of their users are in another country and therefore would benefit from translated documentation.

Finally, continually check around to see what other companies with successful APIs are doing with their documentation. Then produce a plan for incorporating these new ideas into the developer portal to benefit customers, partners, and internal developers.

Tools and Frameworks for Developer Portals

One of the challenges of establishing a developer portal is to select a tool, or a series of tools, that helps produce the developer portal. Outlined here are tools that organizations have used to produce their developer portal:

- **Static site generators:** Tools such as Jekyll, used to power GitHub pages, and Hugo are popular choices for creating and managing developer portals. Pages are authored using Markdown or similar notation and are stored in a code repository. Deployment is typically automated to ensure the latest version of the documentation is published once changes are merged into the main branch.

- **SwaggerUI:** This is the tool that started it all for the Swagger API description format, now separated from the tool as the OAS. This open-source codebase renders any OAS v2 or v3 specification, plus older Swagger specification files, into API reference documents in HTML format.

- **MVP template:** I have collaborated with others to create a GitHub project for starting an API developer MVP that is based in Jekyll. It helps to combine the static site generator with some placeholders for content and integrating SwaggerUI or similar reference documents into a single location. Fork the repository at https://github.com/launchany/mvp-template and customize as needed to get started quickly.

Whatever tools are selected, be sure to provide any machine-readable descriptions, such as OAS files, as part of the portal. This will allow developers to apply their own tooling, such as custom code generators, for speeding up the integration process.

Finally, be sure to research open-source and commercial tools that can assist in the creation and management of the developer portal. Some API management (APIM) layers, detailed in Chapter 15, offer portal management support as well.

Summary

Establishing an API documentation strategy is part of delivering a successful API product, formalized API program, or enterprise API platform. Developer portals must support a variety of personas. It is critical to ensure that documentation is part of the overall API design and delivery lifecycle. Otherwise, it becomes a last-minute task that results in poor documentation that fails to meet the needs of the target personas.

Seek to include documentation and API portal updates as part of the overall delivery schedule. An API should be considered done only when the documentation is updated alongside the release. This approach to documentation will produce a more complete API that encourages rapid adoption by developers and other decision makers.

Chapter 14

Designing for Change

You have to be really consciously careful about API design. APIs are forever. Once you put the API out there, maybe you can version it, but you can't take it away from your customers once you've built it like this. Being conservative and minimalistic in your API design helps you build fundamental tools on which you may be able to add more functionality, or which partners can build layers on top of.

— Werner Vogels

Managing change is not easy, yet it is an inevitable part of maturing an API. For developers working within a single codebase, change can be difficult but is manageable. Refactoring tools and automated test coverage are leveraged to assess the impact of a change.

When the change involves Web-based APIs, change becomes even more challenging. Some teams may have a direct relationship with every API consumer, allowing for changes to be introduced gradually and in coordination with all parties. However, that is usually not the case. Instead, most consumers of an API have no personal relationship with the team that owns the API. Extra care is required to manage changes to an API design to avoid customer churn. This chapter presents some considerations to determine the impact of change and strategies to introduce change to API designs that minimize the impact to API consumers.

The Impact of Change on Existing APIs

The Align-Define-Design-Refine (ADDR) process will work for any organization, whether an early-stage startup or an organization with hundreds of existing APIs. The process surfaces the outcomes and activities needed by customers, partners, and the workforce. This approach is useful whether a team is designing their first or fiftieth API.

The fictional online bookstore example used throughout this book assumes that the APIs identified throughout the process did not already exist, resulting in a greenfield project. The reality is that organizations already have APIs in production for a variety of purposes, and any proposed API designs must fit the reality that brownfield development will be required.

These brownfield initiatives are forced to reconcile the findings from the ADDR process with any existing API designs to determine the best path forward. This chapter details some considerations for handling change when APIs already exist.

Perform an API Design Gap Analysis

Teams should perform a gap assessment of the ideal API design identified during the process with the way it is designed today. The team must then determine whether to follow the same style and design decisions of the API design for consistency, mix the new design alongside the older design decisions, or consider other alternatives.

Factors to consider when performing this design gap analysis include the following:

- Introduction of differing terminology for resources and resource properties during the design process
- A shift from data-centric to resource-centric API design styles
- Change in vision and direction for the API product compared to what exists today

Using these factors as a starting point, itemize the differences between existing APIs and the ideal API design created as a result of the ADDR process. Assign a sizing for the value provided to API consumers by the new API design and the size of the impact in API design change. Using t-shirt sizing (e.g., small, medium, large, extra-large) ensures the measurement is an effective way to size the value and impact. Then determine what is best for API consumers.

Determine What Is Best for API Consumers

Making an API design decision, particularly when breaking changes will be required, involves more than the direct impact to the organization. It must also include what is best for API consumers.

Consider the following questions to determine the impact of API changes to current and future API consumers:

- **Who are the API consumers?** Internal consumers may offer easier change coordination, whereas partners may be resistant to making changes to integrations. Customers and third parties acting on behalf of customers may be unable to make changes because of limited or no development resources available.

- **What kind of relationship has been established with API consumers?** An internal or external party that the team knows personally can more easily negotiate for breaking changes. API consumers that have no relationship may be more challenging. API consumers that are heavy influencers in the marketplace may have a negative impact on current and future customer prospects if they are cornered into adopting unnecessary API changes.

- **What value is being delivered to API consumers as a result of the change?** API changes that improve the use of the API may be well received. Changes may also unlock new capabilities that consumers have been requesting, even with the cost of change. For others, it may give them pause to consider moving to a different vendor, resulting in customer churn.

How an organization manages change with its API consumers tells a lot about who and what it values. If the API provider prefers to deliver API design elegance at the cost of constant breaking changes, API consumers may soon start shopping for alternatives. If, however, the API provider values the API consumer above having the perfect API design, it may just find itself the leader in the marketplace.

Strategies for Change

Proceeding with an existing design style may require compromises in the API design that are less than ideal. These compromises may include minor annoyances, such as continuing forward with a misnamed resource that doesn't necessarily reflect the insights gained during the ADDR process.

Compromises such as supporting the old message formats alongside the new are commonly found in the real world. In this case, the server first checks for the new request message format, falling back to the older message format when necessary. The versioning responsibility is placed on the server rather than on the API consumers, ensuring that no breaking changes are introduced.

Another example is adding the new design style alongside the older style. New operations use the new design style, and the older ones remain as-is for a time. Gradually, older operations are replaced by newer operations using a deprecation strategy that encourages existing integrations to migrate to the new operations one at a time.

However, some compromises may be more significant, such as an existing API design that is too low level. This issue is common for APIs that opt to expose database tables directly compared to the new proposed API design that would apply a more coarse-grained design with an outcome-based focus. Mixing low-level and high-level APIs may create too much cognitive dissonance for developers and therefore are less than ideal.

Teams must determine if they wish to add the new design to an existing API, start a new API as if it were a brand-new product offering, or deliver the new design as a new version of the existing API. Each option will have an impact both on the organization and on current and future API consumers.

If the existing API design impedes the API consumer's ability to use the API effectively, a more greenfield approach may be required. Keep in mind that if the team chooses to release a new API product or version, additional resources will be required to maintain both APIs for some amount of time in the future. The next section discusses API versioning strategies and considerations.

Change Management Is Built on Trust

The most important thing is that the ADDR process helps to align business and API teams in a unified understanding of the problem space. A unified understanding may create a vision of the design target state of the API design and reality. Work through the process using the recommendations provided in this chapter. Doing so ensures that enhancements to an existing API or the delivery of a new API meets the needs of the API consumers and that the trust between API provider and consumer is not lost.

> ### Principle 5: APIs are forever, so plan accordingly
>
> Thoughtful API design combined with an evolutionary design approach makes APIs resilient to change. Extra care is required to manage changes to an API design. This helps to avoid frustrating developers who are required to stay updated with the latest changes.

API Versioning Strategies

APIs are contracts established between the providers of an API and their consumers. Ideally, they will never have to alter this contract. However, the ideal may not be the reality. There may be times when a change to the contract is required. When this happens, teams should try to ensure that they do not introduce breaking changes that will force their API consumers to fix code. For some API consumers, updating code to adapt to an API change may not be an option at all. Therefore, it is important to understand what may constitute a breaking change, then establish an API versioning policy that encourages the evolution of an API over time without breaking existing API consumers.

Common Nonbreaking Changes

Nonbreaking changes tend to be additive in nature, although this isn't always the case. These kinds of changes may include

- Adding a new API operation. Existing client code won't use the operation, so no harm is done to existing integration.

- Adding an optional field to a request message. In this case, existing client code will not be forced to add the new field.

- Adding a required field to a request message with a default value. For client code written prior to the addition, the server will apply the default value because it would be missing from the request.

- Adding a field to a response message. Existing client code should safely ignore the new field(s) unless they opted to use a mapping library that raises an error if the newly added field cannot be found in the destination object. This is an antipattern for API consumption but may be encountered in some circumstances, so use caution.

- Adding a value to an enumeration field type. A new enum value that is deserialized on the client may not have a known display string associated to it. To be a nonbreaking change, older clients must run correctly when receiving a new enum value. Not all clients may be designed in this way, so caution is advised.

Incompatible Changes

Changes that are incompatible with existing integration code include, but are not limited to, the following:

- Renaming fields and/or resource paths, as existing client code will require a code change to adapt to the renamed value

- Renaming or removing fields in a request or response

- Removing API operations used by existing API client code

- Changing fields from a single value to a one-to-many relationship (e.g., moving from one email address per account to a list of email addresses for an account)
- Changing the HTTP method or the response codes returned by an API operation

Remember that once an API is released into production and has at least one integration, the design decisions are permanently a part of the API. This is why the ADDR process is so important—it helps teams to validate design decisions before an API goes into production. However, a proper API versioning strategy can assist in mitigating some of these issues while allowing an API design to evolve over time.

API Versions and Revisions

There have been many discussions, articles, and debates about API versioning. The most critical aspect of every discussion must be the differentiation between safely evolving an API design and introducing breaking changes that force code modification as a result. One of the biggest tools in the API versioning toolbox is the introduction of API versions and revisions.

API versions represent a grouped set of API operations. Within each version, all modifications to an API should be backward compatible. However, across versions there is no guarantee of compatibility. Each version of an API is often treated as a separate product with differing behaviors and capabilities. API consumers opt into a specific version and write code against that version. They migrate to a new version only when they are ready, which may be a long time after the new version is released— or perhaps never. Versions may be numbers or strings (e.g., v1 or 2017-01-14). For those familiar with semantic versioning (semver), this is the same thing as a major version. Figure 14.1 illustrates two versions of an API, each offered as a different product that the API consumer selects when making the API request.

An API revision identifies an internal enhancement that should have no negative impact to API consumers of a specific API version. Revisions should be transparent to the API consumer, as consumers should be subscribed to a specific version only. The provider opts to release a new revision of a specific API version with or without the knowledge of the API consumer. Internally, a team may release v1.2, but API consumers only know that they are using v1 of the API (see Figure 14.2). API consumers may review changelogs for each revision to see if an enhancement would be useful but otherwise take no action when the provider releases a new API revision. This is equivalent to increasing the minor version number when using semver.

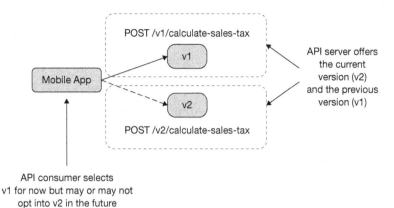

Figure 14.1 *API versions are selected by the API consumer, and the API server offers both the current version (v2) for new applications and the previous version (v1) for existing applications until they migrate their code to v2.*

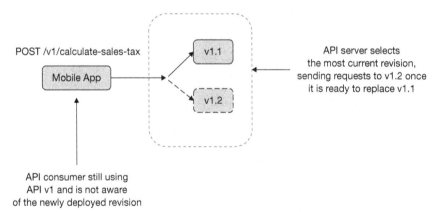

Figure 14.2 *API revisions are not exposed to API consumers, allowing the API provider to upgrade to the latest revision without explicit knowledge by the application.*

API Versioning Methods

There are three popular methods of implementing API versioning: header-based, URI-based, and hostname-based versioning.

Header-based versioning places the desired version as part of the Accept header in the HTTP request (e.g., Accept: application/vnd.github.v3+json). Many consider it the preferred form of versioning, as the URI remains the same across versions, and the media type defines which version of the resource representation is desired.

URI-based versioning includes the version as part of the URI, either as a prefix or as a suffix. Examples include /v1/customers. This method of versioning tends to be the most commonly encountered, as it works across a variety of tools that may not support customizing request headers. The downside is that resource URIs change with each new version, which some consider counter to the intent of supporting evolvability through a resource URI that never changes.

Hostname-based versioning includes the version as part of the hostname rather than the URI (e.g., `https://v2.api.myapp.com/customers`). This approach is used when technology limitations prevent routing to the proper backend version of the API based on the URI or `Accept` request header.

No matter which option is selected, API versions should include only the version number. Minor numbers should not be used; otherwise, code changes are required and thus cause typically nonbreaking changes to become breaking changes. For example, code changes would be required to move from `/v1.1/customers` to `/v1.2/customers`, even if the only difference between versions is the addition of a new operation.

Business Considerations of API Versioning

Each time a new version is released, customers must decide whether or not they wish to opt in. The decision is based on the cost versus the reward. Is the effort to migrate worth the cost it will take to migrate?

Moving to a new API version is a forcing factor. Just because an API design isn't perfect doesn't mean the team should release a new version with breaking changes to get the design exactly right. Every time a new version is released to accommodate a desired breaking change, the organization risks introducing customer churn because the customer must weigh the cost of migration versus moving to a competitor.

In addition, introducing a new version often requires keeping the current API version around for some indeterminate period of time. While some organizations may have the leverage to force customers to upgrade by some period of time, this isn't always the case. Consequently, any previous versions of an API must be supported for the foreseeable future.

Every new API version is like a completely new product that requires additional infrastructure, support, and development costs to maintain. Keep this in mind when the temptation arises to release a new API version to fix that annoying design decision that crept in last year.

Deprecating APIs

Nothing will ruin a team's week more than scrambling to find a replacement to an API that has been shut down overnight. To avoid this kind of impact on existing API consumers, teams must define their deprecation policy and communicate it to their API consumers.

Deprecating an API operation or product provides an opportunity for an API provider to maintain a level of trust with its API consumers. But this requires a clear policy and planning to deprecate and eventually sunset an API. When executed properly, API consumers are notified early and often of the deprecated API and are given a chance to move to an alternative solution prior to the retirement of the API.

Establish a Deprecation Policy

The organization should have a clearly documented deprecation policy and process as part of the API program standards and practices. This policy should include

- Details on when deprecations are allowed
- Steps to establish a deprecation process
- The minimum duration of the deprecation period prior to retirement of the API or operation
- A requirement to establish a migration path for consumers, even if that includes other vendors that provide a solution similar to the deprecated operation or product
- A clear definition of the organization's deprecation policy in the API's terms of service

Organizations that establish a deprecation policy will be better equipped to deprecate an API operation or product while maintaining the trust of their API consumers.

Announcing a Deprecation

Communicating a deprecation is a significant factor in maintaining API consumer trust. The methods of communication vary, but should include

- Well-written emails that address the deprecated operation(s) or product(s)
- Notification banners at the top of a Web-based dashboard
- Warnings embedded in all related API documentation
- Blog posts or a dedicated landing page for deprecations that discuss the decision and address frequently asked questions
- Frequent social media notifications with a link to the blog post

The announcement strategy should include most or all of these methods of communication. Keep in mind that employee turnover may result in email addresses that are not current, so using a variety of methods ensures the most effective communication possible.

For APIs using OpenAPI descriptions, use the `deprecated: true` indicator, resulting in the rendering of a deprecation warning in generated HTML documentation. GraphQL and gRPC-based APIs have similar provisions for their schema and interface definition language (IDL) formats.

Use the Sunset Header RFC[1] to programmatically communicate when it will be retired. Consider including a step-by-step guide to using the Sunset Header as part of the API documentation. It will help API consumers receive automated notification of deprecated API operations.

Finally, if API helper libraries are offered, include a warning in the log file or console regarding the existence of the Sunset Header. Backend code that uses the library may redirect log files to log aggregators, resulting in internal alerts in monitoring dashboards.

Establishing an API Stability Contract

As the quote at the start of this chapter indicates, an API design isn't finished until someone is using it. So, how can teams design an API that lasts forever if the design isn't finished until after it is being used? This requires a few disciplines that encourage evolutionary API design, including listening to early feedback, continually seeking additional insights, and establishing expectations through an API stability contract with developers.

The ADDR process is designed to engage with stakeholders early and often to ensure that the API design meets the needs of its target audience. API designers must be willing to listen, learn, and adjust their API designs according to the feedback they receive. Anything short of this will only serve the needs of the API owners rather than serve the needs of current and future API consumers.

Not only must teams listen to feedback during the initial design process, but they must continue to listen after the initial release. Seek to better understand how the API is being used beyond its original intent. Conduct interviews with customers and developers to see how API design and documentation improvements can help them. Communication must be continuous rather than a one-time discussion at the start of the API design process.

---

1. E. Wilde, "The Sunset HTTP Header," February 3, 2016, https://tools.ietf.org/html/draft-wilde-sunset-header-01.

An API stability contract is a method of establishing expectations of change between the API provider and its API consumers. The contract defines the level of support and longevity of API operations or entire API-based products. Following is a recommended starting point for organizations:

- **Experimental:** This is an early release for experimentation and feedback. There is no guarantee that it will ever be supported. The design may change, or it may be removed completely in a future release.

- **Prerelease:** The design has been prereleased for feedback and will be supported in the future. However, the design is not frozen and therefore may introduce a breaking change.

- **Supported:** The API is in production and is supported. Any design changes must not break existing consumers.

- **Deprecated:** The API product or API operation(s) is still supported but will soon be retired.

- **Retired:** No longer available or supported.

Applying an API stability contract gives API providers the freedom to introduce new API operations or experimental APIs early for design feedback prior to supporting it on a long-term basis.

Summary

Changes to API design cannot be avoided. Whether internal or external, consumers depend on the API to remain stable in the face of improvements. Introducing changes to an API's design provides an opportunity for the owning team and the organization to maintain the trust of their API consumers. By applying an appropriate API versioning strategy, taking appropriate steps to deprecate APIs when they are no longer needed, and establishing an API stability contract, teams are able to manage change while avoiding negative impacts to their API consumers.

Chapter 15

Protecting APIs

Organizations must apply an integrated approach to API security or else leave the door open to further threats.

— D. Keith Casey

API design doesn't stop at HTTP methods, paths, resources, and media types. Protecting APIs from malicious attackers is an essential part of API design. If left unprotected, an API will become an open door that can do irreparable damage to an organization and its customers. An API protection strategy involves the implementation of the right components, selection of an API gateway solution, and integrating an identity and access management to tie it all together.

This chapter outlines some foundational principles and provides guidance on common practices along with antipatterns to avoid when approaching an API protection strategy. Resources are provided for further reading and research on the journey.

The Potential for API Mischief

Some API providers may choose to implement no API security or only basic API security measures using passwords or API keys. Mischievous attackers prefer to seek out poorly secured APIs and exploit them as the means to gain access to data and internal systems.

Recent API security breaches show some of these key vulnerabilities and the consequences that can occur when using APIs:

- Gaining access to a user database via an unsecured API, allowing the bad guy to confirm the identities of 15 million accounts on Telegram while remaining undetected.

273

- Exploiting a password reset API that returns the reset token, allowing the confirmation email to be bypassed and accounts to be taken over, exposing sensitive health and personal details.

- Combining large data sets from previous hacks to confirm authorization of users, resulting in the ability to pass security screening and download tax returns from the US Internal Revenue Service.

- Reverse-engineering undocumented APIs intended for internal, private use by a company for its mobile apps, allowing the bad guy to access data easily with minimal or no implemented protective measures. This security risk is common for many API vendors that consider an undocumented API as secure, such as Snapchat.

- Exposing the exact location, by latitude and longitude, of users because a previously private Tinder API was opened for end users. A thorough security review prior to opening the API to developers would have identified that the mobile app, not the API, was responsible for hiding the actual physical location of their users.

These recent breaches span from low-reward results, such as disclosing business intelligence as a competitive advantage, to high-reward results that can disclose extremely sensitive data. One even jeopardized the safety of individuals by disclosing their exact location!

Unfortunately, some API providers may take shortcuts in securing their internal APIs. Perhaps they mistakenly think that if they do not document the potential access to the API, no one will go looking for it. This misguided belief is naïve at best and risks exposing the organization to various attack vectors that it could otherwise avoid.

Essential API Protection Practices

Whether the API is available for use by public developers or hidden for private use, protecting the API is important. API protection requires a variety of practices that are essential to an overall API security strategy:

- **Authentication (authn):** Used to determine the identity of callers and verify their identity. Using username and a password is most common for Web apps but is not recommended for API use because passwords may change often. Instead, use OpenID Connect or similar solution to ensure the identity of the caller is verified before allowing API requests to be processed.

- **Authorization (authz):** Prevents unauthorized access to individual or groups of API operations based on the caller's assigned scopes. API keys, API tokens, and/or OAuth 2 are commonly used authorization techniques for APIs.

- **Claims:** Assigns access controls at a finer-grained level than authorization allows, ensuring that API resource instances are protected.

- **Rate limiting (throttling):** Restricts API request thresholds to prevent traffic spikes from negatively impacting API performance across consumers. Also prevents denial-of-service attacks, either malicious or perhaps unintentional due to developer error. Rate limits are typically based on an IP address, API token, or a combination of factors and are limited to a specific number over a period of time.

- **Quotas:** Limits an application or device from using the API more than permitted within a specific time frame. Quotas typically have a monthly limit and may be established on the basis of the assigned subscription level or through formal agreements between organizations.

- **Session hijack prevention:** Enforces proper cross-origin resource sharing (CORS) to allow or deny API access based on the originating client. Also prevents cross-site request forgery (CSRF), which is often used to hijack authorized sessions.

- **Cryptography:** Applies encryption in motion and at rest to prevent unauthorized access to data. Keep in mind that encryption requires additional precautions to protect private keys used to encrypt data elements; otherwise, attackers will easily decrypt the data from API responses using a compromised private key.

- **Mutual TLS:** Mutual TLS, or mTLS, is used when a guarantee of client identity is required. mTLS may be applied when communicating between services or when HTTP-based callbacks using webhooks are used to prevent malicious parties from attempting to forge their identity.

- **Protocol filtering and protection:** Filters requests from API clients that may be used for malicious purposes. This security measure detects invalid combinations of the HTTP method and path, enforces the use of secure HTTP via Transport Layer Security (TLS) for encrypted communications, and blocks known malicious clients.

- **Message validation:** Performs input validation to prevent submitting invalid data or overriding protected fields. It may also prevent parser attack such as XML entity parser exploits, SQL injection, and JavaScript injection attacks sent via requests to gain access to unauthorized data.

- **Data scraping and botnet protection:** Detects intentional data scraping via APIs, online fraud, spam, and distributed denial-of-service (DDoS) attacks from malicious botnets. These attacks tend to be sophisticated and require specialized detection and remediation.

- **Review and scanning:** Manual and/or automated review and testing of API security vulnerabilities within source code (static reviews) and network traffic patterns (real-time reviews).

Not all of these practices are included in a single solution. Instead, several components must be considered as a necessary part of an API protection strategy.

Components of API Protection

There are several components that may be used to protect APIs. When combined, these components form the foundation of a security strategy for APIs.

API Gateways

API gateway is both a pattern and a classification of middleware. The API gateway pattern involves the addition of an extra network hop that the client must traverse to access the API server.

API gateway middleware is responsible for externalizing APIs across network boundaries. They may act as a pass-through or perform protocol transformation as part of the process. The API gateway becomes a central gatekeeper for all traffic in and out of the API.

API gateway middleware may be standalone products or a component within a larger product offering, such as an API management layer. While API gateways may be built from the ground up, some gateways are composed from building blocks such as a reverse proxy and plug-ins to realize the features needed. API gateways rarely address more advanced features needed to manage APIs as products. These concerns are offered by API management layers.

API Management

API management layers, or APIMs, include an API gateway but also extend their capabilities to include a complete API lifecycle management solution. The solution includes publishing, monitoring, protecting, analyzing, and monetizing APIs. It may also include community engagement features.

Subscription-level support involves defining the API operations to be included or excluded at each level. It also allows for more advanced rate limiting and quota support based on the assigned subscription level for a registered application.

APIMs may also offer extended security measures not found in most API gateways. As a result, they may overlap with the duties of Web application firewalls (WAFs).

Service Meshes

Service meshes shift the needs of network reliability, observability, security, routing, and error handling away from each process to separate out-of-process infrastructure. This new infrastructure is portable and independent of any specific programming languages and frameworks selected by each process, making it portable. Service meshes have grown in popularity due to the introduction of microservices but may be used for any architecture or combination of architectural styles.

Service meshes replace the direct communication of processes with a series of proxies that direct the communication and error handling on behalf of the process. A proxy is deployed alongside each running process to eliminate any central point of failure. Deployment is often to a single virtual machine (VM) or alongside each container as a sidecar. A centralized management control plane is used to configure the proxies, communicate outages, and oversee the network health. The controller, however, does not involve itself with network data communications.

The components of a service mesh are shown in Figure 15.1.

Service meshes may be seen as a competitor to API gateways and APIMs. However, this is not the case. While service meshes manage on OSI layer 4 (TCP/IP) and OSI layer 7 (HTTP), they are often paired with an API gateway or APIM. This offers the best of both worlds by providing resilient, observable network communications using a service mesh, with API product and lifecycle management offered by an APIM or API gateway.

Service meshes introduce additional network hops and therefore may have a negative impact on network performance. However, the capabilities offered by a service mesh may offset the negative impact and may produce a net gain when factoring in the many separate network management elements that have to be coordinated when a service mesh is not present.

Finally, bear in mind that smaller organizations may not see the need for the added complexity of a service mesh. However, larger organizations managing many developer teams producing a multitude of services across one or more cloud environments may benefit from the use of a service mesh.

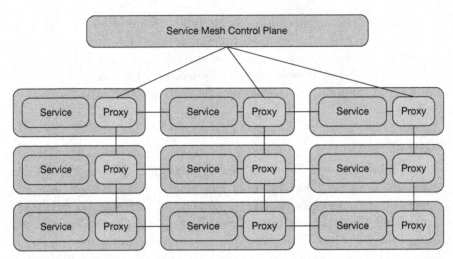

Figure 15.1 *The components of a service mesh, including the proxy instances, each connected to a central control plane for oversight and configuration.*

Web Application Firewalls

WAFs protect APIs from network threats, including common scripting and injection attacks. Unlike API gateways, they monitor OSI layer 3 and layer 4 network activity, allowing for deeper packet inspection than what is possible with API gateways that focus on the HTTP protocol only. As such, they can detect more attack vectors and prevent common ones before request traffic reaches backend API servers.

WAFs offer an additional layer of protection against DDoS attacks that may be sourced from a variety of locations and IP addresses.

It is important to note that while the capabilities offered by WAFs are important, they are sometimes merged into APIMs, content delivery networks, and other layers that may eliminate the need to install an explicit WAF.

Content Delivery Networks

Content delivery networks (CDNs) distribute cacheable content to servers spread across the world, reducing load on API servers. They improve application performance by responding with cached data to API clients more quickly than waiting for API servers to handle the request.

Some CDN vendors are taking on many of the aspects of a WAF by acting as a reverse proxy for dynamic content alongside caching static content. This reduces unwanted traffic on APIs and Web applications. Some CDNs also offer an additional layer of protection against DDoS attacks before they ever reach cloud infrastructure.

Intelligent API Protection

Even with one or more of these components in place, API providers are still vulnerable to automated attack vectors, sometimes referred to as *botnet attacks*. These attacks are often coordinated across multiple hosts and even multiple IP ranges, resulting in attacks that may go undetected. Botnet attacks are difficult to detect because most components evaluate an incoming request in isolation. They aren't designed to evaluate incoming traffic across multiple clients spread across the Internet.

Data scraping is also a risk for APIs that surface an entire catalog of data at once. API quotas and rate limits might be large enough to support an attacker scraping all data at once, even if the related API operations are protected by an API gateway, APIM, and WAF.

Therefore, it is becoming more essential to have advanced detection techniques in place to analyze API traffic across multiple originating IP addresses. This capability is delivered through more advanced versions of the components described previously or by dedicated components that monitor and assess traffic for more complex attack vectors. This protection goes beyond traditional WAFs by extending beyond single IP address rules to a more comprehensive traffic assessment that includes multiple IP addresses.

API Gateway Topologies

Every organization will require a specific API topology that includes one or more API gateway or APIM instances. The topology should seek to make the API platform or product easily managed and flexible to handle the various functional and nonfunctional requirements demanded by the marketplace, regulatory requirements, and business goals.

This section outlines some considerations and common topologies from the field. Keep in mind that not all organizations may fit one of these specific scenarios. When a deviation is identified, seek to verify that the business and operational aspects of the intended scenario merit the need for an uncommon approach.

API Management Hosting Options

There are three primary options for hosting an API gateway or APIM layer: hosted, on-premises, and hybrid. Each one offers advantages and disadvantages to the organization.

Hosted APIMs are offered as a software-as-a-service (SaaS)–based solution by vendors. Some vendors may offer a hosted solution up to a maximum number of requests per second before they recommend self-hosting. Other vendors may support

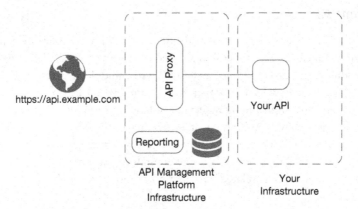

Figure 15.2 *The hosted API management option.*

a large number of API requests, with a variety of subscription levels and service-level agreements (SLAs) offered to customize the solution. Hosting an APIM is a great option for smaller organizations or for organizations beginning to embark on the API journey. However, they may become costly and are often moved on-premises as the API program matures. Figure 15.2 illustrates the hosted APIM option.

On-premises APIMs are installed in a data center or cloud infrastructure. They place more burden on the operations teams to ensure proper reliability and availability than hosted APIMs but also offer more customization options. In addition, on-premises installations allow organizations to install multiple instances of the gateway to isolate APIs involved in regulatory audits or to isolate the impact of API usage across partners and customers. They are also useful when API gateways are desired to manage internal-facing APIs that are not externalized to the public Internet. Figure 15.3 illustrates the on-premises APIM option.

The third type of APIM management option is hybrid. Hybrid installations use a hosted dashboard and reporting infrastructure offered by the vendor while supporting API gateway instances to be deployed using an on-premises model. This is the option that is seen least in the field. The primary advantage is to reduce the burden of supporting the various processes involved in analysis and reporting systems, particularly if the organization lacks in-house expertise for some of the related components or database vendors. Figure 15.4 illustrates the hybrid APIM model.

Keep in mind that some cloud infrastructure providers offer their own API gateway or APIMs. While this may be useful in the short term, some organizations may find the customization effort required to be too great. Organizations that are required to take a multicloud approach may opt to select a third-party APIM vendor rather than try to support multiple cloud-provided API gateways. Whatever the case, select the best fit for the current stage of the API program, reevaluating to ensure the best option continues to be in use.

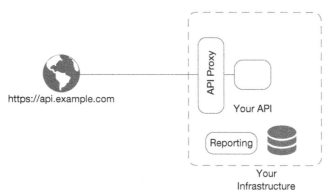

Figure 15.3 *The on-premises API management option.*

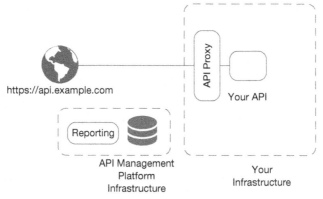

Figure 15.4 *The hybrid API management option.*

Multicloud API Management Retail Case Study

Multicloud strategies aren't new. In fact, anyone delivering solutions in the retail space may have encountered challenges when using a competitor's cloud. One example is Walmart, who prefers that hosted SaaS offerings not use AWS. The initial assumption to this demand may be concerns about placing data on a competitor's cloud. However, the real reason is simpler than that: Walmart doesn't want operational revenue to go toward its competitor. As such, those using AWS for their primary cloud provider may be required by retail companies to use another cloud provider, such as Azure.

> This preference had a considerable impact on the organization's choice for API management deployment. It also forced the organization to consider an independent APIM vendor to avoid supporting two separate API gateways, one for each cloud vendor.
>
> Be sure to factor such considerations into an API management strategy architecture to avoid vendor lock-in and losing potentially lucrative business.

API Network Traffic Considerations

It is important to include network communication considerations as part of establishing an API security strategy. The traffic entering an existing data center requires different treatment than traffic moving within the data center. This difference has an impact on how organizations manage their API network traffic.

To better understand the decisions involved in API network traffic protection, it is important to review network topology concepts. When in doubt, consult a network engineer to establish a secure and efficient network topology for an on-premises or cloud-based infrastructure.

North–south traffic describes the flow of data in and out of the data center. Northbound traffic is data exiting the data center. Southbound traffic is data entering the data center. East–west traffic denotes the flow of data within a data center.

In the case of request/response API styles, all API requests from applications outside the data center are considered southbound traffic, and API responses are northbound. The traffic between an API and a database, or service-to-service communications, is east–west traffic.

Note that with the introduction of zero trust architecture (ZTA), the differentiation between north–south and east–west traffic is decreasing. In ZTA, all public traffic, corporate network traffic, and virtual private network (VPN) traffic is viewed with no initial trust factors. Instead, all devices and services are required to establish their trust through per-request access decisions. This places even greater emphasis on establishing well-architected access policies that incorporate identity and access management, authentication, and authorization services combined with a comprehensive access control policy for every API, service, and application. More details on ZTA may be found in the NIST special publication on Zero Trust Architecture.[1]

---

1. Scott Rose, Oliver Borchert, Stu Mitchell, and Sean Connelly, *Zero Trust Architecture* (National Institute of Standards and Technology (NIST) Special Publication 800-207, August 2020), https://nvlpubs.nist.gov/nistpubs/SpecialPublications/NIST.SP.800-207.pdf.

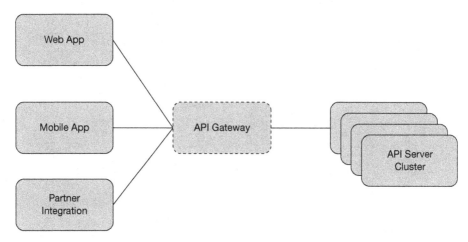

Figure 15.5 *API topology 1 showing an API gateway routing to a monolith.*

Topology 1: API Gateway Direct to API Server

The most common topology for standalone API products is the direct routing of incoming requests through the API gateway to the API backend. The API backend is often a cluster composed of a load balancer and multiple API server instances. In this scenario, there is no need for a service mesh. Figure 15.5 demonstrates this traditional approach to API management.

Topology 2: API Gateway Routing to Services

Another option is to compose an API of multiple backend services. The API gateway uses the path of the request to determine which service is responsible for handling the request. Services may be managed behind a load balancer or may be part of a service mesh, allowing the API gateway to leverage the service mesh to communicate with an available instance. Figure 15.6 demonstrates how an API gateway is used to route incoming requests to multiple backend services.

Topology 3: Multiple API Gateway Instances

For organizations that have regulatory requirements with frequent audits, or for those that must handle a variety of customer, partner, and Web/mobile app deployments, multiple API gateway instances may be required. Each gateway instance may route to a single monolith, as demonstrated in topology 1, or to multiple backend services, as shown in topology 2. Alternatively, API gateway instances

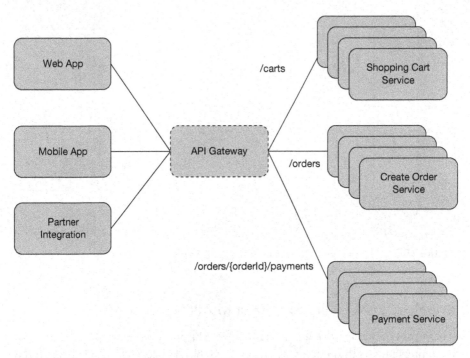

Figure 15.6 *API topology 2 showing an API gateway routing to multiple backend services based on the base path of the incoming API request.*

may be dedicated to one or several tenants of a multitenant SaaS. Issues with availability of one gateway instance should not negatively impact the other gateway instances, limiting the impact during peak usage scenarios. This topology is shown in Figure 15.7.

Identity and Access Management

So far, the assumption has been that there is an API client, an API server, and now an API gateway and perhaps other middleware that helps to prevent malicious attack vectors. There is one more important ingredient to protecting an API product or platform: identity and access management (IAM). IAM provides authentication and authorization services, often through the integration with other vendors using industry standards. It also includes the generation of API tokens that take the place of passwords when representing a user and the user's assigned access controls. IAM is the glue that ties together all other API protection components.

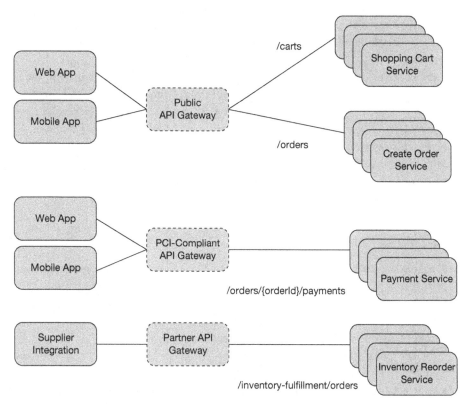

Figure 15.7 *API topology 3 showing multiple API gateway instances that support various internal and external API clients, including the isolation of payment processing for PCI compliance and auditing.*

Passwords and API Keys

Some APIs choose to allow API clients to provide their username and password credentials that are used to log in to the Web or mobile application. While this is an easy way to get started, it is highly discouraged for several reasons:

- Passwords are fragile because they change often, which would render any code unable to use the API until it is updated with the new password.

- Delegating access to some or all data to third parties requires sharing the password with them.

- The use of username and password does not support multifactor authentication.

To avoid these challenges, the use of API keys or API tokens is preferred for most situations. These two concepts are often used interchangeably but are quite different.

API keys are simple replacements for a password and have no expiration date. They are often found in a user profile page or in the settings page for a Web application. An API key may be a long alphanumeric value (e.g., `15vza8ua896maxhm`). Because API keys have no expiration date assigned, anyone who obtains the key maliciously may be able to use the API to access data and backend systems for an indefinite period of time. Resetting an API key usually requires a manual step within the same user profile or settings page, assuming that the API provider offers API key reset capabilities at all.

API Tokens

API tokens are a robust alternative to API keys. They represent a session where a user is authorized to interact with an API. While they may be alphanumeric and look similar to an API key, they are not the same. An API token may represent a user or a third party who has been given limited or full access to the API on the user's behalf. API tokens also have an associated expiration time.

An API token's expiration time may vary from a few seconds to a few days depending on various configuration elements. With an API token also comes a refresh token, which allows the API client to request a new API token when the previous one has expired or is no longer valid.

An API token may have one or more access controls associated with it. These controls are often referred to as *scopes*. Multiple API tokens may be generated on behalf of a user, including one with an assigned scope for read-only access of a specific API resource, another with assigned scopes for read/write access to all resources, and yet another that offers a single scope assignment for limited API resource access by a delegated third-party application. API tokens are illustrated in Figure 15.8.

APIs often use a variety of methods for passing an API token to the server, including as a query argument on the URL, as a POST parameter, and through an HTTP header. Avoid using query arguments in the URL, as the API token will be logged by Web servers and reverse proxy servers, and JavaScript code may also be allowed to access the API token easily. POST parameters tend to be more secure, but the location of the token will vary across APIs.

Therefore, it is recommended to use the standardized HTTP Authorization header. Access to HTTP headers can be limited through the use of CORS response headers, and headers are less likely to be logged by intermediary servers.

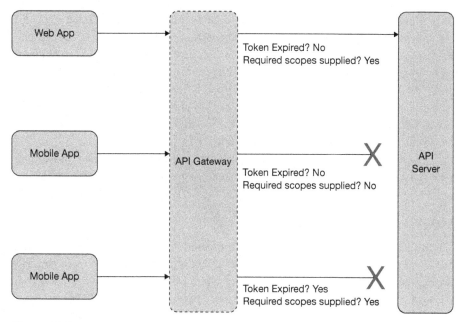

Figure 15.8 *Three separate API tokens, only one of which is valid and allowed to pass to the API server by the API gateway.*

Pass-by-Reference versus Pass-by-Value API Tokens

Pass-by-reference API tokens do not contain any content or state, only a unique identifier for dereferencing on the server side. For example:

```
GET https://api.example.com/projects HTTP/1.1
Accept: application/json
Authorization: Bearer a717d415b4f1
```

It is the responsibility of the API server to dereference the API token to determine the specific user making the API call, along with any other details.

Pass-by-value API tokens contain name/value pairs included within the token. This reduces the number of lookups required to dereference a token to its associated values by the API server.

API tokens that use pass by value typically allow the API client to access the same name/value pairs that are available to the API server. Therefore, pass-by-value API tokens should embed feature flags or other sensitive data that could be used to compromise a system. Instead, use them to convey minimal details, such as opaque identifiers.

A popular pass-by-value API token standard is the JSON Web Tokens (JWTs), typically pronounced "jot." JWTs are composed of three elements: a header, payload, and signature. Each element is Base64 encoded and dot-separated to compose an opaque token that may be used as an Authorization bearer token between client and API. JWTs are signed to ensure they haven't been tampered with by the client before being sent to the server. Using a private key signature provides further protection against tampering and verifies the identity of the client. The JWT.io[2] Web site is an excellent resource for learning more about JWTs.

JWTs tend to be more popular for communicating authorization details for east–west traffic, while pass-by-reference API tokens are used for north–south traffic.

OAuth 2.0 and OpenID Connect

The workflow to authenticate a user, generate an API token, and support delegated access to third-party applications requires a complex workflow between the data owner, the API server, an authorization server, and the third party. OAuth 2.0 is an industry-standard framework designed to prevent every API server from implementing a different form of this workflow. It offers specific authorization flows for Web applications, desktop applications, mobile phones, and devices. These flows support multiple grant types, integrated or third-party authorization servers, a variety of token formats, authorization scopes, and support for extensions.

This complex workflow is commonly seen with Web sites that support logging in with a Google, Twitter, Facebook, or other kind of supported account. While the Web site itself isn't owned or managed by any of these vendors, they do provide the login screen for authenticating with a user account on their system. The Web site implements a specific flow to send the user to the login page of the chosen vendor (e.g., Google). Once the login is successful, the Web site user is returned to the Web site and is now authenticated. Behind the scenes, the Web site and the authentication provider exchange sufficient details to verify that the user is who they claim to be. The core components of an OAuth 2.0 interaction are shown in Figure 15.9.

OAuth 2.0 is a complex framework but one that can be understood given sufficient time and effort. As with other API security topics, it merits a dedicated book. For now, more information on OAuth 2.0, including links to resources, can be obtained by visiting Aaron Parecki's excellent OAuth Community[3] Web site.

As mentioned earlier, OAuth 2.0 is focused on the authorization workflow. OpenID Connect is an identity layer on top of the OAuth 2.0 protocol that offers a standard way of verifying and obtaining identity details. It allows Web and mobile

---

2. https://jwt.io
3. https://oauth.net/2

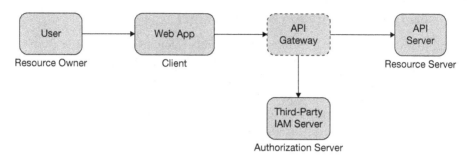

Figure 15.9 *The core components and basic interaction of OAuth 2.0.*

clients to verify the identity of the end user as well as to obtain basic profile information using a REST-like API. Without this protocol, custom integration is required to bridge identity and profile details between the authorization server and the API. The specification details, along with an updated list of OpenID Connect–compliant servers, is available on the OpenID Connect[4] Web site.

Enterprises that require federated identity management across multiple internal and third-party vendors lean heavily on single sign-on (SSO) for their Web applications. Security Assertion Markup Language (SAML) is a standard used to bridge APIs into an existing SSO solution within the enterprise, making the transition better for enterprise users accessing an API through an application. More details are available on the OASIS SAML[5] Web site.

Considerations before Building an In-House API Gateway

Teams often consider building their own API gateway or using a helper library to implement their own authentication and authorization support. While some organizations had to take this on early in their API journey, there is no longer a need to build an API gateway in-house. In fact, building a custom API gateway is highly discouraged for three reasons.

---

4. https://openid.net/connect

5. https://www.oasis-open.org/committees/tc_home.php?wg_abbrev=security

Reason 1: API Security Is a Moving Target

Want to make it easier for an attacker to find and exploit a security hole in an API? Build a custom API gateway. Ask any company that has experienced a breach through its API—security is hard, even with the right components in place.

Applying proper security requires focused attention to detail at every aspect of the organization. Unless the organization has a staff of security experts on hand, building an in-house, secure API gateway will take much longer than it takes to build a proof-of-concept version. And it will require continued resources to keep it up to date with the latest vulnerabilities.

Reason 2: It Will Take Longer than Expected

Building a custom API gateway often starts as a romantic notion. Rationalization begins with "It shouldn't take too long" and continues with "It will do exactly what I need it to do—no more—and it will be much faster as a result," only to end with the dreaded rhetorical question, "How hard could it be?"

The reality is that building and maintaining a production-worthy API gateway isn't trivial. There is a reason why API gateway and APIM vendors are able to charge for their product. Beyond the baseline set of features, deviations by nonstandard clients and proxy servers will force all sorts of troubleshooting throughout the life of the API gateway. In addition, implementing OAuth 2.0, OpenID Connect, SAML, and other specifications is complex and takes considerable time to build, test, and support.

It is important to first ask if the time spent building a custom API gateway is time well spent by the organization. Count the full cost of building and maintaining the API gateway, including patches and improvements to handle new and emerging attack vectors that are not currently handled. Many organizations have gone down this path only to never deliver their intended solution to market.

Reason 3: Expected Performance Takes Time

In software, there are three recommended phases of development: make it work, make it right, and make it fast. Often, developers are good at the first step—make it work. They experiment with code to see if something is possible or perhaps to see what the result might look like before proceeding.

The effort required to go from making it work to making it right for production is vast. The edge cases are numerous and unforeseen. It takes time to make it right. To make it fast requires even more investment. Is the organization ready to dedicate staff on building a solution that already exists?

What about Helper Libraries?

Perhaps a team is considering that the features of an API gateway could be included right inside the source code. Maybe an existing helper library offers API token generation and some basic security features. That might work for today. However, will it be sustainable in the long term?

In addition, many developers assume that the library was written by security experts, designed to address the needs of the organization, and will be maintained in the future against all forms of exploits, bugs, and language/framework major version releases. Unless it is a library offered by a commercial company, at least one of these assumptions will be wrong. Is that a risk the organization is willing to take?

Leverage third-party IAM solutions that offer authentication and authorization services whenever possible. Avoid implementing a custom authentication and authorization solution, as it will expose the API to malicious attacks that take advantage of weak or abandoned code.

Summary

API design requires considering how an API will be protected from malicious attackers. Unprotected APIs are an open door that welcome attackers to damage an organization and its customers. An API protection strategy involves the implementation of the right components, selection of an API gateway solution, and integrating an identity and access management to tie it all together.

Don't leave API protection to someone's side project or to a well-intentioned team within the organization. Select the right approach with vendor-supported components that ensure that the front door of the organization's APIs is barred shut rather than left unlocked.

Chapter 16

Continuing the API
Design Journey

*When done effectively, governance can provide clear direction, remove obstacles,
and allow different parts of the organization to function independently.*

— Matt McLarty

An organization that produces more than one API product must learn to scale its API
design process. Otherwise, designs will lack consistency across the portfolio of APIs
produced by the organization. Authentication and authorization will vary between
APIs. Naming conventions and error responses will deviate. In short, the API program will become a mess.

This chapter explores the factors required to scale API design efforts within
an organization. These factors include establishing a style guide for consistency,
incorporating design reviews, and encouraging a culture of reuse. Once these measures
are applied, teams will be able to function independently while maintaining consistency
across the API portfolio. Finally, the chapter takes a look back at the topics covered in
this book and offers some guidance on how to continue the API design journey.

Establishing an API Style Guide

Many API programs begin as a single API or a few small APIs. Over time, more APIs
emerge across the company. Consistency for all API consumers is an important
component of a great developer experience. A common design approach makes
integration more intuitive and can reduce troubleshooting and support costs.

Great style guides go beyond basic design decisions to include common error
strategies, applying patterns consistently across APIs, and even suggest common
architecture styles for teams looking to get started quickly.

An API style guide commonly includes the following topics:

- **Introduction:** The scope of the style guide, who to contact for questions, clarifications, or enhancements

- **API fundamentals:** Used to educate and coach those less familiar with the basics; may consist of links to internal or external training materials

- **Standards:** Naming conventions, guidance for selecting HTTP methods and response codes, organizing resource paths, resource lifecycle design, payload and content formats, when and how to use hypermedia

- **Design patterns:** Common patterns encountered, including pagination, error responses, bulk processing, singleton resources

- **Lifecycle management:** Recommendations for moving an API into production, along with deprecation and sunset procedures

- **Tools and technologies:** List of tools that are recommended, including those with site licenses already available

- **Operational recommendations:** Recommended API management tools, configurations, processes, marketing recommendations, and common practices for highly available, robust, and resilient APIs

- **Further reading:** Additional resources that may be interesting to the reader, including both internal and publicly available papers, articles, and videos

Too often, style guides are used to push an agenda. Full compliance, or else. That isn't what style guides should be about. Their goal should be to advise teams designing APIs toward a more consistent API with other APIs across the organization. A newly hired developer should be able to work with a variety of APIs across the organization without realizing that different teams designed them.

Methods for Encouraging Style Guide Adherence

Style guides, without some kind of incentive to adhere to the recommendations, will be ignored. There are three common methods to enforcing style guide compliance:

1. **Incentivized:** A centralized team oversees and enforces the guide. Reviews are conducted by the centralized team for any new API prior to production deployment. API teams are incentivized to adhere to the style guide to gain

access to shared services and support (e.g., API management layer, operational and infrastructure support) rather than being forced to implement it themselves.

2. **Federated:** A centralized team oversees and maintains the style guide, but coaches, embedded locally within the business unit and/or region, are available to address their specific needs. This method avoids the ivory tower problem of a committee designing standards without understanding the needs of specific business units.

3. **Clone and customize:** A single group manages the style guide. Teams clone the standards as a starting point, making minor enhancements locally for business unit consistency. For organizations that have many independent teams within and/or across business units, this is the most effective method.

These methods may be used independently or in combination to achieve the desired results that best meet the needs of the organization.

Selecting Style Guide Tone

Some style guides are informal, and others are very formal, including the use of RFC 2119[1] for requirement levels. Deciding upon a tone and formality for the style guide depends upon the answers to three questions:

- Will the organization be enforcing the standard? If so, then use RFC 2119 recommendations to enforce what MUST, SHOULD, and MAY be implemented.

- Will enforcement be deferred to a future date? Then go ahead and start using RFC 2119, but keep the wording to lowercase (e.g., must, should, may) until it is enforced. This demonstrates expectations and likely future enforcement but with less of a formality during the initial introductory period.

- Is the guide shared across business units, limiting the organization's ability to control or strictly enforce the guidelines? Then soften the tone and focus on design consistency by encouraging teams to adopt as many of the guidelines as possible rather than using a more formal tone.

---

1. S. Bradner, "Key Words for Use in RFCs to Indicate Requirement Levels," March 1997, https://datatracker.ietf.org/doc/html/rfc2119.

Tips for Getting Started with an API Style Guide

- Browse Arnaud Lauret's (aka the API Handyman) *API Stylebook*.[2] *API Stylebook* aims to help API designers to solve API design matters and build their API design guidelines. Browse other publicly available style guides as well for insights.

- Start small. The scope of an API style guide may be too much for one individual or a small team to take on initially. Start simple and expand over time.

- Socialize the style guide. Just because the style guide exists doesn't mean people in the organization know about it. Spend time evangelizing the style guide with teams. Gain their insights from early release candidates before releasing an official version.

Remember

The goal of an API style guide is to advise teams designing APIs toward consistency with other APIs across the organization.

Supporting Multiple API Styles

While most organizations may suggest or mandate a single API style, this won't always be the case. As new API styles emerge, API portfolios become challenged with the push for new ways of interacting with the enterprise. Remember, it was only a decade ago that most organizations stopped developing SOAP-based Web services. API programs must consider how new API styles will be evaluated, approved, and supported as they gain popularity.

API programs must consider async APIs, such as Webhooks, WebSockets, Server-Sent Events (SSE), data streaming, and internal messaging as part of the API portfolio. Like the design of synchronous APIs, the design of async APIs must be governed and managed as part of the overall API portfolio.

The API style guide must address each of these API styles as they are introduced into the organization. While it is possible to share elements of the style guide between different API styles, it is highly recommended to write a style guide for each API style at the start.

Over time, common recommendations such as naming conventions and reserved words may be shared between API style guides. However, most organizations find

---

2. *API Stylebook: Collections of Resources for API Designers,* maintained by Arnaud Lauret, accessed August 24, 2021, http://apistylebook.com.

that there is significant deviation in standards and common practices across API styles. Remember that it is better to follow common practices for each API style than to try to unify all API styles into a single set of recommendations.

Finally, keep in mind that there is a cost to supporting each API style. Take time to understand the needs for the new API style. Then determine if the needs outweigh the cost required to build and support yet another API style guide.

Conducting API Design Reviews

API design reviews seek to improve the design of APIs through constructive review and feedback. Implementing a healthy API design review process helps to capture insights, patterns, and lessons learned into a repeatable process, guiding organizations toward a more consistent design and a better developer experience.

API design reviews offer an organization a chance to

- Share knowledge of upcoming APIs.

- Incorporate design feedback before coding begins.

- Become an advocate for the many developers who will use the API once it is released.

- Offer a more consistent developer experience through consistently designed APIs.

- Catch missing or incorrect assumptions before code changes become more expensive or time is limited.

Following are some tips and insights on conducting healthy API design reviews.

A Word of Caution about Design Reviews

Design reviews can go two ways: constructive or destructive. A constructive design review provides an opportunity to coach those newer to API design and build up and edify the entire organization. Destructive design reviews are the opposite, typically sowing the seeds of frustration and mistrust. Worst case, design reviews will be a cause for team attrition as caustic team members invade an otherwise healthy and useful process.

Therefore, use caution when conducting an API design review. Seek to ask questions first. Too often, biases and assumptions are incorporated into design reviews. Instead, seek to first understand by asking questions and listening. Don't claim to know everything about API design—everyone can benefit from learning something new. Never accuse someone of deliberately designing a poor API—no one sets out to do so. Assume good intentions, listen carefully, seek to understand, then provide some recommended next steps for design improvement.

Remember: Everyone starts out as a newbie API design reviewer. Model the proper reviewer behavior that encourages improvement in a constructive way.

Start with a Documentation Review

API design reviews are not code reviews. API design reviewers are acting as an advocate for the developers who will consume the API. Therefore, it is important to start with the API documentation.

APIs exist for a variety of reasons, including data access, customer automation, system-to-system integration, marketplace creation, and workforce automation. An API's introduction should be clear about why the API exists and how it might collaborate with other APIs to accomplish more complex workflows or outcomes.

Use the following as a review checklist for all areas of documentation:

- **API name:** The name should be descriptive and make it easy to determine the scope of the API when first discovered.

- **API description:** The description should be comprehensive, starting with an overview of the API and including a list of use cases it solves.

- **API operations:** Each operation should offer a summary of what task, activity, or outcome it produces along with a description that includes detailed usage instructions. Ensure all input and output values are captured and properly described, including expected formats that could cause errors if violated.

- **Example usage:** Examples of API usage are often the most important, yet missing, element of an API's documentation. These examples do not need to be in a specific programming language (although that helps when trying to offer an API to a broad audience). Simple HTTP request/response examples, perhaps complemented with Postman collections, will go a long way toward accelerating developer understanding and completing the integration effort.

- **Avoid internal references:** Great documentation assumes that readers have no idea about any of the internal systems or implementation choices behind the scenes. They just want to get something done and they want to find out if the API will help them achieve their goals.

Check for Standards and Design Consistency

One of the common challenges for many mid- to large-sized organizations is API design consistency. It is easy to spot APIs that were independently designed by teams without any cross-organization consistency applied. Commonly, lack of consistency is associated with organizations that lack a design review process. Even with a review process in place, inconsistencies may creep in from time to time.

Part of the API design review should be to verify that the standards and design choices match any established style guides and standards. This task may be performed by a combination of a manual review and the use of an API linter such as Spectral.

Finally, look for opportunities to apply common design patterns consistently. Examples include create-read-update-delete (CRUD), consistent use of pagination techniques, multipart MIME for file uploads, and so on. While these common patterns may be captured as part of the style guide, identifying deviations and discussing them with the team will help to provide consistency whenever possible and making exceptions when appropriate.

Review Automated Test Coverage

While an API design review does focus on the design, reviewing test coverage is important as well. Including test coverage review ensures that the testing strategies for the API have been considered as part of the design. It also helps to ensure that the API's operations can be used in combination to produce the desired outcomes identified during the align phase.

If the review is conducted early in the process, there may not be any specific code or test coverage in place. In this case, review test plans to surface missing or incorrect design assumptions. A good starting place is to review job stories, API profiles produced during modeling, and other artifacts. This will help surface any missing test plans and ensure the test coverage will be sufficient to verify operational functionality along with acceptance tests that will verify intended outcomes.

Add Try It Out Support

Nothing provides a better review of an API design than interacting with it. If code already exists for the API, go ahead and try out the API. This will help to exercise the documentation, the API design, and the implementation.

If the team took a design-first approach, little or no code exists yet. Mocking tools help to address this issue. Mocking tools are a great way to fill the gap and catch bad design decisions or missing endpoints sooner rather than later in the delivery process. These tools often accept a definition in OpenAPI Specification, API Blueprint, and other description formats to produce a mock version of the API design. While the mock API won't be fully formed, it will provide a basic understanding of how the API will be used once completed and catch suboptimal design decisions early.

Developing a Culture of Reuse

API consumers are an essential ingredient of any program. However, many organizations focus on strategy, objectives, and governance to create APIs without addressing the need to make adoption of APIs easy through discovery.

For most organizations, API documentation is an afterthought. This is unfortunate, as it leads to serious consequences for API discovery and adoption, resulting in reduced reuse of valuable APIs. Organizations implementing effective API discovery subscribe to the following mantra: Discover digital capabilities when possible; build them when necessary.

API documentation is the first encounter most developers will have with an API, so providing great documentation is essential to helping them understand what the API offers, how to use it, and what to do when they are ready to start integrating. This topic is addressed in detail in Chapter 13, "Documenting the API."

Developers who are new to an API platform do not have an easy journey. In fact, development teams go through several phases as they evaluate and integrate the API, as shown in Figure 16.1.

To ensure developers can quickly get started with using the API, define a clear onboarding process. Set the expectations for the path from discovery to mapping and integrating their solution to the API. Don't stop with winning developers

Consumption	Goal
Onboarding	Register for portal and API access
Discovery	Identify API capabilities
Mapping	Map solution to platform API capabilities using reference documentation
Exploration	Prototype consumption ("try-it-out")
Integration	Consume via code
Certification	Obtain approval for production API access
Usage monitoring	Production access monitoring and throttling for compliance
Platform improvement	Request platform API enhancements to meet the needs of the solution
Platform updates	Update notifications for new API endpoints, enhancements, case studies

Figure 16.1 *The API consumption lifecycle, showing the phases that a development team experiences when they find a new API.*

with an API—stay in contact with them through newsletters or distribution lists. Announce new and upcoming improvements, success stories, and common use cases through consistent developer communication. Highlight the teams that are responsible for building and supporting APIs to demonstrate their commitment to meeting developers' needs.

The Journey Has Only Begun

The focus of this book has been on principles of Web API design that produce a repeatable, collaborative API design process that helps to deliver value using an outcome-based focus. These principles are as follows:

- **Principle 1:** APIs should never be designed in isolation. Collaborative API design is essential for a great API. (Chapter 2)

- **Principle 2:** API design starts with an outcome-based focus. A focus on the outcome ensures the API delivers value to everyone. (Chapters 3–6)

- **Principle 3:** Select the API design elements that match the need. Trying to find the perfect API style is a fruitless endeavor. Instead, seek to understand and apply the API elements appropriate for the need, whether that is REST, GraphQL, gRPC, or an emerging style just entering the industry. (Chapters 7–12)

- **Principle 4:** API documentation is the most important user interface for developers. Therefore, API documentation should be first class and not left as a last-minute task. (Chapter 13)

- **Principle 5:** APIs are forever, so plan accordingly. Thoughtful API design combined with an evolutionary design approach makes APIs resilient to change. (Chapter 14)

The principles are the foundation for a four-phase process: Align-Define-Design-Refine (ADDR). The ADDR process focuses on aligning stakeholders, defining the digital capabilities required, designing the API to produce the outcomes, and then refining the design based on feedback.

The process recognizes that an API should never be designed in isolation. It requires the collaboration of a variety of roles, including subject matter experts. When those involved in API design are aligned on the outcomes first, the API remains focused on the value delivered. Along the way, stakeholders are aligned in their understanding using collaborative techniques such as EventStorming and API modeling prior to designing the API. The API is then designed and refined through feedback with those who will integrate the API into their solution.

While some may think that the journey has been completed, this is only the beginning. The API design will now be delivered and managed. It will meet real-world usage, perhaps even encountering new use cases never considered. The ADDR process will be used once again as the API grows and matures. For larger organizations, this API design lifecycle will be repeated for many new APIs, requiring the ADDR process to be scaled for use by multiple teams. The journey has only begun.

Appendix

HTTP Primer

To better understand how Web APIs work, it is important to start with an understanding of HTTP, the language of the Web. While the HTTP protocol can be hidden behind various libraries and frameworks, understanding the protocol provides a foundation for troubleshooting API integrations and improved API design.

This primer offers an introduction to the HTTP protocol, the elements that are involved in using HTTP for interacting with Web APIs, and some advanced features that help to shape more powerful API interactions.

Overview of HTTP

The HTTP protocol is a client/server protocol. An HTTP client sends a request to a server. The HTTP server then determines if it can service the request with the information given. The server then returns a response that includes a code indicating success or failure, along with a response payload containing the information requested or details about the error. This request/response flow is illustrated in Figure A.1.

HTTP is comprised of several elements:

- The Uniform Resource Locator (URL) where the request is sent
- The HTTP method that informs the server how the client wishes to interact with the resource
- The request headers and body
- The response headers and body
- A response code that indicates whether the request was successfully processed or an error was encountered

Figure A.1 *An overview of the HTTP protocol.*

The Uniform Resource Locator

HTTP uses a URL as a unique address where data or services are located. Requests are sent to the URL, where the server processes the request and sends a response back to the client. The URL is commonly seen in the location bar in a browser. Examples include:

- https://www.google.com
- https://launchany.com/effective-api-programs/
- https://deckofcardsapi.com/api/deck/new/shuffle

A URL is comprised of the following items:

- **Protocol:** The protocol used to connect (e.g., http [unsecure] or https [secure]).
- **Hostname:** The server to contact (e.g., api.example.com).
- **Port number:** A number ranging from 0 to 65535 that identifies the process on the server where the request is to go (e.g., 443 for https or 80 for http).
- **Path:** The path to the resource being requested (e.g., /projects). The default path is /, which indicates the homepage.
- **Query string:** Contains data to be passed to the server. Starts with a question mark and contains name=value pairs, using an ampersand as a separator between them (e.g., ?page=1&per_page=10).

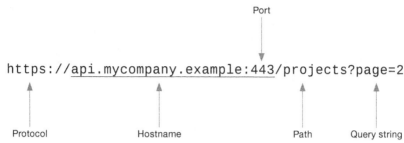

Figure A.2 *The elements of a Uniform Resource Locator (URL).*

Figure A.2 demonstrates the elements of a URL.

HTTP Request

An HTTP request is composed of several parts: the HTTP method, the path, the header, and the message body.

The HTTP method informs the server what kind of interaction the client would like to request. Common HTTP methods are GET, to request data, and POST to submit data. The methods commonly used for Web-based APIs are detailed later in this appendix.

The path is the portion of the URL that references a resource on the server. The resource may be a static file, such as an image, or a piece of code that performs dynamic request processing.

The header tells the server about the client and specifics about the request. The header is comprised of header fields in name:value format. Common HTTP request headers used with Web-based APIs include the following:

- **Accept:** Informs the server what content types the client is able to support. Examples may include image/gif and image/jpeg. If the client is willing to accept any kind of response, */* is used. This header is often used with content negotiation, detailed later.

- **Content-Type:** Informs the server the content type of the request message body. Used when submitting data using a HTTP method that requires a message body (e.g., POST).

- **User-Agent:** Provides a free-form string indicating the kind of HTTP client that is making the request. This may indicate a specific browser type and version or may be customized to indicate a specific helper library or command-line tool.

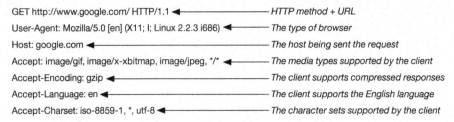

GET http://www.google.com/ HTTP/1.1 ◄————————————— HTTP method + URL

User-Agent: Mozilla/5.0 [en] (X11; I; Linux 2.2.3 i686) ◄———— The type of browser

Host: google.com ◄——————————————————— The host being sent the request

Accept: image/gif, image/x-xbitmap, image/jpeg, */* ◄———— The media types supported by the client

Accept-Encoding: gzip ◄————————————— The client supports compressed responses

Accept-Language: en ◄——————————————— The client supports the English language

Accept-Charset: iso-8859-1, *, utf-8 ◄————————— The character sets supported by the client

Figure A.3 *A line-by-line examination of an HTTP request to https://www.google.com.*

- **Accept-Encoding:** informs the server what, if any, compression support the client is able to process. This allows the server to compress the response using gzip or compress formats to reduce the byte size of the response.

The message body provides details to the server when data is being submitted and may be human-readable or binary, as required by the server. For a retrieval request using GET, the message body may be empty.

Figure A.3 shows an example of an HTTP request sent to Google to request the homepage that contains the search form, documented line by line.

HTTP Response

Once the request is received by the server, the server processes the request and sends a response. The response is composed of three parts: the response code, the response header, and the response body.

The response code is a number that corresponds to a success or error code indicating whether the request could be fulfilled. The response code sent must be one of the those outlined in the HTTP specification and are detailed later. Only one response code is allowed per response.

The response header tells the client specifics about the result of the request. The header is comprised of header fields in name:value format. Common HTTP response headers used with Web-based APIs include the following:

- **Date:** The date of the response.
- **Content-Location:** The fully qualified URL of the response. Useful if the request resulted in redirects that may require the client to update its URL for the resource.
- **Content-Length:** The length, in bytes, of the response message body.
- **Content-Type:** Informs the client of the content type of the message body.

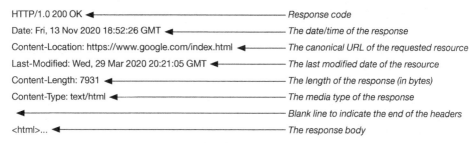

Figure A.4 *A line-by-line examination of an HTTP response to a request sent to https://www .google.com.*

- **Server:** A string that provides details about the vendor and version of the server that processed the request (e.g., nginx/1.2.3). The server may choose to provide little or no detail to avoid exposing details that might indicate a possible vulnerability exists.

The response message body provides the content back to the client. It may be an HTML page, an image, or data in XML, JSON, or another format, as indicated by the Content-Type response header.

Figure A.4 shows an HTTP response sent back from Google based on our earlier request for the homepage.

It is important to note that the response in Figure A.4 includes only the HTML in the response and not additional images, stylesheets, JavaScript, and so on. The HTTP client is responsible for parsing the HTML, identifying the tags that reference these additional assets, and sending subsequent HTTP requests for each one. For a Web page with 20 images, 21 separate HTTP requests are required to gather all of the files necessary to render the Web page—one request for the HTML page, along with the 20 requests necessary to retrieve each image.

Common HTTP Methods

HTTP methods inform the server what kind of operation or interaction the client would like to perform. Common interactions include retrieving a resource, creating a new resource, performing a calculation, and deleting a resource.

The following HTTP methods are commonly encountered when using Web-based APIs:

- **GET:** Retrieves a resource from the server—response may be cached by the server or an intermediary caching server

- **HEAD:** Requests only the response headers but not the actual response body

- **POST:** Submits data to the server, often for storage or for calculations—response not cacheable

- **PUT:** Submits data to the server, often as a replacement of existing data—response not cacheable

- **PATCH:** Submits data to the server, often as a partial update of existing data—response not cacheable

- **DELETE:** Deletes an existing resource on the server—response not cacheable

HTTP methods have additional semantics that are important for clients to take into consideration: safety and idempotence.

A safe method indicates that the HTTP method used will not generate side effects, such as altering data. This is common for GET and HEAD methods, as they are intended for resource retrieval and do not alter data. APIs that implement data-altering operations using safe HTTP methods risk generating unpredictable results, especially when middleware servers, such as caching servers, are involved.

Idempotent methods ensure that the same side effects are produced when identical requests are submitted. This is true for GET and HEAD retrieval methods because no data is altered. PUT and DELETE are guaranteed by the HTTP specification to be idempotent, as PUT replaces the resource with a completely new representation and DELETE removes the resource from the server.

POST is not guaranteed to be idempotent, as it may create new resources on each subsequent request or alter data in some way that is not guaranteed to produce the same results (e.g., incrementing a value). Likewise, PATCH is not idempotent, as only a subset of fields, rather than the entire representation, is altered.

Figure A.5 summarizes the semantics of the common HTTP methods used for Web-based APIs.

Method	Safe	Idempotent
GET	Yes	Yes
POST	No	No
PUT	No	Yes
PATCH	No	No
DELETE	No	Yes
HEAD	Yes	Yes
OPTIONS	Yes	Yes

Figure A.5 *Common HTTP methods used with APIs, including safety and idempotency traits that help to guide the client on how to recover from errors.*

HTTP Response Codes

HTTP responses include a response code that indicates to the API consumer whether the request succeeded or failed. HTTP provides a series of response codes that the API server can send back to the client to indicate the result.

HTTP response status codes belong to four primary response code families:

- **200 codes** indicate that the request was processed successfully.

- **300 codes** indicate that the client may need to take additional action(s) to complete the request, such as follow a redirect.

- **400 codes** indicate a failure in the request that the client may wish to fix and resubmit.

- **500 codes** indicate a failure on the server that is not the fault of the client. The client may attempt a retry at a future time, if appropriate.

Table A.1 offers a list of the common response codes from the HTTP specification that are used by REST-based APIs.

Table A.1 *Common HTTP Response Codes Used in API Design*

HTTP Response Code	Description
200 OK	The request has succeeded.
201 Created	The request has been fulfilled and resulted in a new resource being created.
202 Accepted	The request has been accepted for processing, but the processing has not been completed.
204 No Content	The server has fulfilled the request but does not need to return a body. This is common for delete operations.
304 Not Modified	The server determined that the content has not changed since the last request as determined by the client-provided If-Modified-Since or If-None-Match request header.
400 Bad Request	The request could not be understood by the server due to malformed syntax.
401 Unauthorized	The request requires user authentication.
403 Forbidden	The server understood the request but is refusing to fulfill it.
404 Not Found	The server has not found anything matching the requested URL/URI.
412 Precondition Failed	The client submitted a request with a condition based on the last modified timestamp or ETag, and the condition failed. The client should refetch the resource and attempt the change again, if desired.

Table A.1 *(continued)*

415 Unsupported Media Type	The server was unable to respond with any of the client-supplied media types supported as specified in the `Accept` header.
428 Precondition Required	The server requires that a precondition header be supplied before the request may be processed. Often enforced where concurrency control headers are required.
500 Internal Server Error	The server encountered an unexpected condition that prevented it from fulfilling the request.

Content Negotiation

Content negotiation allows clients to request one or more preferred media type(s) for the server response. With content negotiation, a single operation may support different resource representations, including CSV, PDF, PNG, JPG, SVG, and others.

The client requests the preferred media type using the `Accept` header. This example demonstrates an API client requesting a JSON-based response:

```
GET https://api.example.com/projects HTTP/1.1
Accept: application/json
```

More than one supported media type may be included in the header, as shown in this example:

```
GET https://api.example.com/projects HTTP/1.1
Accept: application/json,application/xml
```

The asterisk may be used as a wildcard when selecting media types. A `text/*` indicates that any subtype of the text media type is acceptable. Specifying a value of `*/*` indicates that the client will accept any media type in the response. This is a common scenario for browsers, which will prompt the user whether to save the file or launch a chosen application when encountering an unknown media type. However, for clients working with an API, it is important to be explicit to avoid runtime errors that could occur when encountering an unknown or unsupported content type.

Requests may specify preference for specific media types supported within the `Accept` header through the use of quality factors. Quality factors are expressed as a qvalue between 0 and 1 that helps to assign a preferred order of media types. The API server reviews the header values and return the response using the content type that matches both what the server supports and what the client requested. If the server cannot respond with an accepted content type, it returns a 415 Unsupported Media Type response code.

Here is an example of using qvalues to specify a preference for XML, with JSON also supported if XML is unavailable:

```
GET https://api.example.com/projects HTTP/1.1
Accept: application/json;q=0.5,application/xml;q=1.0
```

The use of qvalues allows API client code to support a specific type, perhaps XML for improved transformation capabilities and JSON as a fallback.

Because API clients may specify more than one media type, they must pay special attention to the Content-Type response header to determine which parser is appropriate. The following is a response that provides XML based on the previous example request:

```
HTTP/1.1 200 OK
Date: Tue, 16 June 2015 06:57:43 GMT
Content-Type: application/xml

<project>...</project>
```

Content negotiation extends the media type support of an API beyond a single type, such as JSON or XML. It allows some or all operations of an API to respond with the content type that best meets the needs of the API client.

Likewise, language negotiation allows APIs to support multiple languages in a response. The approach is similar to content negotiation using the Accept-Language request header and Content-Language response header.

Cache Control

The fastest network request is the one that doesn't need to be made. A cache is a local store of data to prevent re-retrieval of the data in the future, thereby optimizing network communications. Developers familiar with the term have likely used server-side caching tools such as Memcached to keep data in memory and reduce the need to fetch unchanged data from a database to improve application performance.

HTTP cache control allows for cacheable responses to be stored locally by API clients or intermediary cache servers. This moves the cache closer to the API client and reduces or removes the need to traverse the network all to the way to the backend API server. Users experience better performance and reduced network dependence.

HTTP makes available several caching options through the `Cache-Control` response header. This header declares whether the response is cacheable and, if so, for how long it should be cached.

Here is an example response from an API operation that returns a list of projects:

```
HTTP/1.1 200 OK
Date: Tue, 22 December 2020 06:57:43 GMT
Content-Type: application/xml
Cache-Control: max-age=240

<project>...</project>
```

In this example, the max age indicates that the data may be cached for up to 240 seconds (4 minutes) before the client should consider the data stale.

APIs may also explicitly mark a response as not cacheable, requiring a new request each time the response is required:

```
HTTP/1.1 200 OK
Date: Tue, 22 December 2020 06:57:43 GMT
Content-Type: application/xml
Cache-Control: no-cache

<project>...</project>
```

Applying thoughtful use of the cache control header to APIs reduces network traffic and speeds up Web and mobile applications. It also is the building block for conditional requests.

Conditional Requests

Conditional requests are a lesser known but powerful capability offered by HTTP. Conditional requests allow clients to request an updated resource representation only if something has changed. Clients that send a conditional request will either receive a 304 Not Modified response if the content has not changed or a 200 OK response along with the changed content.

There are two precondition types for informing the server about the client's local cached copy for comparison: time-based and entity tag–based preconditions.

Time-based preconditions require that the client store the `Last-Modified` response header for later requests. The `If-Modified-Since` request header is then be used to specify the last modified timestamp that the server will use to compare against the last known modified timestamp to determine if the resource has changed.

Following is an example of a client/server interaction that uses the last modified date in a subsequent request to determine if the resource has changed on the server:

```
GET /projects/12345 HTTP/1.1
Accept: application/json;q=0.5,application/xml;q=1.0


HTTP/1.1 200 OK
Date: Tue, 22 December 2020 06:57:43 GMT
Content-Type: application/xml
Cache-Control: max-age=240
Location: /projects/12345
Last-Modified: Tue, 22 December 2020 05:29:03 GMT


<project>...</project>


GET /projects/12345 HTTP/1.1
Accept: application/json;q=0.5,application/xml;q=1.0
If-Modified-Since: Tue, 22 December 2020 05:29:03 GMT


HTTP/1.1 304 Not Modified
Date: Tue, 22 December 2020 07:03:43 GMT



GET /projects/12345 HTTP/1.1
Accept: application/json;q=0.5,application/xml;q=1.0
If-Modified-Since: Tue, 22 December 2020 07:33:03 GMT


Date: Tue, 22 December 2020 07:33:04 GMT
Content-Type: application/xml
Cache-Control: max-age=240
Location: /projects/12345
Last-Modified: Tue, 22 December 2020 07:12:01 GMT


<project>...</project>
```

The entity tag, or ETag, is an opaque value that represents the current resource state. The client may store the ETag after a GET, POST, or PUT request, using the value to check for changes via a HEAD or GET request.

An ETag is a hashed value of the entire response. Alternatively, servers may provide a weak ETag, which is semantically equivalent but perhaps not an exact byte-for-byte equivalency.

Here is a client/server interaction but using ETags rather than the last modified date:

```
GET /projects/12345 HTTP/1.1
Accept: application/json;q=0.5,application/xml;q=1.0


HTTP/1.1 200 OK
Date: Tue, 22 December 2020 06:57:43 GMT
Content-Type: application/xml
Cache-Control: max-age=240
Location: /projects/12345
ETag: "17f0fff99ed5aae4edffdd6496d7131f"


<project>...</project>

GET /projects/12345 HTTP/1.1
Accept: application/json;q=0.5,application/xml;q=1.0
If-None-Match: "17f0fff99ed5aae4edffdd6496d7131f"


HTTP/1.1 304 Not Modified
Date: Tue, 22 December 2020 07:03:43 GMT



GET /projects/12345 HTTP/1.1
Accept: application/json;q=0.5,application/xml;q=1.0
If-None-Match: "17f0fff99ed5aae4edffdd6496d7131f"


HTTP/1.1 200 OK
Date: Tue, 22 December 2020 07:33:04 GMT
Content-Type: application/xml
Cache-Control: max-age=240
Location: /projects/12345
ETag: "b252d66ab3ec050b5fd2c3a6263ffaf51db10fcb"


<project>...</project>
```

Conditional requests reduce the effort required to validate and refetch cached resources. ETags are opaque values that represent the current internal state, whereas last modified timestamps rather than ETags may be used for time-based comparison. They may also be used for concurrency control when making modifications to resources.

Concurrency Control in HTTP

Concurrency control with HTTP is a challenge encountered by teams that need to support APIs that modify data by different users at the same time. Some API designers find clever ways to implement resource-level locking over HTTP. However, HTTP has built-in concurrency control that prevents teams from building it themselves.

Conditional requests are also used to support concurrency control in HTTP. By combining ETags or last modified dates with state change methods such as PUT, PATCH, or DELETE, we can ensure that data is not overwritten accidentally by another API client via a separate HTTP request.

To apply a conditional request, the API client adds a precondition to the request to prevent modification if the last modified timestamp or ETag of the resource has changed. Should the precondition fail, a `412 Precondition Failed` response is sent by the server. API servers may also enforce the requirement of a precondition header to enforce concurrency control by responding with a `428 Precondition Required` response if neither of the conditional headers was found in the request.

Following is an example in which two API clients are trying to modify a project. First, each client retrieves the project resource using a GET request, then each attempts a change, but only the first API client is able to apply the change:

```
GET /projects/12345 HTTP/1.1
Accept: application/json;q=0.5,application/xml;q=1.0


HTTP/1.1 200 OK
Date: Tue, 22 December 2020 07:33:04 GMT
Content-Type: application/xml
Cache-Control: max-age=240
Location: /projects/12345
ETag: "b252d66ab3ec050b5fd2c3a6263ffaf51db10fcb"


<project>...</project>
```

```
PUT /projects/1234
If-Match: "b252d66ab3ec050b5fd2c3a6263ffaf51db10fcb"


{ "name":"Project 1234", "Description":"My project" }



HTTP/1.1 200 OK
Date: Tue, 22 December 2020 08:21:20 GMT
Content-Type: application/xml
Cache-Control: max-age=240
Location: /projects/12345
ETag: "1d7209c9d54e1a9c4cf730be411eff1424ff2fb6"


<project>...</project>

PUT /projects/1234
If-Match: "b252d66ab3ec050b5fd2c3a6263ffaf51db10fcb"


{ "name":"Project 5678", "Description":"No, it is my project" }

HTTP/1.1 412 Precondition Failed
Date: Tue, 22 December 2020 08:21:24 GMT
```

The second API client that received the failed precondition response must now refetch the current representation of the resource instance, inform the user of the changes, and request whether the user wishes to resubmit the changes made or leave it as-is.

Concurrency control may be added to an API through HTTP preconditions in the request header. If the ETag/last modified date hasn't changed, then the request is processed normally. If it has changed, a 412 response code is returned, preventing the client from overwriting data as a result of two separate clients modifying the same resource concurrently. This is a powerful capability built in to HTTP, preventing the need for teams to invent their own concurrency control support.

Summary

HTTP is a powerful protocol with a robust set of capabilities, including some that are less known. Using content negotiation allows API clients and servers to agree on a supported media type. Cache control directives provide client-side and intermediary caching support. HTTP preconditions can be used to determine if expired caches are still valid while protecting resources from overwriting changes. By applying these techniques, teams are able to build robust APIs that drive complex applications in a resilient and evolvable way.

Index

M